高职院校数字商贸系

跨文化商务交际实务

INTERCULTURAL BUSINESS COMMUNICATION PRACTICE

主　编 ◎ 梁志华　广州城建职业学院

温舒蕾　广州城建职业学院

副主编 ◎ 孙晓佳　广州城建职业学院

史佳慧　广州城建职业学院

参　编 ◎ 邹菊花　广州城建职业学院

刘　婕　广州城建职业学院

Hartley Michael Joseph　广州城建职业学院

李征华　网易有道智慧教育事业部

首都经济贸易大学出版社

Capital University of Economics and Business Press

·北 京·

图书在版编目（CIP）数据

跨文化商务交际实务 / 梁志华，温舒蕾主编.
北京 ： 首都经济贸易大学出版社，2025. 1. -- ISBN
978-7-5638-3798-4

Ⅰ．F7

中国国家版本馆 CIP 数据核字第 2024MX2773 号

跨文化商务交际实务

KUAWENHUA SHANGWU JIAOJI SHIWU

主　编　梁志华　温舒蕾

副主编　孙晓佳　史佳慧

责任编辑　杨丹璇

封面设计　砚祥志远·激光照排
　　　　　TEL：010-65976003

出版发行　首都经济贸易大学出版社

地　　址　北京市朝阳区红庙（邮编 100026）

电　　话　（010）65976483　65065761　65071505（传真）

网　　址　http://www.sjmcb.cueb.edu.cn

经　　销　全国新华书店

照　　排　北京砚祥志远激光照排技术有限公司

印　　刷　唐山玺诚印务有限公司

成品尺寸　185 毫米×260 毫米　1/16

字　　数　528 千字

印　　张　22.25

版　　次　2025 年 1 月第 1 版

印　　次　2025 年 1 月第 1 次印刷

书　　号　ISBN 978-7-5638-3798-4

定　　价　49.00 元

Culture is "to know the best that has been said and thought in the world".

—Matthew Arnold, *Literature and Dogma*

My creed is this:

    Happiness is the only good.

    The place to be happy is here.

    The time to be happy is now.

    The way to be happy is to make others so.

—Robert G. Ingersoll, Motto

前 言
PREFACE

我们正处在一个全球化浪潮此起彼伏与科技发展突飞猛进的时代。近年来,在"一带一路"倡议与中华文明国际影响力日益提升的推动下,跨文化商务交际在全球化的经济与社会交往中扮演着越来越重要的角色。随着企业跨国经营、国际旅游与商务活动的不断兴起,人们必须与不同文化背景的客户、合作伙伴以及员工进行有效的跨文化沟通,促进信任和理解,从而建立长期的业务关系,提高谈判的成功率,在全球市场中获得竞争优势;同时,得体的跨文化商务交际可以降低发生误解和冲突的风险,提高团队协作效率,让拥有不同文化背景的商务人士理解和认同中国文化,共同构建国际准则和规则,增进互信与友谊。鉴于此,跨文化商务交际的有效开展和与之相关的人才培养至关重要。

《普通高校商务英语专业教学指南》提出,要培养"拥有良好的人文素养、中国情怀与国际视野"、"具备较强的跨文化能力、商务沟通能力与创新创业能力,适应国家与地方经济社会发展、对外交流与合作需要"的国际化复合型人才。跨文化商务交际课程作为国际经济与贸易高水平专业群的核心课程,对于本专业乃至专业群的人才培养发挥着不可忽视的重要作用。也正是为了达成这一目标,我们编写了《跨文化商务交际实务》这部教材。

本教材以商务英语、国际贸易、跨境电商、电子商务等专业的培养目标、培养规格为依据,对标《商务英语专业教学指南》,聚焦跨文化交际课程所提出的教学目标与教学内容要求。本教材具备实用而精细的教学设计、多维度的教学任务、数字化的教学资源支撑,旨在帮助学习者系统学习并掌握跨文化商务交际的理论知识,并通过真实的跨文化交际案例分析培养学习者的跨文化交际意识,从而实现理实结合、提高思辨能力的教学目标。

编写说明 INSTRUCTIONS

教材内容

本教材从跨文化交际理论体系、国际商务专业能力和理解当代中国文化三个维度实施三层共济的教学模式,旨在体现课程思政、融合学习、能力导向、立足中国、放眼世界的全球视角(Global Perspectives),全方位培养学习者的跨文化商务交际能力。教材内容主要涵盖以下几个方面:

中国智慧的思政引领:在单元首位,引导学习者赏析中国先哲的名言与译文,理解并思考其在学习跨文化商务交际过程中带给我们的启迪。

跨文化交际理论学习:系统学习国际商务语境下的文化比喻、文化定义、跨文化交际内涵、交际与文化的关系、文化模式、跨文化交际障碍、言语与非言语交际等理论知识,旨在使学习者搭建起跨文化商务交际的理论体系。

国际商贸的实践应用:定位于国际经济与贸易高水平专业群,本教材分析了跨文化商务管理、跨文化商务营销、跨文化商务谈判、跨文化商务礼仪等诸方面的实际应用以及真实的、体验感鲜活的案例,从而构建起国际经贸往来中真实的情境,旨在提高学习者解决现实跨文化交际问题的意识和能力。

中西文化的探源思辨:本教材通过对中西方文明、中西文化现象的描述、释义与探究,培养学习者跨文明、跨文化视角下的多元比较与思辨,旨在促进其变被动学习为主动感悟,变单纯的知识积累为主动参与文化差异的思辨,进而实现客观、系统、全面地理解跨文化差异,应用跨文化交际理论,提高跨文化交际能力的目标。

教材特点

理论引领,牢固搭建系统知识结构:与传统的商务英语专业教材不同的是,《跨文化商务交际实务》不仅系统介绍了跨文化交际理论知识,同时还融合了语言知识的理解与阅读。

中外比较,全方位提升跨文化能力:《跨文化商务交际实务》从始至终贯彻务实的能力导向的思路,每个单元均设有"中国古代智慧"名言赏析等板块,要求学习者理解中外文化在思维方式、生活方式、交往方式、价值取向、风土习惯、历史背景、社会结构等方面的异同。

理实一体,系统培养商贸实战技能:《跨文化商务交际实务》共分11个单元,各单元均设有输出驱动、输入促成、理实结合、综合产出、跨文化交际真实案例等板块,聚焦跨文化商务语境下的实际问题,循序渐进地为学习者最终完成"产出任务"搭建起脚手架;在此基础上,通过真实案例分析,进一步深化学习者对单元内容的理解,激发学习者对单元产出成果的跨文化反思(Intercultural Reflection)。

AI赋能,数字化构建立体资源:《跨文化商务交际实务》在整体设计上,利用人工智能等数字技术,构建了一整套教学资源。

单元结构

本教材每个单元分为"中国古代智慧"名言赏析、教学目标、学习情境、导入练习、Part A — E(不等)、学习评价、单元项目、案例分析、拓展阅读和单元小结共 10 个环节。

每个单元设置的栏目介绍如下:

1. "中国古代智慧"名言赏析(Ancient Chinese Wisdom):在单元伊始,通过对我国古代贤哲的名言赏析与翻译,引发学习者从跨文化商务交际的角度对本单元跨文化理论或实践进行思索;有机融入中国古代商务文化元素,选用中国古代文化精髓,有效增强学习者的家国情怀,激发其爱国热忱和民族自信。

2. 教学目标(Learning Objectives):在思政引领主题之后,将本单元要学习的跨文化商务交际理论知识与实践技能、文化反思与思辨能力、文化现象分析与阐述能力、跨文化交际项目和案例展示与分析能力等详细列举出来,供教师和学习者参照讲授和学习。

3. 学习情境(Project Scenario):以中国古代智慧名言和鲜活的视频材料进行导入与热身练习,初步激发学习者的兴趣与思考,为接下来的单元项目提供总体的学习场景。

4. 导入练习(Lead-in):包括一段辅助的听力活动,介绍优秀的中华文明、文化遗产等视频材料和针对单元主题的问题,旨在激活相关背景知识,帮助学习者把握单元项目的主要思想。

5. 检验学习(Part A — E 不等):这一板块属于教材的主体,采用理论学习与理解性任务、单元项目子任务等多样化讲练结合的模式,检验学习者对各部分知识的掌握程度,积极引导学习者不断思考,为最终完成单元项目搭建"脚手架"。

6. 学习评价(Assessment):这个板块是完成单元项目前的最后一项学习评价测试,旨在检验学习者对于单元主体内容的掌握程度,通过多种形式的测试,进一步巩固知识,为顺利完成下一个环节的单元项目奠定基础。

7. 单元项目(Unit Project):在前面几个环节的"输入促成"内容和教学活动充分完成之后,这一环节组织学习者开展基于前期情境的单元任务,旨在引导学习者进一步巩固阶段学习成果,完成综合性的单元产出任务,深化学习者对单元所学内容的理解,同时增强其对单元产出成果的展示和反思能力。

8. 案例分析(Case Analysis):这是单元教学内容的最后一个板块,通过生动的案例及案例分析,不仅可展示学习者对单元情境的综合应用水平,同时可培养其多样化的能力。学习者应积极利用本教材设计的各种跨文化、跨学科、思辨性、合作性、探究性案例分析活动,打破自己的思维定式和认知局限,不断提高跨文化交际能力、思辨能力、创新能力、合作学习能力,促进自身全面发展。

9. 拓展阅读(Further Reading):在单元教学内容结束后,通过更加宽泛的阅读题材,丰富学习者对跨文化知识、跨文化意识、跨文化理解等方面的深入学习和探究,拓展他们的知识体系与视野。

10. 单元小结(Summary):为了让学习者更好地理解各个单元的要点,单元最后设置了中文版的单元小结。

分工与致谢

《跨文化商务交际实务》是全体编者精诚合作的结晶。本教材由梁志华、温舒蕾担任主编并提出教材编写理念，设计教材框架与单元结构，领导编写团队完成样课设计，负责各单元审校与定稿，撰写前言和编写说明；孙晓佳、史佳慧担任副主编。各单元编者分别为：梁志华（Unit 1，Unit 2），温舒蕾（Unit 5，Unit 9，Unit 10），孙晓佳（Unit 3，Unit 4，Unit 11），邹菊花（Unit 6），史佳慧（Unit 7，Unit 8）。刘婕和爱尔兰专家 Hartley Michael Joseph 共同参加了大纲编写、样课修改、格式规范以及整体校对等工作。

由于编者水平与经验有限，书中难免有不足之处，敬请读者批评指正。

编　者

2024 年 7 月

CONTENTS

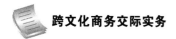

Unit 1   Culture

Ancient Chinese Wisdom

Explain the following quote and reflect on its contemporary relevance.

Plants with strong roots grow well, and efforts with the right focus ensure success. (万物得其本者生,百事得其道者成。)

From *Garden of Stories* (《说苑》)

Learning Objectives

After learning this unit, you shall be able to:

- Understand culture through cultural images or models.
- Describe the features of culture.
- Distinguish the stages of the formation of cultural identity.
- Analyze the culture embodied by the Great Wall and introduce it to the international audience.

Project Scenario

After learning this unit, finish the unit project on the basis of the following scenario.

Suppose you are an assistant in a Chinese auto company. Your company wants to cooperate with an Irish auto import company, and an Irish representative will come to China to negotiate. In order to present our Chinese hospitality and sincerity, the office manager asks you to accompany the Irish representative to the local cultural sites. The representative is very interested in Chinese culture and you need to introduce the sites and tell him the Chinese culture they embodies.

Lead-in

Watch the video clip about the Great Wall and answer the following questions.

- What cultural values do you think the architecture in the Great Wall reflects?
- As the assistant in the scenario, what other aspects of the Great Wall do you plan to introduce to your guests?

The Great Wall

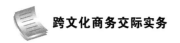

Part A　What is Culture?

Culture is <u>multifaceted and interconnected</u>. Individuals often <u>segment</u> culture into different components to examine each section independently. <u>Analogies</u> such as an iceberg or an onion can aid in comprehending the concept of culture.

1. Culture is Like an Iceberg

The iceberg model for culture is a commonly used comparison. We know that only a small part of an iceberg is visible above the water, while the larger part hidden underwater is not seen. In terms of culture, the visible aspects include things like clothing, food, and buildings. However, the invisible part beneath the surface includes the deeper cultural elements like norms, values, and beliefs, which have a stronger influence.

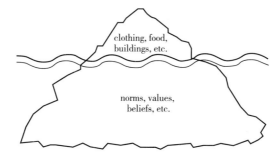

In the movie "Titanic", as the so-called unsinkable Titanic approached an iceberg, the two lookouts warned the crew upon sighting it. Nevertheless, the fate of the Titanic and its passengers was sealed. This was because the Titanic had collided with the massive underwater base of the iceberg. Similarly, a cultural iceberg is composed of two parts: the part above water and the part below water. The culture of a company can also be analyzed using the iceberg model. The top of the iceberg includes the buildings, offices, desks, coffee bars, and the fashion style of a company. The foundation of the iceberg consists of the corporate culture, rules, discipline, and the relationships between colleagues.

Task 1: Understanding the Concepts

According to the features of the iceberg model, fill in the two boxes with the serial numbers of the following words.

(1) architecture　　(2) values　　(3) history　　(4) clothing　　(5) objective

(6) subjective　　(7) visible　　(8) invisible　　(9) spiritual　　(10) material

Above the water: _____

Below the water: _____

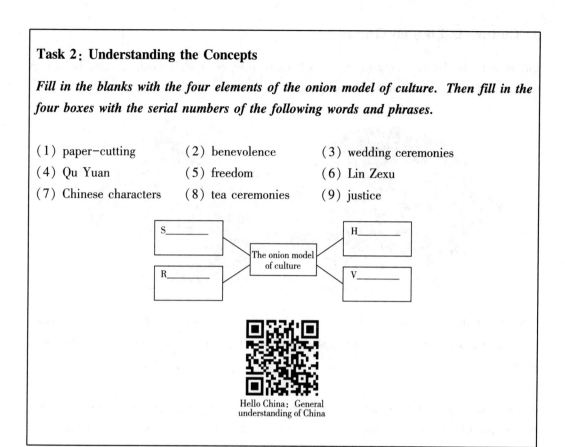

Task 2: Understanding the Concepts

Fill in the blanks with the four elements of the onion model of culture. Then fill in the four boxes with the serial numbers of the following words and phrases.

(1) paper-cutting (2) benevolence (3) wedding ceremonies
(4) Qu Yuan (5) freedom (6) Lin Zexu
(7) Chinese characters (8) tea ceremonies (9) justice

S_____

R_____

The onion model of culture

H_____

V_____

Hello China: General understanding of China

2. Definitions of Culture

People are different throughout the world, culturally, religiously, ideologically and racially, actually different in almost every aspect, therefore we are supposed to know about their differences as much as possible, just for a smooth communication among the Homo sapiens, the people in the global village. You will make it by coming to Intercultural Communication.

Cross-cultural communication studies have been profoundly influenced by anthropologists. In 1952, American anthropologists Alfred Kroeber and Clyde Kluckhohn categorized about 150 definitions of culture. Some definitions emphasize culture as a pattern of thoughts and beliefs; others view culture from the perspective of behavior; still others focus on the non-material aspects of human life or the material aspects of society. Dutch social psychologist Geert Hofstede conducted pioneering research on the cultures of different countries, defining culture as "the collective programming of the mind that distinguishes the members of one group or category from another". Culture is the "software of the mind". From the perspective of social psychology, the definition of culture is rooted in the individual's mind.

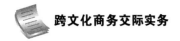
3. Culture is Like an Onion

Culture can also be compared to an onion because both are multilayered. Culture is like an onion with four layers: symbols, heroes, rituals, and values.

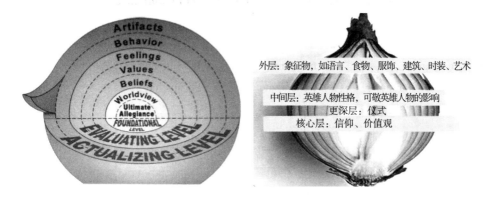

Symbols are the most visible and easily noticed aspects of a culture. They include language, clothing, national flags, etc. These symbols represent the first layer, much like the outer skin of an onion.

The second layer consists of heroes, who are revered for their qualities. In Western cultures, figures like Christopher Columbus are celebrated for their bravery, while Abraham Lincoln is honored for his commitment to justice. In Chinese culture, Confucius is admired for his wisdom, Yue Fei for his loyalty, and Yuan Longping for his dedication to agriculture and food security.

Moving further into the onion analogy, the third layer is made up of rituals. These are important community activities that reflect cultural traditions. For instance, China's Dragon Boat Festival and Mid-Autumn Festival involve specific foods, decorations, and activities that celebrate cultural values and history.

At the heart of the onion are values, which are the foundational beliefs and principles of a culture. In Chinese traditional culture, this includes religious and philosophical systems such as Buddhism, Taoism, and Confucianism. Key virtues like benevolence (仁), righteousness (义), propriety (礼), wisdom (智), and faithfulness (信) are deeply rooted in Chinese society and guide individuals' behavior and ethics.

According to the Oxford English Dictionary, culture is "the name given to the totality of the arts and other manifestations of human intellectual achievement". It includes elements such as music, art, exhibitions, dance, etc. When people talk about Picasso and Beethoven, they are talking about culture. The same goes for when people discuss brands or trademarks, these also belong to a specific culture.

In this book, culture encompasses knowledge, experiences, beliefs, values, actions, attitudes, meanings, roles, artifacts, and more, which are acquired through the efforts of individuals and groups, passed down from generation to generation by a group of people.

Task 3: Preparing for the Unit Project

1. Applying the Concepts

The Great Wall is a manifestation of Chinese Culture. Use the iceberg model or the onion model introduced in Part A and draw a cultural model of the Great Wall.

2. Critical Thinking

Besides the iceberg model and the onion model, what other models do you know?

Please conduct AI research to find more about cultural models, and make a group presentation before your class.

Part B   Culture is Learned

Actually, culture is not innate sensibility, but a learned characteristic. Children begin learning about their own culture at home with their immediate family and how they interact each other, how they dress, and the rituals they perform. When the children are growing in the community, their cultural education is advanced by watching social interactions, taking part in cultural activities and rituals in the community, forming their own relationships and taking their place in the culture.

Even though different countries have their own unique cultures, there are some basic things that most cultures have in common, such as being learned, dynamic and pervasive. These include the fact that culture is something we learn, it's always changing, it's found everywhere in society, it combines many different aspects, and it can adjust to new situations. In this lesson, we focus on two key features of culture: it's learned and it's ever-changing.

Culture isn't something we're born with. Instead, it's a set of shared symbols that people within a particular group understand. The only way to become part of this group is by learning about these symbols. We start learning about our culture from a young age, whether we're aware of it or not, through the process of becoming part of our society. How do we learn our culture?

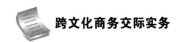

It's not just from our parents and friends that we learn our culture. There are three main ways we learn about our culture: through wise sayings, stories, and art.

1. Learning Culture Through Proverbs

In nearly every culture, proverbs are conveyed using <u>vibrant</u> and lively language. They <u>embody</u> "words of wisdom". Because proverbs can be learned easily and repeated regularly, they soon become part of an individual's belief system. Many of the same proverbs appear throughout the world because all people, regardless of their culture, share common experiences.

Task 4: Cross Cultural Comparison

Work in group of three and have a discussion with your team members: What cultural values do you think the following proverbs reflect?

- All roads lead to Rome.
- 吃一堑长一智。
- Give a dog bad name and hang him.
- 海内存知己，天涯若比邻。

---

2. Learning Culture Through Stories

Learning about culture through stories is a powerful way to gain insights into the values, traditions, and ways of life of different people. Here's how you can approach learning about culture through stories:

Choose appropriate stories: Select stories that are culturally significant and representative of the group you want to learn about. These could be <u>folktales</u>, <u>myths</u>, <u>legends</u>, or <u>contemporary</u> narratives that have cultural relevance.

Understand the context: Before diving into the story, research the historical, social, and geographical context in which the story is set. This will help you understand the <u>nuances</u> and underlying meanings of the story.

Analyze the story: Pay attention to elements like characters, plot, settings, and themes. Look for cultural norms, beliefs, and values that are reflected in these aspects. For example, a story might emphasize the importance of community over individualism, or the respect for elders.

Discussion and reflection: After reading or watching the story, engage in discussion with others. Talk about what you learned, what surprised you, and how the story relates to your own culture. Reflect on the similarities and differences between cultures.

Connect to real life: Try to observe how the lessons from the stories <u>manifest</u> in real life. If possible, interact with members of the culture you are studying to see firsthand how their behaviors and decisions reflect the stories and cultural values you've learned about.

<u>Empathy</u> and open-mindedness: Keep an open mind and try to empathize with the characters in the story. This can help you understand the emotional and psychological experiences of people from different cultural backgrounds.

Examples of learning culture through stories:

<u>Greek mythology</u>: Reading about the myths of ancient Greece, such as the stories of <u>Zeus</u>, <u>Hera</u>, and other gods and heroes, can teach you about the origins of Western civilization, the importance of fate, and the Greek view of the world and its <u>inhabitants</u>.

Native American <u>folktales</u>: Stories like *Coyote and the Man in the Moon* can provide insights into the relationship Native Americans have with nature and the trickster figure common in many of their stories.

Chinese legends: The story of "The Monkey King" from *Journey to the West* offers insights into Chinese <u>Buddhism</u>, morality, and the value of <u>loyalty and perseverance</u>.

Shakespearean plays: Works like *Romeo and Juliet*, *Hamlet*, and *Macbeth* can teach about the societal norms, power dynamics, and personal <u>dilemmas</u> in Elizabethan England.

By engaging with stories from different cultures, you can develop a deeper understanding of the world and its diverse people. It's a journey of discovery that not only educates but also broadens your perspective and <u>fosters empathy</u>.

Task 5: Telling China's Stories in English

1. Translate the following story into English. And share with your classmates what you have learned from this story.

孔融让梨

孔融字文举，鲁国人，孔子二十世孙也。融四岁，与诸兄食梨，辄引小者。人问其故，答曰："我小儿，法当取小者。"

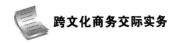

2. *Translate the following story into Chinese. And share with your classmates what you have learned from this story.*

The Odyssey is one of two major ancient Greek epic poems attributed to Homer. It is believed to have been composed between the 8th and 6th centuries BC. The story follows the adventures of a hero named Odysseus as he tries to return home to Ithaca after the Trojan War.

Task 6: Telling China's Stories in English

Divide the class into four or five groups, then discuss the following stories.

3. Learning Culture Through Arts

Arts are a powerful medium for learning about different cultures. The art is another method of passing on a culture. They provide insights into the history, traditions, beliefs, and values of a particular culture. Through arts, we can learn about the way of life, customs, and rituals of different societies. It helps us understand and appreciate the diversity of human experience.

Art also plays a significant role in cultural exchange and understanding. It transcends language barriers and communicates ideas and emotions in a universal language. By appreciating and understanding art from different cultures, we can develop empathy and respect for people from diverse backgrounds.

Moreover, learning about culture through arts can foster creativity and innovation. It exposes us to new ideas, perspectives, and ways of thinking. This exposure can inspire us to create new works of art that reflect our own cultural identity while incorporating elements from other cultures.

In conclusion, learning about different cultures through arts is essential for promoting cultural understanding, appreciation, and respect. It encourages us to embrace diversity and appreciate the richness of human experience. Therefore, it is crucial to include arts education in our curriculum to develop well-rounded individuals who can contribute positively to society.

Task 7: Furthering Your Understanding

Watch the video clip about Western painting and discuss with your partner the charm of this form of arts.

《清明上河图》（局部）

Part C   Culture is Dynamic

Culture is subjective to change over time. Some cultures are more open and <u>embrace</u> change; others tend to resist it. Four major <u>aspects</u> account for the change of cultures: technological invention, disasters, cultural contact, and environmental factors.

1. Technological Invention

Technological inventions have had a profound impact on culture throughout history. Here are some ways in which they have changed culture: Technological invention, like the invention of communication. The invention of the printing press made it possible for books to be <u>mass-produced</u>, leading to an increase in <u>literacy</u> and knowledge sharing. The development of the internet and social media has also revolutionized the way people communicate and share information.

In the field of entertainment, inventions such as the television, radio, and movie <u>projector</u> have transformed the way people consume entertainment. They have made it possible for people to <u>access</u> a wide variety of media from anywhere in the world.

In the education world, Technological advancements have transformed education by making it

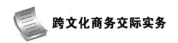

more accessible and efficient. Online learning platforms, <u>digital</u> textbooks, and educational apps have made it possible for people to learn at their own pace and from anywhere in the world.

In the business world, E-commerce has <u>thrived</u> owing to the development of technology. Take the tourism for instance, travelers could make any international hotel reservation and train tickets booking through a simple app, all they need to do is to input their ID number. Technology has changed the way people work by making it possible to <u>automate</u> many tasks and improve efficiency. It has also created new industries and job opportunities.

2. Disasters

Disasters, including human <u>calamities</u> and natural disasters, can have a <u>profound</u> impact on culture, shaping beliefs, values, and practices in various ways. As for cultural traditions and practices, disasters can <u>disrupt</u> or destroy cultural traditions and practices, leading to their <u>adaptation or replacement</u>. For example, after the 2010 <u>Haiti earthquake</u>, many traditional musical instruments were lost or damaged, leading musicians to adapt their music using new materials and techniques.

Some environmental disasters can highlight the importance of environmental stewardship and sustainability. For example, after the 2011 <u>Fukushima</u> nuclear disaster in Japan, there was a renewed focus on renewable energy sources and reducing dependence on nuclear power. Similarly, the 2017 hurricanes in <u>Puerto Rico</u> led to increased awareness of climate change and its impacts on vulnerable communities. Some plagues like <u>Black Death</u>, can be extremely destructive on the population, psychology, and politics as well.

In the same time, disasters can also <u>spur</u> innovation and creativity, as people develop new technologies, strategies, and solutions to cope with the challenges they face. This can lead to lasting cultural changes, as these innovations become <u>integrated</u> into everyday life.

3. Cultural Contact

The world today is characterized by an ever-growing number of contacts resulting in communication between people with different linguistic and cultural backgrounds.

Cultural contact is a process by which individuals or groups from different cultures interact, exchange ideas, and influence each other. This can occur through various means such as trade, travel, <u>migration</u>, <u>conquest</u>, education, media, and the internet. Cultural contact can lead to changes in language, religion, customs, values, and social structures.

When two cultures benefit from their interaction, such as through trade or marriage, a sort of symbiotic convergence occurs; when elements of two cultures blend together to create a new culture, hybridization of cultures takes place.

Since the late 1980s in which the reform and opening-up policy was made in China, a great number of foreign companies have set up joint-venture enterprises in China.

4. Environmental Factors

Environmental factors can significantly influence and shape culture in various ways. The natural resources available in a particular environment can greatly impact the culture that develops there. For instance, areas rich in forests may develop woodworking traditions, while those near the sea may have a strong fishing culture.

As to climate and weather patterns, climate can affect everything from clothing and housing styles to agricultural practices and festivals. For example, colder climates might lead to the use of fur clothing and the construction of insulated homes, while hotter climates might promote outdoor activities and social gatherings.

In conclusion, culture is always changing due to technological innovation, disasters, cultural contact, and environmental factors. Some can be avoided and some can be developed. While some of these changes can be difficult and painful, they can also lead to greater resilience, adaptation, and growth. Others have had a significant impact on culture by changing the way people communicate, consume entertainment, learn, receive healthcare, and work.

Task 8: Understanding the Concepts

Filling in the blanks with four elements why culture is dynamic. Then fill in the four boxes with the serial numbers of the following words or phrases.

(1) Black Death   (2) World War II   (3) climate change

(4) Olympic Games   (5) China Export Commodities Fair

(6) virtual conference   (7) Chat GPT   (8) unmanned aerial vehicle

T		C
	Culture is dynamic	
D		E

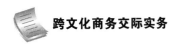

Task 9: Understanding the Concepts

Complete the following sentences by filling in each blank with an appropriate word or phrase from the box below. Change its form if necessary.

prosperity polarization enjoy leave fair capital follow achieve see history cooperate able modern develop

The Chinese modernization is for the (1) _____ of all people. While Western modernization's primary driver was (2) _____ which resulted in enlarging wealth inequality and social (3) _____; Chinese-style modernization, a people-centered modernization, aims to bring common prosperity to all Chinese people and enable all of them to (4) _____ the fruits of development in (5) _____ a way. The CPC will allow no one in China to be (6) _____ behind in the process of advancing China's socialist modernization. (from *Understanding Contemporary China*, *A Reading & Writing Course*, p120)

The Chinese modernization features peaceful development and win-win cooperation. China will not (7) _____ the Western path of aggression, colonization and expansion to (8) _____ its modernization. Marek Hrubec, director and senior fellow of the Center of Global Studies in Prague, points out that "China's development can be (9) _____ as a unique kind of modernization continuing the tread of constant interactions between itself and other civilizations for thousands of years particularly via (10) _____ Silk Road. China's Belt and Road Initiatives revitalizes and updates the historical Silk Road, presenting opportunities for many people and countries to (11) _____ with China on the basis of mutual respect and multilateral cooperation. "

Task 10: Intercultural Reflection

1. Listen to the story of Zhang Qian, the pioneer of the Silk Road in Han Dynasty. Compare him with Christopher Columbus, one of the greatest explorers in the West. How do their adventures differ?

2. Prepare a group presentation of five minutes to illustrate the differences. You may focus on three major perspectives: purpose, experience, and results. (video clip)

The Silk Road

Part D   Cultural Identity

Cultural identity refers to the <u>sense of belonging</u> and shared values, beliefs, traditions, and practices that are characteristics of a particular cultural group. It is the aspect of our identity that is shaped by our cultural background and experiences, and it can include elements such as language, religion, <u>ethnicity, nationality</u>, and social class. However, some people may get confused about their cultural identity when they grow up in a <u>multicultural</u> background. In our life, we all have different identities at the same time. For example, a university teacher could also be a mother, a wife, a daughter, and a Chinese woman, etc. Cultural identity is very important for people. It is the <u>central, dynamic, and multifaceted</u> component of one's self – concept. These qualities are the three major characteristics of cultural identity.

Here are some tips to help you to identify your identities.
Identifying one's cultural identity involves exploring and understanding the various cultural influences that have shaped who we are.

<u>Step1 Reflect on your upbringing</u>: Think about the traditions, customs, and values you were raised with. Consider the language (s) you speak, the religion you practice (if any), and the cultural celebrations you participate in.

<u>Step2 Explore your family history</u>: Learn about your ancestors and their cultural backgrounds. This can provide insight into the cultural influences that have shaped your family and, by extension, your own identity.

<u>Step3 Consider your experiences</u>: Your cultural identity is not solely determined by your background but also by your experiences. Think about the different environments you have lived in, the people you have interacted with, and the challenges you have faced.

<u>Step4 Embrace diversity</u>: Recognize that cultural identity is complex and <u>multifaceted</u>. You may identify with <u>multiple</u> cultures or feel a stronger connection to certain aspects of your <u>heritage</u> than others. It's okay to have a <u>fluid and evolving</u> understanding of your cultural identity.

<u>Step5 Connect with others</u>: Join communities or groups that share similar cultural backgrounds or interests. This can help you learn more about your cultural identity and find a sense of belonging.

<u>Step6 Educate yourself</u>: Read books, watch films, and attend cultural events that explore

13

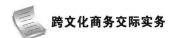
different cultures and perspectives. This can broaden your understanding of cultural identity and help you better identify your own.

Step7 Reflect and self－assess: Take time to reflect on your cultural identity and how it has influenced your life. Consider how you want to express and share your cultural identity with others.

Task 11: Understanding the Concepts

Who are these people in the following pictures? Write down their names and cultural identities with the help of the descriptions.

Nelson Mandela   Christopher Columbus   Barack Hussein Obama

Henry Ford   Michelangelo   Leonardo da Vinci

Jane Goodall   Zhu Di   Yuan Long－ping

Discovery of the New World

Founder of an American car company

_____   _____

Father of modern South Africa

Father of Hybrid Rice

_____   _____

Task 12: Understanding the Concepts

What are these cultural identities in the following pictures? Write down their names and differences with the help of the descriptions.

 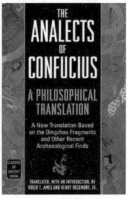 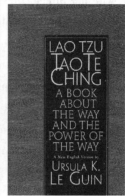

Laozi and Confucius are two great representatives of ancient Chinese philosophy, whose thoughts and writings have had a profound impact on both Chinese culture and world culture. Laozi, traditionally known as Li Er, with the honorific title "Old Master", is considered the founder of Taoism and is revered as the progenitor of religious Taoism. He lived during the Spring and Autumn Period, around the 6th century BCE. Laozi's primary work, the *Tao Te Ching* (also known as the *Classic of the Way and Virtue* or *Laozi*), consists of 81 chapters that expound on central Taoist concepts such as the Tao (the Way), De (Virtue), Wu Wei (non-action), and naturalness. The *Tao Te Ching* is one of the oldest and most influential philosophical texts in the world and has had a profound impact on subsequent generations.

Confucius, whose given name was Kong Qiu and courtesy name was Zhongni, founded the Confucian school of thought and is venerated as the master of Ruism. He lived during the Spring and Autumn Period, approximately between 551 BCE and 479 BCE. Confucius's main educational ideas included Ren (benevolence), Yi (righteousness), Li (propriety), Zhi (knowledge), and Xin (integrity), emphasizing personal cultivation, family harmony, governance of the state, and peace in the world. His teachings, known as "Confucianism", deeply influenced Chinese society for many generations. Confucius's disciples compiled his sayings into the *Analects*, which became one of the classic texts of the Confucian school.

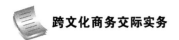

Task 13: Understanding the Cultural Identity

Read each of the following questions and choose the best answer.

1. Jiang Wei is a freshman in China International Airline. She is supposed to take part in a conference with her director to negotiate with Singapore Airlines on a new route program in Singapore. As soon as the conference is over, could you imagine what shall be the most appropriate way for Jiang Wei to say goodbye to the participants from Singapore?

    A. She shakes hands with them with a slight bow.

    B. She gives them a tight hug.

    C. She bows low to them.

    D. She waves hands to them.

2. Liu Tao invites her American colleague Micheal who believes in Judaism to her apartment for the Labor's Day holiday. Which of the following do you think is probably NOT appropriate?

    A. Liu Tao offers Micheal a cup of hot water.

    B. Liu Tao cooks beef for Micheal.

    C. Liu Tao prepares forks and knives for Micheal.

    D. Liu Tao removes pin bones from fish fillets.

3. Liu Jie and Su Lei have been working in Dublin for two years. Today they are about to celebrate Su's birthday at a bar with several friends. Their friend, Micheal, brings along a new friend Jessica who is a Muslim. When Liu Jie and Su Lei greet Jessica, which of the following action would be probably the most appropriate?

    A. They kiss her on the cheek.

    B. They walk up to her and bow.

    C. They shake hands with her using both hands.

    D. They place their hands on their chest.

4. Lin Yi and his boss have a business negotiation with an Indian company in Bombay. During the negotiation, which of the statements below is probably NOT appropriate?

    A. Lin gets down to business quickly at the beginning of the meeting.

    B. Lin has a casual conversation with Indian counterparts before starting negotiation.

    C. Lin receives the business cards from the Indian guests using the right hand.

    D. Lin receives the business cards from the Indian guests using both hands.

5. As a Chinese scholar, Li Xiong has been seeking his master degree in Heidelberg for nearly two years. His German friend Leon has invited Li to a small dinner party at his apartment this Sunday. Which of the following do you think is the most appropriate for Li if he goes to Leon's apartment?

    A. Li brings a bunch of lilies.

B. Li arrives at Leon's apartment a quarter ahead of the agreed time.

C. Li brings a bottle of whisky with him.

D. Li arrives at Leon's apartment a quarter later than the agreed time.

Part E   Culture is Integrated and Based on Symbols

In order for the culture to be transmitted from one person to the next, and from one generation to the next, a system of symbols needs to be created that translates the ideals of the culture to its members. This is accomplished through language, art, religion and money.

For the sake of keeping the culture, functioning all aspects of the culture must be integrated. For example, the language must be able to describe all the functions within the culture in order for ideas and ideals to be transmitted from one person to another. Without the integration of language into the fabric of the culture, confusion and dysfunction would reign and the culture would fail.

Chinese culture is rich in symbols that have been developed over thousands of years and are deeply embedded in various aspects of Chinese life. These symbols reflect the history, traditions, beliefs, and values of the Chinese people. Following are some examples.

Chinese characters (Hanzi): The written language itself is a significant cultural symbol. Each character often has a meaning based on its structure and components, which can reflect aspects of natural phenomena, abstract concepts, or culturally significant objects.

In Chinese culture, the dragon is a powerful symbol of good fortune, power, and wisdom. It is closely associated with the emperor and is considered a protector of the nation. Often paired with the dragon, the phoenix is a symbol of harmony, femininity, and rejuvenation. It represents the ideal partner to the dragon, symbolizing the perfect union of Yin and Yang.

One of the most iconic symbols of China, the Great Wall represents strength and perseverance, as well as the country's long history and enduring power.

In the field of belief, the Yin-Yang, this ancient symbol represents the complementary nature of opposites in the universe, such as light and dark, male and female, and the balance between them. As for the Chinese Zodiac based on a 12-year cycle, each year is associated with an animal sign (rat, ox, tiger, rabbit, dragon, snake, horse, goat, monkey, rooster, dog, and

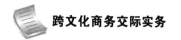

pig). These animals are believed to influence the personality traits of people born in those years.

Other symbols such as the Lunar New Year (Spring Festival), the Welcoming Cat (Cai Shen Ye), and Qipao/Cheongsam, are just a fraction of the many that constitute China's vast cultural tapestry. They continue to play a vital role in contemporary Chinese society and are celebrated both domestically and around the world where Chinese communities exist.

Task 14: Understanding the Concepts

1. *You are an assistant in a branch of MILANO in China. In order to celebrate the successful fulfillment of a important project, your boss asks you to prepare gifts for the Italian partner to thank for their sincere support. What would you do when preparing gifts for them? (　　) Discuss with your partner to cite more examples.*

 A. Prepare gifts with purple wrapping.

 B. Prepare gifts without price stickers.

 C. Prepare knives or scissors as gifts.

 D. Prepare bunches of chrysanthemums as gifts.

2. *These questions focus on assessing the understanding that culture is not an inherent quality but is learned through various forms of expression such as arts, stories, proverbs, and daily life activities, which are all instrumental in preserving cultural knowledge and heritage.*

(1) Which of the following statements best reflects the characteristic of culture being "dynamic"?

 A. Culture remains static and unchanging over time.

 B. Culture is passed down genetically from one generation to another.

 C. Culture is a collection of beliefs, values, and practices that are constantly evolving.

 D. Individuals have no influence on the cultural norms of their society.

(2) How do arts contribute to the transmission of culture from one generation to another?

 A. Arts provide no significant role in cultural learning.

 B. Arts serve as a medium for cultural expression and communication, reflecting and shaping cultural values and identity.

 C. Arts only influence individuals who pursue artistic careers.

 D. Arts are exclusively used for entertainment purposes and have no cultural significance.

(3) Which of the following best describes how stories can convey cultural knowledge?

 A. Stories are merely fictional narratives with no educational value.

 B. Stories are a powerful means of passing down history, moral lessons, and cultural beliefs from one generation to another.

C. Stories only contain factual information and cannot represent cultural perspectives.

D. Stories are only written texts and cannot be conveyed through oral traditions.

（4）Through which of the following means can culture be learned?

A. Only through formal education in schools.

B. Through observation and participation in daily life activities.

C. Exclusively through written documents and historical records.

D. Solely through interactions with government officials.

（5）Why is it important for different forms of cultural expression to be preserved?

A. Because they have no impact on contemporary society.

B. Because preserving them ensures that cultural knowledge and heritage are not lost over time.

C. Because they only appeal to a limited audience.

D. Because they should be replaced with modern forms of expression.

Task 15: Telling China's Stories in English

1. *Translate the following story into English, and share with your classmates what you have learned from this story.*

　　太极是中国文化史上的一个重要概念和范畴。《易传》中这样说道："易有太极，是生两仪。两仪生四象，四象生八卦。""太极观"这种"迷离恍惚"地看待万事万物的现象和本质的人生态度以及这种思维方式本身，实则包含着清醒睿智的哲思，其终极目的是让人类活动顺应大道至德和自然规律，不为外物所拘，"无为而无不为"，最终到达一种有容乃大、无所不包的宁静和谐的精神领域。

2. *Translate the following story into Chinese. And share with your classmates what you have learned from this story.*

The story of the "Apple of Discord"（不和的金苹果）is an allegorical tale from Greek mythology（希腊神话）that has been interpreted in various ways. It is most commonly associated with the judgment of Paris, a prince of Troy（特洛伊王子），who was asked to decide which of three goddesses — Aphrodite, Athena, or Hera — was the fairest. Each goddess attempted to bribe Paris with gifts, and it was Aphrodite's promise of the most beautiful woman in the world that swayed him.

The "Apple of Discord" itself is not explicitly mentioned in Homer's epic poems, but later writers and artists have used it as a symbol for the cause of strife and discord. In these later interpretations, the apple was inscribed with the words "for the fairest" and was thrown into a gathering of the goddesses by Eris, the goddess of discord, as a provocation. This event led to the Trojan War, hence the apple became a symbol of the conflict and its disastrous consequences.

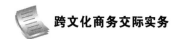

Assessment

1. *Decide whether the following statements are true (T) or false (F).*

_____ (1) Culture can be compared to an iceberg and the part below the water is relatively difficult to understand.

_____ (2) Cultural identity refers to one's sense of belonging to a particular culture or ethnic group.

_____ (3) The stories in different cultures may tell us the same cultural values.

_____ (4) We are born with culture.

_____ (5) New inventions in communication and transportation result in the change of culture.

2. *Read each of the following statements and choose the best answer.*

(1) The Olympic Rings can be considered as a _____ , representing the five inhabited continents in the world.

    A. hero   B. symbol   C. ritual   D. value

(2) People who go to the Forbidden City can mainly learn culture through _____ .

    A. Proverbs   B. stories   C. arts   D. teachers

(3) Truman is a good example of a person who reached the stage of _____ .

    A. unexamined cultural identity

    B. the search for cultural identity

    C. the achievement of cultural identity

    D. unknown cultural identity

(4) Which of the following does NOT belong to Finnish cultural customs?

    A. Tips are necessary for restaurants and taxis.

    B. Kiss of peace reflects intimate relationship.

    C. Appointments should be arranged in advance.

    D. Business trips to Finland are inappropriate in June and July.

Unit Project

Re-examine the scenario of this unit and play the role of the tour guide for the Irish representative. Introduce the Great Wall and tell him the Chinese cultural elements it embodies. Record your introduction and present it in class. Your introduction may include the following points:

- Apply the iceberg model or the onion model to analyze the Great Wall.
- Introduce the architecture, paintings, and other forms of art in the Great Wall.
- Introduce the popular cultural and creative commercial products in the Great Wall.
- Introduce the change of the Great Wall as a symbol for Chinese people.

Case Analysis

Analyze the following case with the cultural models and theories learned in this unit.

A Land Cruiser is running along a rugged and steep mountain path in Kekexilin, dragging with <u>shackles</u> behind it a heavy and clumsy truck looking like Dongfeng. The ad says: Nothing can prevent it from advancing (征途无限).

Some Chinese get angry. They think that the truck behind is Dongfeng. Being dragged by the Land Cruiser implies that China is backward, which hurts the national dignity of the Chinese people.

The Toyota company in China published a public letter of apology: they apologized for publishing such advertisement, and decided to stop it immediately. It emphasized that they did not mean to hurt the Chinese. Their original intention was just for business. Nothing more.

Further Reading

Cultural Difference and Cultural Competence

The first years of life are marked by observational learning, but the subsequent cultural rules of a society are primarily learned through communication. Culture also influences communication beyond language. The way of formulating a request or asking for directions is strongly influenced by culture. Perception, thinking, and acting are guided by cultural affiliation. Assumptions, values, and behavior patterns can lead to mistaken assignments of meaning and misinterpretations. Misunderstandings also occur in an intercultural communication between two obviously similar cultures, due to a false assumption of a common background.

"Cultural competence" is generally defined as what one can learn from a particular group of relevant attitudes, values, beliefs, and behaviors as a non-member of that culture. It is often subdivided according to ethnicity, race, religion, or into national groups such as "Europeans", "African Americans", "Hispanics", or "Asians". This disregards the fact that culture is multidimensional and dynamic. Some people in an ethnic group may have a different understanding of disease and its condition (their "model of explanation") than others in the same group. It is important to keep in mind that culture is not just a single aspect, but encompasses multiple aspects, all of which influence behavior. Cultural processes often differ within the same ethnic or social group because of differences in age cohort, gender, political association, religion, ethnicity, and even personality. Similarities in physical appearance and racial or ethnic affiliation must not lead to the assumption that these people have the same beliefs, values, and behaviors, i. e. , that they automatically share "cultural concepts". This approach can result in stereotypical thinking rather than cultural competence. International patient care should therefore not be reduced to "cultural categories", but instead competencies should focus on foundational communication skills.

Cultural awareness requires people to be aware of how their culture and that of others affect their behaviors. Even if a person does not know much about other cultures, they should know about their own culture and how it shapes them. Being culturally aware can also mean to respect others' cultures even if we do not understand every detail and every motivation affecting how to handle things. This is the starting point for intercultural understanding. The basis of an intercultural life is the awareness of cultural differences and how they affect the behavior of each individual. These influences affect both a person's private and professional life. However, intercultural awareness alone does not provide the ability to communicate across cultures. It is just the first step in a process.

单元小结

1　什么是文化

文化是多维度且相互连接的。人们通常将文化细分为不同的组成部分，以独立地审视每一个部分。学者们常常把文化与冰山、洋葱、水里的鱼以及电脑中央处理器（CPU）等联系起来，这些比喻有助于学习者理解文化的概念。

1.1　学习目标

在学习本单元后，你将能够：
- 通过文化符号或模型理解文化；
- 描述文化的特征；
- 区分文化身份形成的阶段；
- 分析万里长城所体现的中国文化特质，并向国际观众介绍相关场景。

1.2　学习情境

在学习本单元后，基于以下场景完成单元项目：

假设你是一家中国汽车公司的助理。你的公司希望与一家爱尔兰汽车进口公司合作，一位爱尔兰代表将到中国来进行谈判。为了展现我方的好客和诚意，办公室经理要求你陪同爱尔兰代表参观当地的文化景点。这位代表对中国文化非常感兴趣，你需要向他介绍这些景点并讲述它们所体现的中国文化。

2　文化比喻

2.1　文化冰山

文化就像一座冰山。文化冰山模型是一个常用的比喻。我们知道，冰山只有一小部分露出水面，而冰山的大部分是隐藏在水下的，是平常所看不见的。就文化而言，可见的方面包括服装、食物和建筑等。然而，表面之下不可见的部分包括更深层的文化元素，如规则、价值观和信仰，这些元素具有更强的影响力。

2.2　文化洋葱

文化也可以被比作一颗洋葱，因为它们都是多层的。文化包括象征、英雄、仪式和价值观等四种层面。象征是文化中最明显且最容易被注意到的方面。它们包括语言、服装和国旗等。这些象征代表着第一层，就像洋葱的外皮一样。第二层由英雄组成，他们因其品格而受到尊敬。在西方文化中，像克里斯托弗·哥伦布这样的人物因其勇敢而被纪念，而亚伯拉罕·林肯则因其对正义的承诺而受到尊敬。在中国文化中，孔子因其智慧而受到钦佩，岳飞因其忠诚而受到敬仰，袁隆平因其对农业和粮食安全的贡献而受到尊敬。第三层由仪式组成。这些是反映文化传统的重要社区活动。例如，中国的端午节和中秋节涉及特定的食物、装饰和活动，这些活动反映着文化价值和历史。洋葱的核心是价值观，这是文化的基础信仰和原则。在中国传统文化中，这包括宗教和哲学体系，如佛教、道教和儒家思想；关键美德如仁、义、礼、智、信深深植根于中国社会，并指导个人的行为和道德。

3　文化定义

世界各地的人们，在文化、宗教、意识形态和种族上都是不同的，几乎在每个方面都存在差异。因此，我们应该尽可能了解人们之间的这些差异，在地球村实现顺畅的交流。通过学习跨文化交际，你将做到这一点。跨文化交流研究受到了人类学家的深刻影响。1952 年，美国人类学家阿尔弗雷德·克鲁伯和克莱德·克拉克洪对大约 150 个关于文化的定义进行了分类并指出：一些人强调了文化作为一系列思维和信仰的模式，一些人则从行为的角度来看待文化，还有人专注于人类生活的非物质方面或社会的物质方面。荷兰社会心理学家吉尔特·霍夫斯泰德对不同国家的文化进行了开创性研究，他将文化定义为"区分一个群体或类别成员与其他人的集体心智编程"。文化是"心智的软件"。从社会心理学的角度来看，文化的定义植根于个体的心智中。

根据《牛津英语词典》，文化是"艺术和人类智力成就的其他表现形式的总称"，它包括音乐、艺术、展览、舞蹈等元素。当人们谈论毕加索和贝多芬时，谈论的其实是文化。当人们谈论品牌或商标时，这些也一样属于特定的文化。在这本书中，文化包括知识、经验、信仰、价值观、行动、态度、意义、角色、工艺品等，这些要素通过个体和集体的努力，由一群人在世代传承中所获得。

4　文化特性

4.1　文化是可以习得的

尽管存在差异，不同的民族文化仍然有一些基本的共同特征。文化是后天习得的，它是动态的、无处不在的、综合性的，并且具有适应性。在本单元中，我们详细探讨了文化的两个重要特征：文化是习得的，以及文化是动态变化的。文化并非与生俱来的，它是在一个相对较大的人群中共享的象征系统；群体成员进入这个系统的唯一方式是学习。我们从早期生活开始，在社会化的过程中有意识地和无意识地学习我们的文化。我们如何学习文化？除了从父母和熟人那里获得文化外，还有三个主要途径：谚语、故事和艺术。

4.2　文化是动态的

文化随着时间的推移而发生变化。有些文化更加开放并接受变化，有些文化则倾向于抵抗变化。文化变迁的四个主要因素分别为技术发明、灾难、文化接触和环境。

4.2.1　技术发明

历史上，技术发明对文化产生了深远的影响。以下是它们改变文化的一些方式：新通信方式的发明，如印刷术的出现使得书籍能够大量生产，导致文盲率下降和知识共享的增加。互联网和社交媒体的发展也彻底改变了人们交流和分享信息的方式。在娱乐领域，电视、收音机和电影放映机等发明改变了人们消费娱乐的方式。它们使人们能够在世界任何地方接触到各种各样的媒体。

在教育界，技术进步通过使教育更加易于获取和高效来改变教育方式。在线学习平台、数字化教科书和教育应用程序使人们能够按照自己的节奏在世界任何地方学习。

在商业世界中，电子商务得益于技术的发展而蓬勃发展。以旅游业为例，旅行者可以通过一个简单的应用程序预订任何国际酒店和火车票，他们所需要做的就是输入自己的身份证号码。技术通过使许多任务自动化并以此提高效率，改变了人们的工作方式，并创造了新的行业和就业机会。

4.2.2 灾难

包括人为灾难和自然灾害在内的灾难，可以以各种方式深刻影响文化，塑造信仰、价值观和实践。就文化传统和实践而言，灾难可能会中断或破坏文化传统和实践，引起它们的适应或替代。例如，2010 年海地地震后，许多传统乐器遗失或损坏，由此许多当地音乐家使用新材料和新技术来改编他们的音乐。

一些环境灾难可以突出环境保护和可持续性的重要性。例如，2011 年日本福岛核灾难后，人们重新关注可再生能源和减少对核能的依赖。同样，2017 年波多黎各的飓风提高了人们对气候变化及其对脆弱社区影响的认识。像黑死病这样的瘟疫在人口、心理和政治上也可能是极具破坏性的。

同时，灾难也可以激发创新和创造力，因为人们会开发新的技术、策略和解决方案来应对他们面临的挑战。这可能引发持久的文化变革，因为这些创新融入了日常生活。

4.2.3 文化接触

当今世界的特点之一是人们的接触次数不断增长，这促进了具有不同语言和文化背景的人们之间的交流。

文化接触是不同文化的个体或群体相互作用、交换思想并相互影响的过程。这可以通过贸易、旅行、迁移、征服、教育、媒体和互联网等各种方式发生。文化接触可以引起语言、宗教、习俗、价值观和社会结构的变化。当两种文化从它们的互动中受益时（如通过贸易或婚姻），一种互利共生的现象就会发生；当两种文化的元素融合在一起创造新文化时，就会发生文化的交互。

4.2.4 环境

环境可以以各种方式显著地影响和塑造文化。特定环境中可用的自然资源可以极大地影响那里发展的文化。例如，森林资源丰富的地区可能会发展出木工传统，而靠近海洋的地区可能会产生浓厚的渔业文化。

至于气候和天气模式，气候可以影响从服装、住房风格到农业实践和节日庆典的一切。例如，寒冷的气候可能促使人们使用皮草衣物和建造保温房屋，而炎热的气候可能促进户外活动和社交聚会。

总之，由于技术发明、灾难、文化接触和环境等因素，文化总是在变化之中的。有些变化可以也应当避免，有些则可以进一步发展。虽然这些变化中有些可能是困难和痛苦的，但它们也可以促进更强的韧性、适应能力和更快的成长。其他变化通过改变人们交流、消费娱乐、学习、接受医疗保健和工作的方式，对文化产生了重大影响。

5　文化是综合的、基于符号的

为了让文化能够从一个人传递给另一个人，从一代人传递给下一代人，需要创建一个符号系统，将这些文化理念翻译给其成员。这往往通过语言、艺术、宗教和货币等方式来实现。为了保持文化的运作，文化的各个方面必须是综合的。例如，语言必须能够描述文化中的所有功能，以便将想法和理念从一个人传递给另一个人。如果语言没有融入文化的结构中，混乱和功能失调将盛行，文化将遭遇失败。中国文化在符号方面非常丰富，这些符号经过数千年的发展，深深地植根于中国生活的各个方面。这些符号反映了中国人民的历史、传统、信仰和价值观。

＊本单元智慧职教线上课程：https：//zyk. icve. com. cn/courseDetailed？ id＝obbaaaqvo4doejfjffeicq&openCourse＝obbaaaqvw79e5opp1bwbg.

Unit 1　习题参考答案

Unit 2　Intercultural Business Communication

Ancient Chinese Wisdom

Explain the following quote and reflect on its contemporary relevance.

Oceans do not reject any water, so that they can become extremely large. Mountains do not reject any earth or stone, so that they can become extremely high. （海不辞水，故能成其大，山不辞土石，故能成其高。）

From *Guan Zi*（《管子》）

Learning Objectives

After learning this unit, you shall be able to:

- Recite the main definition of communication and intercultural communication.
- Understand the elements involved in the process of communication.
- Distinguish the forms of the intercultural communication.
- Apply intercultural business communication skills and strategies.
- Work out a group presentation on a newly developed items and deliver it to a global business partner.

Project Scenario

The unit project is based on the following scenario.

Suppose you work in a German company, which is focusing on three items of bread, coffee cooker, and beer. As a director of sales department, you will deliver a business presentation on your new product, a brand new item to your international partners. You will be aware of the methods to cope with the aspects of cross-culture communication such as channels, contexts, receiver, encoding, and noise. Besides, you are to guarantee the communication is effective in the process of your presentation. Make a list of essential elements you need to take into consideration.

Lead-in

Watch the video clip about miscommunication and answer the following questions.

- What cause the miscommunication in the video?
- How could you avoid such kind of miscommunication?

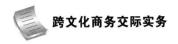

Part A　Communication

Communication is the process of conveying information, ideas, and feelings through a common system of symbols, signs, or behaviors. It can take many forms, such as spoken, written, visual, or non-verbal (e. g. gestures). To improve your communication skills, you can focus on developing your ability to articulate thoughts clearly, practicing active listening, being aware of non-verbal cues, and seeking feedback from others. Continuous learning and practice can make you a more effective communicator.

Sun Tzu Comments on Conflict

1. Definitions of Communication

Communication can be defined from various perspectives, each highlighting different aspects of the complex process of exchanging information, ideas, and emotions between individuals or groups. Here are some definitions of communication:

The definition of communication given in the *Webster's Dictionary* is "sending, giving, or exchanging information and ideas", which is often expressed verbally and non-verbally. Functionally the definition of communication can be described as "a sender who encodes a message using a certain medium (verbal, written, non-verbal), which is then transmitted through a channel to a receiver who decodes the message".

Interpersonal definition of communication refers to the interchange of thoughts, feelings, and ideas between and among people, which is central to the development and maintenance of interpersonal relationships.

Sociologist defines communication as "the process by which social entities (individuals, groups, organizations) create and share meaning through the exchange of information".

In the modern world, digital communication has become increasingly prevalent. This includes social media, instant messaging, video conferencing, and other forms of electronic communication.

2. Cultural Aspects of Communication

Culture plays a significant role in how people communicate. Different cultures have different norms around what is considered appropriate or respectful in communication. Good communication skills involve <u>clarity, brevity, relevance</u>, and timeliness. They also include <u>empathy,</u> active listening, and the ability to adapt your communication style to different situations and audiences.

Effective communication is vital in resolving conflicts. It involves understanding the <u>perspectives</u> of others, expressing one's own views clearly and <u>calmly</u>, and finding mutually acceptable solutions. Some barriers to communication shall be avoided. These can include language differences, cultural differences, personal biases, emotions, and physical barriers like noise <u>interference</u>.

3. The Context of Communication

The context of communication refers to the environment or circumstances that surround and influence the way individuals or groups communicate. Context plays a significant role in how messages are interpreted and understood. It includes both the immediate setting of the communication event and the broader social, cultural, and historical factors that shape the interaction. Below are some elements that constitute the context of communication:

<u>Physical context</u>: The physical environment where the communication is taking place can affect the way people interact. This includes factors such as noise level, spatial arrangements (proximity between participants), and even the layout of a room or the use of technology.

<u>Cultural context</u>: Cultural norms, values, beliefs, and customs greatly impact the way people communicate. They influence what topics are appropriate to discuss, how to address others, and the use of certain verbal and non-verbal behaviors.

<u>Social context</u>: The social roles and status of individuals involved in the communication process affect the way they communicate. For example, communication between a manager and an employee may be influenced by their respective roles within an organization.

<u>Emotional context</u>: The emotional state of the communicators — such as mood, attitude, or emotions like anger, happiness, or sadness — can color the interpretation of a message. Emotions can also influence the choice of words, tone, and non-verbal cues used during communication.

<u>Situational context</u>: The specific situation or event in which the communication is occurring can shape the message. For instance, a job interview is a different context than a casual conversation, leading to different styles and content of communication.

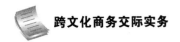

<u>Historical context</u>: Past experiences and interactions between communicators can influence current communication dynamics. Trust built over time or previous misunderstandings can color how messages are delivered and received.

<u>Relational context</u>: The nature of the relationship between the people communicating — whether it's personal or professional, close or distant — will affect the communication style and content.

<u>Temporal context</u>: The timing of the communication can be crucial. A message delivered at a time when the receiver is under stress or in a hurry might not be received in the same way as when delivered in a calmer moment.

<u>Political/Legal context</u>: When communication occurs within organizations, political dynamics and legal considerations can heavily influence what is said, how it is said, and what information is withheld.

Understanding the various layers of context in which communication takes place is essential for effective interaction. Miscommunication can often occur when one or more <u>aspects</u> of the context are <u>overlooked or misinterpreted</u>. Being aware of these contextual factors helps communicators to tailor their messages appropriately, enhancing the likelihood of successful communication.

Task 1: Understanding the Concepts

Choose the best answer from the four choices. Then check and discuss your answers with your group members.

1. What could be a potential barrier to effective communication?
   A. Using clear language
   B. Active listening
   C. Cultural differences
   D. Speaking loudly
2. Which of the following is an example of non-verbal communication?
   A. Written report
   B. Raised voice
   C. Body language
   D. The opening speech
3. What is the primary purpose of feedback in communication?
   A. To initiate a conversation
   B. To confirm that the message was received and understood
   C. To end a conversation
   D. To change the subject

---

4. Which of the following is a model that describes the process of communication?

    A. Maslow's Hierarchy of Needs   B. Shannon−Weaver Model

    C. Theory X and Y   D. SWOT Analysis

5. Understanding and recognizing the types of noise is important for both improving personal communication skills and designing effective communication systems in organizations. Which of the following belongs to Psychological Noise?

    A. sounds from construction work   B. room temperature

    C. confusion between similar−sounding   D. anxiety, stress

---

Task 2: Understanding the Concepts

Watch a TED speech given by Jane Goodall. Some people argue that we should respect the rights of indigenous people to preserve their traditional way of life. Others disagree, saying that we should introduce modernization to theses primitive culture. What do you think? Prepare a group presentation of three minutes to illustrate your ideas.

TED Lecture

Task 3: Preparing for the Unit Project

1. Applying the Concepts

How to deliver a message effectively by means of proper channels and medium?

2. Critical Thinking

Watch a program entitled *Jane Goodall and Her Chimps*. How do you understand what Jane said: "We are part of the animal kingdom, not separated from it. "

Part B   Intercultural Communication

In today's globalized world, intercultural communication has become increasingly important, as people from diverse cultural backgrounds interact more frequently in various settings, such as business, education, and social media. The ability to communicate effectively with people from different cultures can lead to better relationships, increased understanding, and greater success in both personal and professional contexts.

According to Milton J. Bennett, intercultural communication is "the ability to communicate effectively with individuals from different cultures". Edward T. Hall, who is considered one of the founding fathers of intercultural communication studies, defines intercultural communication as "the way people from different cultures interact with one another". The ICA (International Communication Association) defines intercultural communication as "the study of how people from different cultural backgrounds communicate with each other". Ting-Toomey, a prominent scholar in the field of intercultural communication and conflict management, defines intercultural communication as "the process of negotiating shared meanings between people from different cultural backgrounds".

These sources provide valuable insights and perspectives that can help individuals develop their own understanding and approach to intercultural communication.

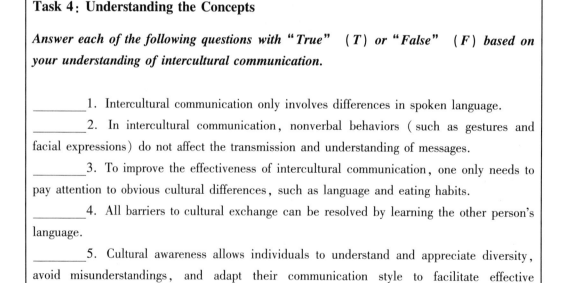

Task 4: Understanding the Concepts

Answer each of the following questions with "True" (T) or "False" (F) based on your understanding of intercultural communication.

_____1. Intercultural communication only involves differences in spoken language.

_____2. In intercultural communication, nonverbal behaviors (such as gestures and facial expressions) do not affect the transmission and understanding of messages.

_____3. To improve the effectiveness of intercultural communication, one only needs to pay attention to obvious cultural differences, such as language and eating habits.

_____4. All barriers to cultural exchange can be resolved by learning the other person's language.

_____5. Cultural awareness allows individuals to understand and appreciate diversity, avoid misunderstandings, and adapt their communication style to facilitate effective interaction.

Task 5: Understanding the Concepts

According to the cultural identity and differences, choose the most appropriate answer for each question.

1. Micheal is attending a ceremony in St. Petersburg, Russia. During the ceremony, the couple's parents give them crystal glasses and the couple break them in front of all the guests. How do you think of the couple's behavior?

A. They break the glasses to indicate the happy ending of the ceremony.

B. They want to arouse the guest's attention and are going to give a speech.

C. They are expressing their respect and gratitude to their parents.

D. They are showing that they are ready to embrace their new life.

2. Which of the following statements about the "OK" sign is NOT true?

A. In Japan, it means "money".

B. In France, it means "zero" or "nothing".

C. In the United States, it symbolize the best wish.

D. In Italy, it conveys that something is acceptable.

3. You are a Chinese employee working at a Sino – German joint venture company in Chengdu, Sichuan Province. Today, you are having an online meeting at ZOOM with your German colleagues. During the speech of a German colleague, it's difficult to catch up and understand his words due to poor network. What's your proper reaction towards such a situation?

A. try to inform him of the problem.

B. Keep listening carefully and take notes.

C. Interrupt his speech directly.

D. Mute him and prepare my speech carefully.

4. Suppose you are working for a Saudi Arabia branch in Guangzhou. Yesterday, you took part in a gathering where your male Saudi Arabia colleague had exchanged cheek kisses three times with another male Saudi Arabia colleague. What do you think about their behavior?

A. They are imitating Western social etiquette.

B. They are close friends.

C. They are a same-sex couple.

D. They are praying for each other.

Part C   Intercultural Business Communication

Intercultural business communication refers to the exchange of information and ideas between individuals or groups from different cultural backgrounds in a business setting. It involves understanding and adapting to different communication styles, customs, traditions, and values to effectively convey messages and achieve <u>mutual</u> understanding.

In today's <u>globalized</u> world, intercultural business communication has become increasingly important as businesses interact with customers, suppliers, and partners from <u>diverse</u> cultural backgrounds. Effective intercultural communication can help build trust, <u>foster</u> relationships, and <u>facilitate</u> successful business transactions.

Having a good command of the language used in business interactions is essential for effective communication. This may involve learning a new language or improving existing language skills. Understanding and adapting to different <u>nonverbal cues</u>, such as body language, facial expressions, and gestures, can help convey the right message and avoid misunderstandings. Being aware of and sensitive to the cultural <u>norms</u>, values, and customs of the people you are communicating with can help you avoid cultural misunderstandings and build <u>rapport</u>.

Being able to adapt your communication style to suit the cultural context and preferences of your audience can help you connect better and achieve your objectives. Active listening and showing interest in the perspectives of others can help build trust and understanding in intercultural business interactions.

Understanding the cultural factors that influence negotiation and conflict resolution can help you find common ground and reach mutually beneficial agreements.
By mastering these skills and adopting a culturally sensitive approach, individuals and organizations can improve their ability to communicate effectively in an intercultural business context and achieve greater success in the global marketplace.

In today's global business world, we are supposed to learn how to achieve effective intercultural business communication with the following skills.

Communication Styles

Intercultural business communication skills are essential for success in today's globalized business environment. These skills involve the abilities to understand and navigate cultural differences, communicate effectively across cultures, and build trust and relationships with people from diverse backgrounds.

1. To Have a Global Mindset

A global mindset involves being open to new experiences, ideas, and ways of thinking. It involves being curious, adaptable, and willing to learn from diverse cultures and perspectives.

2. To be Cultural Aware

Understanding the cultural norms, values, beliefs, and customs of different countries and regions is crucial for effective intercultural communication. This includes knowledge of language, etiquette, social practices, and business protocols.

3. To Conduct Active Listening

Listening attentively and showing interest in what others are saying is crucial for effective communication. This involves not only hearing the words but also understanding the underlying meaning, tone, and context.

4. To be Cultural Empathy

Cultural empathy involves understanding the cultural context of a situation and being able to put yourself in someone else's shoes to see things from their perspective. This helps build trust, foster collaboration, and improve communication.

5. Learn to Acquire Conflict Resolution Skills

Effective conflict resolution skills are crucial for managing disagreements and misunderstandings that may arise in cross-cultural interactions. This involves being able to negotiate, compromise, and find common ground while respecting cultural differences.

Task 6: Understanding the Concepts

1. *Have you ever wondered why you see the world the way you do? Well, Carol Dweck did. In the early 1970s, this American psychologist began to question the whys and hows behind the way people think and react in certain situations. With her research, she coined the terms fixed and growth mindsets and concluded that a person's motivation stems from personal beliefs. So, how motivated are you?*
2. *Tell us which statements you agree and disagree with, and we'll tell you if you have a fixed or growth mindset.*

(1) People can't and won't change.
(2) I'm either good at something or not.
(3) I can learn anything I want to learn.
(4) If a job sounds challenging, I'll sign up for it right away.
(5) Intelligence is something you're born with, and you can't change that.
(6) I fear failure.
(7) The best athletes and artists were born talented.
(8) The harder you work at something, the better you'll be at it.

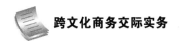
（9）I don't like trying new things. It's stressful.

（10）Smart people don't need to try hard.

（11）I like getting feedback about my performance, whether good or bad.

（12）I can't change who I am, no matter how hard I try.

Task 7: Furthering Your Understanding

Effective intercultural business communication is very important in business. Whether you're trying to communicate something to peers/employees or you're trying to create a successful marketing or informational campaign, you want to do it well. Taking time to measure those communications can help you establish what's working and what you need to reconsider.

After your reading the following passage, exchange your ideas with your classmates.

Things you should know:
Effective communication is about expressing your feelings clearly and concisely while listening to another person's body language and perspectives. Someone with strong communication skills can build positive <u>rapport</u>, strengthen their relationships, and resolve conflicts.

To better your communication in a work or academic setting, organize your thoughts beforehand, keep your audience in mind, and listen attentively to differing ideas.

Improve your communication in personal relationships by using "I" statements to express your feelings and ask questions to show you're listening. Effective communication is the process of expressing your thoughts, opinions, and ideas while listening to the input of others.

Part D   How to Communicate Effectively in the Workplace?

If you are going to prepare for a presentation or talk in the workplace, and to deliver it effectively, your audience will listen and they are likely to remember the points you wish to make. In this part we will show you the basics of preparing a good spoken report or presentation, concentrating on the importance of preparation and conciseness.

Many people are more or less terrified when asked to present a spoken report and some shall try almost anything to avoid it. However, if you want to succeed you should be pleased of each opportunity to present your idea, as you will learn on every fresh occasion. You should aim to enjoy as much practice as possible.

Nearly all excellent speakers tend to stick to simple presentations and to make their points in a short and simple manner. You are supposed to watch them and learn, then give your own presentations.

We are going to start with five elements that you need to follow in your presentations. Read the notes and finish the tasks which follow them.

Intercultural competence involves <u>five</u> elements:
- Attitudes: curiosity and openness, readiness to suspend disbelief about other cultures and beliefs about one's own.
- Knowledge: of social groups and their products and practices in one's own and in one's interlocutor's country, and of the general processes of societal and individual interaction.
- Skills of interpreting and relating: ability to interpret a document or event from another culture, to explain it and relate it to documents from one's own.
- Skills of discovery and interaction: ability to acquire new knowledge of a culture and cultural practices and the ability to operate knowledge, attitudes, and skills under the constraints of real-time communication and interaction.
- Critical cultural awareness /political education: an ability to evaluate critically and on the basis of explicit criteria perspectives, practices and products in one's own and other cultures and countries.

1. It is Essential to Organize Your Thoughts Before Speaking

Before you attempt to communicate ideas, organize your thoughts using key points. A good rule of thumb is to choose three main points to center your conversation around. That way, if you wind up on a <u>tangent</u>, you'll be able to return to one or more of your points without being <u>flustered</u>.

If possible, write your talking points down on your phone's Notes App or an index card for reference. This will help you stay on topic and be <u>crystal</u> clear about your intent. If you're giving a presentation, don't be afraid to use visual aids to get your point across. You can also highlight important keywords or ideas on a whiteboard or PowerPoint. Don't be afraid to use <u>acronyms</u> or phrases that will stick in people's minds. Confident, well-known speakers often reuse their key lines over and over for emphasis and <u>reinforcement.</u>

2. Keep Your Audience in Mind

If you're giving a presentation, consider the interests, commonalities, differences, and <u>anticipated</u> levels of knowledge on the topic you're speaking on. For instance, if you're lecturing a college-level Biology course, students should have a good grasp of <u>evolution</u> and cell theory.

It may help to put yourself in the audience's shoes. Ask yourself, "What kind of information would I want to walk away with?"

Similarly, if you're lecturing students, you may want to opt for visual aids like videos or memes to capture their attention. Use graphs or charts in professional environments when presenting new ideas to clients or stakeholders.

3. Minimize External Distractions to Maintain Focus

When you're having a serious conversation, the last thing you want is to be interrupted by a phone call. Turn your phone on do not disturb, and if you have a radio or television in your office, turn it off. If you're in a public space, like a restaurant, wait until your waiter has taken your order to limit any interruptions.

4. Be Clear and Concise When Speaking

Be clear about your goal so your message comes across in a way that every listener can understand. This requires using simpler words rather than more complex ones.
Similarly, be sure to enunciate clearly to avoid any kind of misunderstanding. You want to speak at a volume level that is guaranteed to be heard and doesn't come across as too quiet or disengaged.

It may be helpful to remember the 5 C's of communication, which include clarity, conciseness, consistency, connection, and confidence.

5. Adjust Your Tone of Voice to Capture Interest

Monotone voices may not always be pleasing to the ear, so good communicators use vocal color to enhance their message. Yale University recommends that you:
— Raise the pitch and volume of your voice when you transition from one topic or point to another;
— Increase your volume and slow the delivery whenever you raise a special point or are summing up;
— Speak briskly but pause to emphasize keywords when requesting action.

6. Maintain Eye Contact

Eye contact builds rapport, helps convince others you're trustworthy and shows interest. During a conversation or presentation, maintain eye contact for as long as it feels natural. Generally, you'll want to aim for 2 to 4 seconds at a time.

Remember to take in all of your audience. If you're addressing a boardroom, look each member in the eye. Neglecting any single person can easily be taken as a sign of offense.
If you're addressing an audience, pause and make eye contact with a member of the audience

for up to two seconds before breaking away and resuming your talk. This helps individuals feel personally valued.

Be aware that eye contact is culturally ordained. In some cultures, it is considered to be unsettling or inappropriate. Ask about this in particular or do research in advance.

7. Practice Active Listening Skills

Communication is a two-way street. By actively listening, you can gauge how much of your message is getting through your listener (s) and whether or not it's being received correctly or needs to be tweaked.

If your audience needs clarification, asking for feedback is often helpful. You can also ask the listener (s) to reflect back on what you said but in their own words. This can help you identify and correct mistaken views. If someone is struggling to understand a topic, be sure to validate people's feelings. This will encourage them to open up and feel better.

8. Pay Attention to Non-verbal Communication

Be conscious of what your hands are saying as you speak. Some hand gestures can effectively highlight your points (open gestures), while others can be distracting and may shut down the conversation (closed gestures). Generally, the most effective gestures are natural, slow, and emphatic. Similarly, be aware of if your eyes wander or if you're constantly sniffling, shuffling, or rocking. These small gestures add up and are all guaranteed to dampen the effectiveness of your message. It's also helpful to be aware of these signs in your audience. Common signs showing someone isn't listening to you include looking bored, yawning, fidgeting, and silence.

Strive to reflect passion and generate listener empathy using soft, gentle, aware facial expressions. Avoid negative facial expressions, such as frowns or raised eyebrows, as this may signal judgment.

9. Be Mindful When Communicating Online

Whether you're communicating through text, email, video, or audio calls, there's plenty of room for miscommunication online. After conducting a meeting, summarize any important details in a follow-up email. Don't forget to respond if you're receiving an email like this, even if it's an informal, "Okay, sounds good!" It lets the other person know you've read and received their message.

(*Wiki How, Effective Ways to Improve Your Communication Skills, Download Article Communicate Clearly and Listen Actively in Any Situation, Co-authored by Gale McCreary and Mason Martinez, BA*)

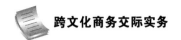

Task 8: Understanding the Concepts

You are asked to give a five-minute talk about potential challenges at a national conference of the regional sales managers of your company to be held in Guangzhou. You are informed to put the emphasis on the new ideas being used in each sales areas. The presentation should be given three weeks from now.

You are introduced by the panel leader and start your presentation.

Good afternoon, ladies and gentlemen. I am very pleased to be asked to explain to you how we in our company might be affected by recent changes in international trade. China's increasing presence in world trade indicates that more opportunities will be offered. Any success will take a lot of consistent work and some adjustments to the way we do things.

I don't have enough time to cover every point in detail but I have written a paper which will be given to you afterwards, so you could check it for further understanding. At the end of this presentation I shall be happy to try to answer questions.

Note how you have clarified what you will do. Now you move on to the main part of your speech.

One of the main benefits to our company of the removal of trade barriers is that it is now easier for us to take advantage of a wider world business environment. We could enter new markets with fewer restrictions and this is , obviously, very exciting.
. . .
However, we are facing challenges that we have never met.
. . .
How are we preparing for these new challenges, and how will our company make the most of the opportunities that are available in years to come?
. . .
We shall consider the regulatory and legal environment. We will talk about how we can improve the way we deal with foreign clients. We will look at new methods of improving quality control.
. . .
Now you have kept the main part of your presentation simple and clear.

Finally you will move to the concluding part of your talk and reinforce your messages.

In this short presentation I have only had time to give you a general introduction to the challenges and opportunities we will meet.

. . .

I am very happy to try to answer any questions that you might have.

Thank you so much.

Task 9: Furthering Your Understanding

Translate the following sentences into Chinese, then discuss the meaning with your partners.

1. Someone with strong communication skills can build positive rapport, strengthen their relationships, and resolve conflicts.

2. If you wind up on a tangent, you'll be able to return to one or more of your points without being flustered.

3. Confident, well-known speakers often reuse their key lines over and over for emphasis and reinforcement.

4. It may be helpful to remember the 5 C's of communication, which include clarity, conciseness, consistency, connection, and confidence.

5. During a conversation or presentation, maintain eye contact for as long as it feels natural. Generally, you'll want to aim for 2 to 4 seconds at a time.

6. Common signs showing someone isn't listening to you include looking bored, yawning, fidgeting, and silence.

Task 10: Telling China's Stories in English

1. Watch the video about the Silk Road and complete the following questions. And share with your classmates what you have learned from this story.

(1) What is the traditional transportation means crossing the desert?

    A. Monkeys   B. Horses   C. Camels   D. Cattle

(2) From the video how many bags can you see on the back of the donkey of Zhang Guolao?

    A. one   B. two   C. three   D. four

(3) What are the music instrument Not mentioned in the video?

    A. Piano   B. Five String   C. Dutar   D. Stattar

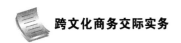

2. Translate the following story into Chinese. And share with your classmates what you have learned from this story.

During the Warring States Period, there was a carpenter named Lu Ban. He was good at making woody tools. One day, a young man passed by a red gate. He held up an axe with his hand and said, "This axe is really good. I can make the greatest tools in the world with it." Hearing this, people around here all laughed. One person asked, "So, can you make a more beautiful gate than this one?" "That's so easy! I was a student of Lu Ban before! Making a similar gate is like a piece of cake!" The young man said arrogantly. "But the gate was made by Lu Ban!" All people said.

Assessment

Read each of the following statements and choose the best answer.

1. Small vermicelli (螺蛳粉) is a local snack in Liuzhou, Guangxi province. Which of the following is NOT true?

    A. It is the intangible cultural heritage of Guangxi province, China.

    B. Its biggest feature is the unique spicy and smelly soup base.

    C. Its soup base must be made from snails.

    D. Its foul smell comes from sour bamboo shoots (酸笋).

2. In *The Chrysanthemum and the Sword* (《菊与刀》) written by Benedict, which is NOT the characteristic of Japanese?

    A. Loyalty to the emperor (天皇).

    B. Emphasis on the honor.

    C. Rigid hierarchy (等级森严).

    D. Free love and be faithful to the wife.

3. People in Nigeria will give others a thumb-up to express their feelings when there is a quarrel. What does thumb-up mean in this circumstance?

    A. Praise   B. Catch a ride   C. Insult   D. Agree

4. Beef Wellington is one of the most popular cuisine in Britain. Which of the following is NOT true?

    A. The major contents include filet steak (菲力牛排) and foie gras (鹅肝酱).

    B. It commemorates the great 1st Duke of Wellington.

    C. It originates in Wellington, the capital city of New Zealand.

    D. The beef is wrapped in pastry and then baked in the oven.

5. Xu Han is a Chinese college student. Today, her new foreign teacher from Ireland came to her class, but her classmates could hardly catch up with the lecture in English. What's your suggestions?

    A. Keep silent and talk to the teacher after class.

    B. Ask her classmates what the teacher has taught.

C. Try her best to listen and use eye contact to respond.

D. Turn on her phone and use the translation apps.

Unit Project

Review the Scenario of this unit and play the role of the Director of Sales Department to deliver a business presentation on your new product to your international partners. Be aware of the methods to cope with the aspects of cross-culture communication to guarantee the communication is effective in the process of your presentation. Complete your checking list of essential elements you have done. Take the following elements into consideration.

- Apply the skills of intercultural communication, such as contrastive analysis, cooperation skill, conflict management skill.
- Apply the presentation skills to ensure effective communication.
- Pay close attention to the different cultural aspects.

Case Analysis

Analyze the following case with the cultural models and theories learned in this unit.

Mr. Liang had traveled 17 hours all the way from Guangzhou to Boston. He was expecting a decent meal. His American friend, Richard, picked him up from the airport. But to his surprise, Richard only offered him a plate of roasted chicken and a glass of lemendade. Mr. Liang had been used to having a main course for dinner, and asked Richard if he had any rice. Richard said he only had fried noodles, and Mr. Liang had to make do with it. Though Mr. Liang knew that Americans didn't care very much about what they ate, he still felt surprised because he had taken Richard to the well-known Gardon Hotel in Guangzhou for a wonderful dinner last year when he visited Guangzhou.

Further Reading

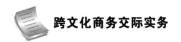

The Course in Intercultural Business Communication offers an opportunity to develop awareness of international business culture, and provides a critical understanding of the role of communication & society in defining that culture.

The course develops necessary skills for undertaking independent research and project management. It offers the knowledge of intercultural sensitivity and awareness of any different contexts. You will gain knowledge of various cultures and communication processes, and how they relate to one another in the world of business.

Communicate across cultures, enhance your skills in intercultural business and seize opportunities for placements within the industry. You will acquire the knowledge and skill sets needed to navigate the modern business industry. Study intercultural and communication theories through a range of taught modules, as well as extended work placement and research training.

Why study with us?
— This course raises awareness of theories of communication, culture, language and society and their applications in business interactions.

— The distinctiveness of the program lies in the focus of the course's three principal components: intercultural and communication theories applied to work – related context, engagement with industry practitioners and placements to increase career prospects.

— Our research – active teaching staff bring research of international standing into your classroom sessions and tutorials. More importantly, you'll have the opportunity to help to develop that research.

What you'll do?
This program offers both part – time and full – time routes in both theory and practice of Intercultural Business Communication, and research training.

— Have opportunities to engage with and work alongside industry specialists to further improve your intercultural business communication skills.

— Secure professional work placement within the industry, acquiring priceless experience within the field and improving your chances of a successful career after completion of the program.

Finally, You'll develop intercultural competence and communication skills by the end of this module and will be introduced to theories of intercultural communication skills through practical applications. Your awareness of cultural differences and their effects on work practice and business will increase.

单元小结

1 学习目标

学习了这个单元之后，你将能够：
- 掌握交际和跨文化沟通的主要定义；
- 理解参与交际过程中的元素；
- 区分跨文化沟通的形式；
- 应用跨文化商务沟通技巧和策略；
- 制定一个关于新开发项目的小组演示，并向全球商业伙伴进行展示。

2 学习情境

在完成这个单元后，根据以下情景完成该单元项目：

假设你在德国公司工作，该公司专营面包、咖啡机和啤酒三种产品。作为销售部门的主管，你将向国际合作伙伴介绍你公司的一个全新商品。你将了解应对跨文化沟通方面的方法，如渠道、上下文、接收者、编码和噪声。此外，你要确保在你的演讲过程中沟通是有效的。列出你需要考虑到的基本要素。

3 交际的定义

交际是通过共同的符号、标志或行为系统传递信息、想法和感受的过程。它可以采取多种形式，如口头、书面、视觉或非言语（例如手势）。要提高沟通技巧，你可以专注于培养清晰表达思想的能力，练习积极倾听，注意非言语线索，并从他人那里寻求反馈。持续学习和实践可以使你成为一个更有效的沟通者。

沟通可以从不同的角度进行定义。每个角度都强调了个体或团体之间交换信息、想法和情感这一复杂过程中的不同方面。以下是一些沟通的定义：

根据韦斯特词典的定义，沟通是"发送、给予或交换信息和想法"，通常通过口头和非口头方式表达。从功能上来说，沟通可以描述为"一个发送者使用某种媒介（口头的、书面的、非口头的）编码一条信息，然后通过一个渠道传输给接收者，接收者再对信息进行解码"。人际交往中的沟通定义涉及人与人之间思想和感受的相互交流，这是人际关系发展和维持的核心。

社会学家将沟通定义为"社会实体（个人、群体、组织）通过信息交换创建和分享意义的过程"。

在现代世界中，数字沟通变得越来越普遍。这包括社交媒体、即时消息、视频会议以及其他形式的电子沟通。

4 交际中的文化因素

文化在人们的交际方式中扮演着重要角色。

不同的文化对于交际中什么是得体的、恰当的或尊重的，有不同的规范。良好的沟通技巧包括清晰、简洁、相关性和及时性。它们还包括同理心、积极倾听，以及根据不同情境和听众调整沟通风格的能力。

有效沟通在解决冲突中至关重要。它涉及理解他人的观点，清晰而冷静地表达自己的观点，并找到双方都能接受的解决方案。应避免一些沟通障碍，这些可能包括语言差异、文化差异、个人偏见、情绪和物理障碍，如噪声干扰等。

交际的情境：交际背景指的是围绕并影响个人或群体沟通方式的环境或情境。背景在信息如何被解释和理解中起着重要作用。它包括沟通事件的即时环境以及塑造互动的更广泛的社会、文化和历史因素。以下是构成沟通背景的一些要素：

- 物理情境：沟通发生的物理情境可以影响人们的互动方式。这包括噪声水平、空间布局（参与者之间的接近度）以及房间布局或技术使用等因素。
- 文化情境：文化规范、价值观、信仰和习俗极大地影响人们的沟通方式。它们影响适合讨论的话题、如何称呼他人以及使用某些言语和非言语行为。
- 社会背景：参与沟通过程的个体的社会角色和地位影响他们的沟通方式。例如，经理和员工之间的沟通可能会受到他们各自在组织中的角色的影响。
- 情感背景：沟通者的情感状态——如情绪、态度或愤怒、快乐或悲伤等情绪——可以影响对信息的解读。情绪还可以影响沟通过程中使用的词汇、语气和非言语线索的选择。
- 历史背景：沟通者之间的过去经历和互动可以影响当前的沟通动态。随时间建立的信任或之前的误解可以影响信息的传递和接收方式。
- 关系背景：人们之间沟通的性质——无论是个人的还是专业的，亲密的还是疏远的——会影响沟通风格和内容。
- 时间背景：沟通的时机可能至关重要。在接收者处于压力之下或匆忙时发送的信息可能不会以同样的方式被接收。
- 政治/法律背景：当沟通在组织内发生时，政治动态和法律背景可能会严重影响所说的内容、说话的方式以及保留的信息。理解沟通发生的各个层面的背景对于有效互动至关重要。当一个或多个方面的背景被忽视或误解时，常常会发生误解。意识到这些情境因素有助于沟通者适当地调整他们的信息，增加成功沟通的可能性。

* 本单元智慧职教线上课程：https：//zyk. icve. com. cn/courseDetailed？ id = obbaaaqvo4doejfjffeicq&openCourse＝obbaaaqvw79e5opp1bwbg.

Unit 2 习题参考答案

Unit 3 Cultural Patterns

Ancient Chinese Wisdom

Explain the following quote and reflect on its contemporary relevance.

Isn't it a joy to have friends come from afar? （有朋自远方来，不亦乐乎?）

From *Analects* （《论语》）

Learning Objectives

After learning this unit, you shall be able to:

- Summarize and contrast the distinguishing features of high-context and low-context cultures.
- Explain the five core value orientations and assess their application across diverse cultures.
- Assess various cultures using the four cultural dimensions framework.
- Examine the corporate culture of a Chinese company and a foreign company, noting what's similar and different.

Project Scenario

After learning this unit, finish the unit project on the basis of the following scenario.

Imagine you're a graduate from a vocational college. You've been invited to participate in a job interview at a multinational corporation, either based in China or in the Western world. This corporation specializes in producing cutting-edge technology such as smart home devices, wearable technology, and virtual reality gadgets. During the interview, the HR manager asks for your insights into the corporate culture of the company.

Lead-in

Watch the movie clips from The Farewell and answer the following questions.

- How does this scene from *The Farewell* illustrate the differences between high-context and low-context cultures?
- How does the family's decision to hide Nai Nai's diagnosis in *The Farewell* reflect collectivist values?

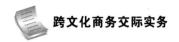

Part A   Culture and Context

Cultures can be analyzed through various lenses, with scholars of intercultural communication often exploring methods to differentiate between them. Edward T. Hall, an American anthropologist credited as a pioneer in this field, introduced the concepts of "high-context culture" and "low-context culture".

Hall's definition of "context" revolves around the information surrounding an event, deeply intertwined with its significance. For instance, a cocktail party serves as a business context where professionals engage in social interactions, while a meeting room represents a context where business negotiations unfold, typically with a more serious tone. People adapt their behavior based on these differing situations, collectively forming what we refer to as context.

In categorizing cultures, Hall proposed the distinction between high-context and low-context cultures. He observed that while most cultures exhibit elements of both, they can generally be positioned along a continuum reflecting their predominance in either high or low contextual communication tendencies.

In terms of higher-context cultures, examples include Japanese, Chinese, South Korean, African American, Native American, Arab, Greek, Latin American, Italian, English, French cultures, etc. These cultures tend to place greater emphasis on implicit communication cues and shared understanding within their social contexts. Conversely, lower-context cultures are characterized by a more explicit communication style. Examples of lower-context cultures include those typically found in English-speaking countries such as English, White American, Scandinavian, and German cultures, where communication tends to rely more heavily on direct verbal expression and less on contextual cues.

1. High-Context Cultures

High-context cultures are characterized by a predominant reliance on the physical context or internalized understanding among participants, where minimal information is conveyed through explicit verbal messages. These cultures depend heavily on shared experiences, information networks, and traditions that provide a stable cultural framework over time. This stability and shared understanding mean that routine interactions often do not require extensive background information because the cultural norms are well-established and widely understood, shaping responses to various situations seamlessly.

In high – context cultures, non – verbal cues, such as gestures, spatial arrangements, and silence, convey significant amounts of information. This mode of communication is efficient within these cultures because individuals are typically adept at interpreting these cues, understanding the underlying context effortlessly. The reliance on non – verbal communication often extends to a heightened awareness of the surrounding environment, which plays a crucial role in the transmission of meaning.

A quintessential example of high–context culture is the traditional Chinese banquet. This event is significant and laden with meaning that transcends mere verbal exchanges. The harmony between hosts and guests is established and maintained through the subtleties embedded in the context. The choice of dishes, the seating arrangement, and the sequence in which food is served are all rich with cultural significance. For instance, specific dishes may be chosen for their symbolic meanings, reflecting good fortune, prosperity, or longevity. The seating arrangement often respects social hierarchy and relationship dynamics, while the order of serving food can denote respect and honor.

Common characteristics of high–context cultures include:

• Heightened awareness of surroundings and environment:
Individuals in high – context cultures are particularly attuned to their surroundings. They pay close attention to environmental cues and use these to inform their understanding and behavior. This sensitivity helps them interpret non – verbal signals accurately and respond appropriately without the need for explicit verbal communication.

• Verbal communication as secondary:
In these cultures, verbal communication is not the primary source of information. Instead, much of the communication occurs through non – verbal means, such as body language, eye contact, and tone of voice. The context in which a message is delivered often holds more weight than the words themselves. This contrasts sharply with low – context cultures, where verbal communication is explicit, detailed, and central to information exchange.

• Effortless grasp of context:
Both the sender and receiver in high–context cultures typically grasp the context of messages effortlessly. This shared understanding stems from a collective cultural background and similar life experiences that reduce the need for detailed explanations. As a result, communication can be more fluid and intuitive, relying on implicit knowledge and mutual understanding.

• Emphasis on interpersonal relationships:

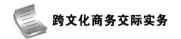

Building and maintaining interpersonal relationships is paramount in high－context cultures. Relationships are often long－term and deeply rooted in mutual trust and loyalty. The communication style reflects this focus, as interactions are more personal and indirect, emphasizing harmony and group cohesion over individual expression.

High－context cultures, such as those found in Native American, Chinese, and Japanese societies, have evolved intricate ways of communicating that reflect their historical and social contexts. For example, in Japan, silence can be as expressive as words, often used to convey respect, contemplation, or disagreement without confrontation. Similarly, in Native American cultures, storytelling and symbolism play vital roles in passing down knowledge and values, with much of the meaning understood through shared cultural narratives.

In these environments, non－verbal communication not only conveys information but also reinforces social bonds and cultural continuity. The ability to interpret non－verbal cues and the subtleties of the environment becomes a crucial skill, expected of all members of the culture. As such, high－context cultures foster a unique communication dynamic that prioritizes context, relationship, and mutual understanding over explicit verbal exchanges.

Task 1: Deepening Understanding

View a video clip showcasing the traditional Chinese banquet and identify its key components.

---

2. Low-Context Cultures

Low－context cultures are characterized by a communication style in which the majority of information is conveyed explicitly through verbal messages. This means that individuals within these cultures tend to communicate in a straightforward and direct manner, relying heavily on spoken or written words to convey their ideas and intentions. Contextual cues, shared understandings, and non－verbal signals play a minimal role in the communication process. This is in stark contrast to high－context cultures, where much of the communication relies on implicit understanding and context.

In low－context cultures, there tends to be less homogeneity among the population, which necessitates the need for detailed background information in each interaction. This diversity means that there is not a large pool of shared experiences or common knowledge to draw upon, so communicators must be explicit to ensure understanding. The necessity for clarity and precision in communication is paramount because assumptions based on shared context cannot be relied upon.

Typical examples of low–context cultures, as identified by anthropologist Edward T. Hall, include German, Scandinavian, and White American cultures. In these cultures, individuals expect messages to be precise, clear, and unambiguous. Ambiguity and vagueness are generally uncomfortable for them, and they prefer to have explicit rules and detailed information. Consequently, individuals in low–context cultures are likely to ask direct and probing questions when they feel that clarity is lacking.

Some common characteristics of low–context cultures are showed as follows.

- Primary communication through language:

In low–context cultures, the primary mode of communication is through language. This means that the spoken or written word is the main vehicle for conveying messages, and there is less reliance on non–verbal cues or contextual hints.

- Explicit articulation of rules and meanings:

In these cultures, rules, norms, and expectations are typically articulated clearly through verbal expression. This explicit articulation helps to reduce misunderstandings and ensures that everyone is on the same page.

- Verbal messages carry the bulk of information:

Since there is limited reliance on contextual or non–verbal cues, the bulk of the information in a message is contained within the words themselves. This contrasts sharply with high–context cultures, where much of the information is embedded in the context surrounding the communication.

Hall noted that individuals from high–context cultures might become impatient or irritated with the detailed information–seeking behavior of those from low–context cultures. High–context communicators often view the reliance on verbal messages as less credible and may place more value on silence or non–verbal communication as a means of conveying meaning. This can lead to misunderstandings if the differences in communication styles are not recognized and accommodated.

A notable example of these differences is observed between Chinese and American communication styles. In Chinese culture, communication often involves implicit meanings that are conveyed through body language, pauses, and the nature of relationships. Silence can be a powerful communicative tool, and messages are often indirect, requiring interpretation based on the context. In contrast, Americans typically emphasize direct and articulate verbal expression. They value clarity and explicitness in communication and are likely to spell out their thoughts and intentions clearly.

Understanding these differences is crucial for effective intercultural interactions. When individuals from low-context cultures interact with those from high-context cultures, they need to be aware that their preference for explicit communication might be seen as overly blunt or even rude. Conversely, individuals from high-context cultures need to recognize that their more implicit communication style might be confusing or frustrating to those who expect clear and direct messages.

By acknowledging and accommodating these cultural communication preferences, individuals can bridge the gap between different communication styles and foster more effective and harmonious intercultural interactions. Recognizing the value in both approaches and striving for a balanced communication strategy can enhance mutual understanding and cooperation in a diverse and interconnected world.

Differences in Business Practices

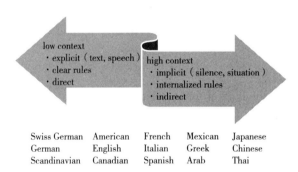

Swiss German	American	French	Mexican	Japanese
German	English	Italian	Greek	Chinese
Scandinavian	Canadian	Spanish	Arab	Thai

Task 2: Understanding the Concepts

According to the features of high – context and low – context cultures, Classify the following words and phrases.

A. Common experiences　　B. German culture　　C. Direct　　　　D. Chinese culture

E. White American culture　F. Detailed　　　　G. Silence　　　H. Japanese culture

I. Ambiguity　　　　　　J. Homogeneous　　K. Non-verbal　L. Explicit

M. Gestures　　　　　　　N. Scandinavian culture　O. Verbal　　　P. Implicit

High-context cultures: _____

Low-context cultures: _____

Task 3: Preparing for the Unit Project

1. **Applying the Concepts**

Select a Chinese multinational company that manufactures advanced technology products and a Western counterpart. Conduct online research to find advertisements from both companies. Use the concepts of high-context and low-context cultures introduced earlier to analyze the contextual elements reflected in these advertisements.

2. **Critical Thinking**

Work in pairs. Provide examples to illustrate that Chinese culture is a high-context culture. Discuss how these cultural characteristics are reflected in communication styles, social interactions, and advertising strategies.

Part B   Value Orientations

Value orientations indeed play a crucial role in shaping cultural frameworks and influencing human behavior and cognition. Clyde Kluckhohn and Fred Strodtbeck, renowned anthropologists, developed a framework to understand cultural values and differences by identifying five fundamental problems that all cultures must address. Their Value Orientation Theory posits that these universal problems are tackled differently across cultures, leading to diverse value systems. The five fundamental problems are showed as follows.

- Human nature orientation:
— What is the nature of people?
— Are they inherently good, evil, or a mixture of both?

- Man-nature orientation:
— What is the relationship between humans and the environment?
— Should humans dominate nature, live in harmony with it, or be subjugated to it?

- Time orientation:
— What is the temporal focus of a society?
— Do they emphasize the past, present, or future?

- Activity orientation:
— What is the modality of human activity?

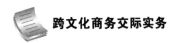

— Are people oriented towards being (living in the moment), doing (taking action and achieving), or becoming (developing and changing)?

- Relationship orientation:
— What is the mode of human relationships?
— Is the primary concern individualistic, collateral (emphasizing group harmony), or lineal (emphasizing hierarchical structure)?

1. Human Nature Orientation

This orientation considers the inherent nature of humans. It explores whether people are fundamentally good, evil, or a mix of both.

Human Nature as Essentially Evil but Perfectible
Rooted in traditional Western beliefs, this perspective acknowledges the inherent darkness within humanity but holds onto the potential for redemption through virtuous actions.

Human Nature as a Balance of Good and Evil
Reflecting the influence of humanism, some cultures recognize the coexistence of positive and negative traits within individuals, advocating for vigilance against corruption and wrongdoing.

Human Nature as Essentially Good yet Susceptible to Corruption
Drawing from philosophical and cultural traditions like Confucianism, this view holds that humanity possesses innate goodness, though it can be tarnished by external influences like greed or power. Role models and moral exemplars play a crucial role in upholding ethical standards and guiding societal behavior.

By exploring these value orientations, we gain deeper insights into the diverse perspectives and priorities that shape cultures worldwide.

Task 4: Enhancing Understanding

Watch a video clip from the movie The Dark Knight that explores the theme of human nature and discuss with your partner the potential influences on human nature depicted in the film.

---

2. Man Nature Orientation

This orientation concerns the relationship between humans and the natural world. It addresses whether humans are seen as subjugated to nature, in harmony with nature, or as having mastery over nature.

Mastery-over-Nature Orientation

In contemporary societies driven by technology and industry, the mastery – over – nature orientation is prominent. This perspective advocates for the relentless pursuit of control over natural forces, viewing them as resources to be harnessed or conquered by human ingenuity. Examples include genetic modification of crops and geoengineering projects aimed at altering climate patterns.

Harmony-with-Nature Orientation

The harmony – with – nature orientation emphasizes a seamless integration between human existence and the natural world. This perspective finds resonance in cultures like the indigenous peoples of Australia, who regard themselves as custodians rather than dominators of the land. Practices such as sustainable agriculture and eco-spirituality reflect this deep reverence for the interconnectedness of all living beings.

Subjugation-to-Nature Orientation

In cultures where reverence for the natural world borders on worship, the subjugation-to-nature orientation prevails. Here, humans acknowledge their vulnerability in the face of nature's immense power and choose to submit to its whims. This can be observed in the beliefs of certain Amazonian tribes who attribute divine qualities to natural phenomena, yielding to the will of the rainforest and its inhabitants.

3. Time Orientation

This orientation looks at a culture's focus on time. Cultures may prioritize the past, present, or future, affecting how they value tradition, immediate experiences, or future planning and innovation.

Past Orientation

Cultures rooted in tradition and ancestral veneration exhibit a past orientation, cherishing the wisdom of bygone eras and maintaining continuity with their heritage. This reverence for the past is evident in rituals performed by the Maori of New Zealand, who honor their ancestors through elaborate ceremonies and oral storytelling traditions, preserving the collective memory of their people.

Present Orientation

In societies where immediacy reigns supreme, a present orientation dominates, prioritizing the experiences of the here and now over historical legacies or future possibilities. The "Carpe Diem" ethos embraced by certain Mediterranean cultures epitomizes this perspective, urging individuals to seize the moment and revel in the pleasures of the present without dwelling on the past or worrying about the future.

Future Orientation

Where progress and innovation are celebrated, a future orientation prevails, envisioning tomorrow as a realm of limitless potential and advancement. This forward-looking mindset characterizes the ethos of Silicon Valley, where technological optimism fuels aspirations of creating a brighter, more technologically-advanced future. As epitomized by visionary leaders like Elon Musk, the mantra "The best is yet to come" encapsulates this relentless pursuit of innovation and improvement.

Task 5: Translation and Discussion

Rephrase the following Chinese expressions into English. Discuss within groups of four and analyze the value orientations conveyed by these sayings.

(1) 人定胜天   (2) 物以类聚，人以群分

(3) 前人种树，后人乘凉   (4) 活在当下

(5) 未雨绸缪   (6) 畏天命，敬天时

(7) 与天地合其德，与日月合其明   (8) 温故知新

---

4. Activity Orientation

This orientation refers to the preferred mode of human activity. Cultures may value being (emphasizing the inherent value of being), doing (emphasizing achievement and action), or being-in-becoming (emphasizing continual development and growth).

Doing Orientation

In cultures with a doing orientation, emphasis is placed on activities with measurable outcomes. Questions like "What did he achieve?" and "What has she completed?" are common. For instance, in a doing-oriented culture, sitting at a desk lost in thought might be seen as unproductive because the results of thinking are not externally visible. Such cultures advocate for taking action and stepping outside of comfort zones. This orientation prioritizes efficiency and tangible accomplishments. An example of a doing-oriented culture is the United States, where business success and personal achievements are highly valued.

Being Orientation

Being orientation contrasts sharply with doing orientation. Here, actions are valued for their intrinsic expression of one's identity. Social status and personal relationships are prioritized over measurable accomplishments. In these cultures, satisfaction comes from enjoying the present and valuing who one is rather than what one does. For example, in Italy, people may spend hours socializing over coffee, valuing the act of being together and conversing as a fundamental pleasure of life.

Being-in-Becoming Orientation

Being-in-becoming orientation is a middle ground between being and doing. It focuses on personal growth and self-development. In these cultures, individuals strive to evolve and improve continually. An example of this orientation can be seen in many Buddhist practices, where meditation and self-reflection are means to achieve higher levels of personal development and enlightenment.

5. Relationship Orientation

This aspect examines the way individuals relate to each other within a culture. It considers whether relationships are hierarchical, group-focused, or individualistic, influencing social structures and interactions.

Individual Orientation

This orientation emphasizes self-reliance and independence. In cultures with a strong individual orientation, personal goals and achievements are paramount. Individuals are seen as distinct and separate from the group. The United States is a prime example of an individual-oriented society, where personal success and self-sufficiency are highly valued.

Group Orientation

In contrast, group orientation prioritizes the goals and identity of the collective. Decisions are made through consensus, and individuals derive their social identity from group membership. Loyalty and interdependence are key values. A classic example of this is found in Chinese culture, where family and community bonds are strong, and individuals often prioritize the needs of their group over their personal desires. Additionally, the concept of teamwork, prevalent in modern corporate environments, reflects group orientation by valuing collaborative efforts over individual achievements.

Hierarchy Orientation

Hierarchy orientation assigns individuals specific roles and responsibilities within a structured hierarchy. Each person's position dictates their privileges and duties. Traditional Indian caste systems exemplify this orientation, where social roles and interactions are heavily influenced by one's caste, establishing clear expectations and societal functions. Similarly, military organizations worldwide operate on a hierarchy orientation, where rank and chain of command are strictly adhered to.

Understanding these cultural orientations offers valuable insights into how basic values and attitudes manifest in work ethics and behavioral patterns. However, it's essential to remember that while these orientations provide a framework for understanding cultural differences, they cannot predict individual behaviors in all circumstances. Each person's actions are influenced by a

Value Orientation Summary

complex interplay of personal experiences, cultural background, and specific situations.

Task 6: Preparing for the Unit Project

1. Applying the Concepts

Time orientation and activity orientation significantly influence work values. Form a group of four, utilize these orientations, select four famous multinational companies and analyze their corporate culture. Share your observations and engage in group discussions.

2. Critical Thinking

In addition to the five orientations mentioned earlier, what other factors do you believe are essential for gaining a deeper understanding of a particular culture?

Part C   Cultural Dimensions

Cultural Dimensions

Cultural dimensions refer to the prevailing values, principles, beliefs, attitudes, and ethics collectively held by a specific cultural group.

Geert Hofstede, a renowned expert in intercultural communication, conducted extensive research involving people from numerous countries and regions throughout his career. With the collaboration of other scholars, he identified six key cultural dimensions: large versus small power distance, individualism versus collectivism, masculinity versus femininity, high versus low uncertainty avoidance, long-term orientation versus short-term orientation, as well as indulgence versus restraint. Hofstede's groundbreaking study remains one of the most influential investigations into work-related values. Below, primary four of these dimensions are explored in detail.

1. Large versus Small Power Distance

Power distance is a concept from Geert Hofstede's cultural dimensions theory. It describes the extent to which less powerful members of a society accept and expect that power is distributed unequally. It reflects the degree of inequality that is considered normal and acceptable within a society or organization.

Large Power Distance

In cultures with a large power distance, there is a significant gap between those who hold power and those who do not. Authority and hierarchy are emphasized, and subordinates are often expected to follow orders without question.

Here are some key characteristics of large power distance cultures.

- Hierarchy and authority reign with a clear, well-defined structure within organizations and society. Leaders, managers, and elders command respect, rarely facing challenges to their decisions.
- Centralized decision-making dominates, where key decisions are primarily made by those at the top of the hierarchy, with minimal input from lower-level employees or subordinates.
- Formal communication is the norm, characterized by structured protocols between different hierarchy levels. Informal interactions between superiors and subordinates are infrequent.
- Respect for elders and superiors is deeply ingrained, starting from a young age and reflected in various social norms and behaviors.
- Limited social mobility is a common feature, where one's social status or class at birth significantly determines life opportunities.
- Acceptance of inequality prevails, with the belief that everyone has a predetermined place in society. Challenging this social order is uncommon.
- Subordinate dependence is pronounced, with subordinates relying on superiors for direction and approval. Lower-level initiative is often discouraged, as subordinates may fear taking responsibility for potential mistakes.

Small Power Distance

In contrast, cultures with a small power distance strive for equality and minimize hierarchical differences. Authority is more decentralized, and subordinates are encouraged to participate in decision-making processes.

Here are several defining traits of cultures with small power distance.

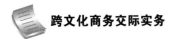

- <u>Equality and inclusiveness</u> are emphasized, with power distributed more evenly and efforts made to reduce hierarchical barriers.
- <u>Decentralized decision – making</u> is practiced, encouraging employees at all levels to contribute ideas and participate in discussions. Leadership tends to be more democratic and participatory.
- <u>Informal communication</u> is prevalent between different hierarchy levels. Superiors are approachable, fostering relaxed interactions.
- <u>Mutual respect</u> is based on individual qualities and achievements rather than formal position or age, promoting respect between superiors and subordinates.
- <u>Social mobility</u> is greater, allowing people more opportunities to improve their status through education, hard work, and achievements.
- <u>Challenge to authority</u> and questioning decisions are common and accepted. Subordinates are encouraged to voice opinions and contribute to decision–making.

Examples and Implications of Large and Small Power Distance

Malaysia, Guatemala, the Philippines, and Russia are examples of cultures with large power distance. These cultures have a more rigid hierarchy and greater acceptance of unequal power distribution. Denmark, Israel, New Zealand, and Austria are examples of cultures with small power distance. These cultures emphasize equality, participative decision – making, and minimize hierarchical differences.

Understanding power distance is crucial for effective cross – cultural communication and management. For instance, in business, managers in large power distance cultures may need to provide clear instructions and maintain a more authoritative presence, while those in small power distance cultures may focus on collaboration and empowering their teams. In education, teaching methods may vary, with more directive approaches in large power distance cultures and more interactive and participative approaches in small power distance cultures. In negotiations, recognizing the power distance dimension can help in understanding negotiation styles and preferences, ensuring more effective and respectful interactions. Recognizing and adapting to the power distance dimension can enhance intercultural understanding and improve interactions in diverse settings.

Task 7: Understanding the Concepts

Read each of the following questions and choose the best answer.

1. In large power distance cultures, authority figures are _____ and their decisions are rarely challenged.

    A. ignored   B. respected   C. questioned   D. undermined

2. Communication in large power distance cultures tends to be more _____ .
   A. formal　　B. informal　　C. casual　　　　D. structured
3. Small power distance cultures emphasize _____ and inclusiveness.
   A. hierarchy　B. equality　　C. centralization　D. formality
4. Social mobility is generally _____ in small power distance cultures.
   A. limited　　B. encouraged　C unchanged　　D. ignored
5. In small power distance cultures, subordinates are encouraged to _____ authority.
   A. challenge　B. respect　　C. ignore　　　　D. undermine

2. Individualism versus Collectivism

Individualism and collectivism are key cultural dimensions identified by Geert Hofstede that describe the relationship between the individual and the group within a culture. These dimensions affect various aspects of social behavior, communication, and organizational dynamics.

Individualism

Individualism emphasizes the importance of individual rights, independence, and personal achievements. In individualistic cultures, people are expected to look after themselves and their immediate family only.

Here are the key characteristics of individualism.

- Self-reliance is highly encouraged, with individuals being expected to be self-sufficient and independent. Personal achievements and initiatives hold significant value.
- Personal goals and individual rights are prioritized over group goals, with people focusing on their own aspirations and interests.
- Autonomy is emphasized, encouraging people to express their opinions and make their own decisions freely.
- Individual responsibility is paramount, with individuals being accountable for their actions and well-being. Success and failure are seen as results of personal effort.
- Direct communication is common, characterized by explicit and straightforward exchanges. People are expected to speak their minds and clearly articulate their needs and desires.
- Privacy is highly valued, with well-defined boundaries between personal and professional life.
- Competition is often encouraged, viewed as a means to achieve personal success and advancement.

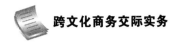

- Relationships are typically formed based on personal choice and mutual benefit, with a focus on the quality of personal connections rather than group affiliations.

Examples of Individualistic Cultures

The United States, Australia, and the United Kingdom share a strong emphasis on individualism, though each country exhibits this trait in unique ways. In the United States, there is a pronounced focus on personal freedom, self-reliance, and individual rights. Australia similarly values independence and personal achievement, along with a preference for direct communication. The United Kingdom, while also prioritizing individual rights, places significant importance on personal privacy and autonomy.

Collectivism

Collectivism emphasizes the importance of groups and collective interests over individual ones. In collectivist cultures, people are integrated into strong, cohesive in-groups, often including extended family and communities, which provide protection in exchange for loyalty.

Here are several defining traits of cultures with collectivism.

- Group reliance is a fundamental aspect, with individuals depending on their in-groups for support and security, prioritizing the group's welfare over individual ambitions.
- Collective goals take precedence, where the importance of group goals and harmony outweighs personal goals, emphasizing collective achievement and success.
- Interdependence is a key trait, as individuals perceive themselves as part of a larger group, with their identity closely tied to group membership, often involving the group in decision-making processes.
- Shared responsibility is evident, with responsibility distributed among the group. Success is credited to collective effort, and failure is also collectively borne.
- Indirect communication is common, characterized by a more indirect and context-sensitive approach. Maintaining harmony and avoiding confrontation are vital.
- Community and family hold significant importance, emphasizing strong community and family ties, along with loyalty. Personal relationships frequently extend into professional contexts.
- Cooperation is highly encouraged to sustain group harmony and cohesion, focusing on group success and mutual support.
- Relationships are typically long-term, grounded in mutual obligations and loyalty. Group membership often dictates social behavior and responsibilities.

Examples of Collectivist Cultures

China, Japan, and India share strong collectivist values with unique cultural nuances. China emphasizes family ties and collective responsibility, prioritizing group harmony. Similarly, Japan values loyalty, interdependence, and group harmony, focusing on collective well-being. In contrast, India stresses family bonds, community support, and collective decision-making, reflecting its own blend of social cohesion and familial interconnectedness.

Implications of Individualism and Collectivism

Understanding whether a culture leans towards individualism or collectivism significantly influences various aspects of interaction, including communication styles and management practices. In individualistic cultures, there is a preference for clear and direct communication, valuing personal expression and clarity. Decision-making tends to be autonomous, prioritizing individual initiative and efficiency. Motivation often revolves around personal achievements and recognition. Conflict resolution typically involves direct confrontation and problem-solving to address issues efficiently.

On the other hand, in collectivist cultures, communication is often more nuanced, emphasizing harmony and maintaining relationships. Decision-making leans towards consensus-building, involving group members to ensure unity and shared responsibility. Motivational strategies focus on team success and loyalty to the group, fostering a sense of collective achievement. Conflict resolution emphasizes mediation and indirect approaches to preserve group harmony and relationships. These cultural orientations shape how people interact, make decisions, and resolve conflicts within their societal frameworks.

Recognizing these cultural dimensions helps in fostering better interpersonal relationships and effective communication in multicultural environments. It also aids in creating more inclusive and culturally sensitive policies and practices in organizations and communities.

Task 8: Understanding the Concepts

Classify the following words or phrases as related to either Individualism or Collectivism based on their characteristics and implications as described in the text.

(1) Independence   (2) Group harmony   (3) Self-reliance   (4) Family ties

(5) Personal privacy   (6) Group reliance   (7) Personal goals   (8) Competition

(9) Mutual obligations   (10) Loyalty   (11) Freedom   (12) Autonomy

(13) Interdependence   (14) Cooperative behavior   (15) Personal achievements

(16) Shared responsibility (17) Direct communication (18) Indirect communication

---

Individualism：_____

Collectivism：_____

3. Masculinity versus Femininity

Masculinity and femininity are cultural dimensions identified by Geert Hofstede that describe the distribution of emotional roles between the genders and the value placed on traditionally male or female qualities within a society. These dimensions influence various aspects of social behavior, work environments, and cultural norms.

Masculinity

Masculinity in Hofstede's framework refers to cultures that value traditionally male qualities, such as competitiveness, assertiveness, ambition, and material success. In these cultures, there is a clear distinction between gender roles, and traditionally masculine traits are emphasized.

Here are the key characteristics of masculinity cultures.

• Achievement and success hold high value, with a strong emphasis on personal accomplishment, success, and winning. Individuals are driven by competition and the desire to excel.
• Assertiveness is encouraged, promoting behaviors that are strong, decisive, and dominant. Aggressiveness is seen as a positive trait.
• Materialism plays a significant role, where material success and the accumulation of wealth are important indicators of success and social status.
• Gender roles are distinctly maintained, with men expected to be ambitious and competitive, while women often focus on nurturing roles and caregiving.
• Performance orientation is prevalent, placing a strong focus on performance, productivity, and results. Success is frequently measured in quantitative terms.
• Work-centric attitudes are common, with work being a central aspect of life. Professional success and career advancement are often prioritized over leisure and personal life.
• Conflict resolution tends to be direct and open, with an emphasis on winning or achieving the best possible outcome.
• Toughness is highly valued, emphasizing the importance of resilience, overcoming

challenges, and demonstrating strength.

Examples of Masculine Cultures

Examples of masculine cultures include Japan, Germany, and the United States. Japan is highly masculine, with a strong emphasis on competition, achievement, and work ethic. Germany values assertiveness, efficiency, and a focus on performance. The United States emphasizes individual achievement, competitiveness, and the pursuit of material success.

Femininity

Femininity in Hofstede's framework refers to cultures that value traditionally female qualities, such as nurturing, cooperation, modesty, and quality of life. These cultures tend to blur gender roles, emphasizing equality and caring for others.

Here are several defining traits of cultures with feminine cultures.

- Quality of life is highly valued, emphasizing well-being and work-life balance. Success is often measured by the quality of social relationships and overall happiness.
- Cooperation is strongly encouraged, with a focus on consensus-building and collaboration. People work together harmoniously and support one another.
- Caring and nurturing are central, with a focus on caring for others, nurturing relationships, and maintaining social harmony. Empathy and compassion are highly valued.
- Gender role flexibility is evident, as gender roles are more fluid and overlapping. Both men and women share responsibilities in both professional and domestic spheres.
- Modesty and humility are encouraged, with boasting about personal achievements being discouraged in favor of showing respect and modesty.
- Interpersonal relationships are a priority, with a strong emphasis on building and maintaining strong social connections. Social support networks are important.
- Conflict resolution is often approached through compromise and negotiation, aiming to maintain harmony and avoid confrontation.
- Social equality is a key focus, with an emphasis on fairness and welfare for all members of society.

Examples of Feminine Cultures

Examples of feminine cultures can be found in countries like Sweden, Norway, and the Netherlands. Sweden is known for its strong emphasis on equality, cooperation, and quality of life, making it a highly feminine society. Norway similarly values social welfare, gender equality, and work-life balance. The Netherlands places a significant emphasis on modesty, egalitarianism, and social harmony.

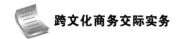

Implications of Masculinity and Femininity

Understanding whether a culture is more masculine or feminine can significantly impact various aspects of interaction, from workplace dynamics to social expectations

In work environments influenced by masculine cultures, competitiveness and performance drive workplace dynamics. Leadership often leans towards assertiveness and decisiveness, emphasizing achieving results. Gender roles tend to be more rigid, with distinct expectations for men and women. Conflict resolution may prioritize winning and optimal outcomes. Social policies often prioritize economic growth and competitiveness over social welfare.

Conversely, in workplaces shaped by feminine cultures, collaboration and employee well-being take center stage. Leaders are characterized by empathy, supportiveness, and a collaborative approach. Gender roles are more flexible and egalitarian, allowing for greater individual expression. Conflict management focuses on compromise and maintaining harmony. Social policies emphasize equality and comprehensive social welfare systems to support all citizens.

Recognizing these cultural dimensions helps in fostering better understanding and cooperation in multicultural settings. It also aids in creating more inclusive and effective policies and practices in organizations and communities.

Task 9: Understanding the Concepts

Decide whether the following statements are True (T) or False (F) based on the concepts of masculinity and femininity in Hofstede's cultural dimensions theory.

_____1. In masculine cultures, work-life balance and quality of life are prioritized over personal achievement and material success.

_____2. Masculine cultures tend to have clear and distinct gender roles, with men being more focused on ambition and competitiveness.

_____3. Feminine cultures value nurturing, cooperation, and quality of life over competitiveness and material success.

_____4. In feminine cultures, conflicts are typically resolved through open confrontation and a focus on winning.

_____5. Feminine cultures often emphasize social equality, modesty, and maintaining strong interpersonal relationships.

---

4. High versus Low Uncertainty Avoidance

Uncertainty avoidance is a concept from cultural dimensions theory, initially developed by Dutch social psychologist Geert Hofstede. It describes the extent to which members of a culture feel threatened by ambiguous or unknown situations and the degree to which they try to avoid these situations by adopting strict codes of behavior, rules, and regulations.

High Uncertainty Avoidance

Cultures with high uncertainty avoidance have a low tolerance for uncertainty and ambiguity. They tend to have strong beliefs in absolute truths and structured circumstances.

Here are some key characteristics of high uncertainty avoidance cultures.

- Strict rules and regulations are a hallmark of these cultures, which often implement detailed rules, regulations, and policies to minimize uncertainty. People in these cultures prefer formal structures and clear guidelines.
- Resistance to change is common, with a preference for stability and continuity. Change and innovation can be perceived as threats rather than opportunities.
- Risk aversion characterizes these cultures, where individuals tend to avoid taking risks. They prefer sticking with the known and familiar rather than venturing into the unknown.
- Emphasis on security is strong, with a focus on job security, long–term employment, and comprehensive social security systems.
- High stress and anxiety levels are prevalent due to the low tolerance for uncertainty. Individuals in these cultures often experience significant stress and anxiety, emphasizing the need to control the future.
- Traditional gender roles may be more pronounced, with clear distinctions between male and female responsibilities.
- Importance of planning is crucial, as detailed planning and forecasting are valued. People in these cultures often prefer predictable situations where outcomes can be anticipated.
- Education and expertise are highly regarded, with a strong emphasis on expertise, qualifications, and education as means to reduce uncertainty and gain control over life situations.

Low Uncertainty Avoidance

On the other hand, cultures with low uncertainty avoidance have a higher tolerance for ambiguity and uncertainty. They are more comfortable with taking risks and less dependent on strict rules and regulations.

Here are several defining traits of cultures with low uncertainty avoidance cultures.

- Flexibility and adaptability are notable traits, as these cultures are more open to change and innovation. People generally show a higher degree of adaptability and a willingness to try new things.
- Risk acceptance is prevalent, with individuals being more inclined to take risks and explore new opportunities. This environment fosters a greater entrepreneurial spirit.
- Tolerance for deviance is higher, leading to greater acceptance of diverse behaviors and ideas. People are more open to unconventional thinking and diversity.
- Lower stress and anxiety are common, as individuals have a higher tolerance for uncertainty. There is less pressure to control the future, resulting in reduced stress and anxiety levels.
- Fluid structures characterize organizational and societal arrangements, which are more flexible with fewer formal rules and regulations. People feel more at ease with informal setups.
- Focus on achievement is emphasized, where success and achievement often hold more value than security. Individuals are encouraged to strive for personal and professional growth.
- Innovation and creativity are highly valued, with a strong emphasis on thinking outside the box. People are encouraged to develop novel solutions and ideas.
- Pragmatic approach is common in problem−solving, as people are more likely to adjust their strategies based on the situation rather than sticking to predetermined plans.

Examples of High and Low Uncertainty Avoidance

High uncertainty avoidance cultures, such as Greece, Portugal, Japan, and France, emphasize stability, clear structures, and the avoidance of risk. These cultures focus on creating strict rules and regulations to manage uncertainty, show a strong preference for avoiding risk and maintaining job security, and often resist change. They value tradition, established norms, and long−term stability, and tend to have complex and detailed legal systems to manage uncertainties. Formal rituals, thorough decision−making processes, and adherence to established guidelines are common.

On the other hand, low uncertainty avoidance cultures, such as Denmark, Sweden, Singapore, and the United States, are more comfortable with ambiguity, change, and taking risks. These cultures embrace change and innovation, often showing a flexible approach to rules and regulations. They encourage entrepreneurship, risk−taking, and exploring new opportunities. Individuals in these cultures are open to new ideas, have a high tolerance for different viewpoints and lifestyles, and emphasize individuality, freedom of expression, and personal initiative.

Implications of High and Low Uncertainty Avoidance

High uncertainty avoidance cultures, such as many in East Asia, emphasize structured environments with detailed rules and procedures in business. Decision-making involves careful risk assessment and consulting with authority figures to minimize uncertainty. Negotiations often focus on consensus-building and addressing all contingencies, leading to longer processes. In education, these cultures favor structured curricula and teacher authority, while in negotiations, they prioritize trust-building and detailed agreements.

Conversely, low uncertainty avoidance cultures, like those in many Western countries, encourage risk – taking and innovation in business. They prioritize flexibility and adaptability, fostering efficiency in negotiations. In education, they promote critical thinking and student – centered learning, valuing questioning authority. Negotiations emphasize informality and exploring creative solutions, prioritizing rapport and mutual understanding over strict adherence to protocols. Understanding these differences is essential for effective cross-cultural communication and management.

Another Two Cultural Dimensions

Task 10: Understanding the Concepts

Fill in the blanks with appropriate words or phrases.

1. Cultures with high uncertainty avoidance have a low tolerance for uncertainty and ambiguity. They tend to have strong beliefs in absolute truths and _____.

2. Key characteristics of high uncertainty avoidance cultures include strict rules and regulations, resistance to change, risk aversion, emphasis on security, high stress and anxiety, traditional gender roles, importance of planning, and _____.

3. Examples of cultures with high uncertainty avoidance are Greece, Portugal, Japan, and _____.

4. In business, managers in high uncertainty avoidance cultures may need to provide clear instructions and maintain a more structured approach, while those in low uncertainty avoidance cultures may focus on fostering creativity and allowing _____.

Assessment

1. *Read each of the following questions and choose the best answer.*

(1) Which of the following is not characteristic of cultures with large power distance?

    A. Decentralized decision-making   B. Formal communication

    C. Emphasis on respecting elders   D. Limited social mobility

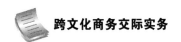

(2) In collectivist cultures, what is emphasized?

    A. Personal achievements   B. Group harmony

    C. Individual autonomy   D. Competition

(3) What are key characteristics of cultures with masculinity?

    A. Emphasis on nurturing relationships   B. High value on quality of life

    C. Competitive behavior   D. Modesty

(4) Which cultures tend to avoid risks and prefer stability?

    A. Low uncertainty avoidance cultures   B. High uncertainty avoidance cultures

    C. Collectivist cultures   D. Individualistic cultures

(5) What is emphasized in low uncertainty avoidance cultures?

    A. Flexible structures   B. Detailed rules and regulations

    C. Resistance to change   D. Formal communication

2. *Decide whether the following statement are true (T) or false (F).*

_____ (1) In large power distance cultures, communication between different levels of hierarchy is typically informal.

_____ (2) Individualistic cultures prioritize personal goals over group goals.

_____ (3) Masculine cultures value nurturing, cooperation, and quality of life.

_____ (4) High uncertainty avoidance cultures tend to have a lower tolerance for ambiguity and uncertainty.

_____ (5) Low uncertainty avoidance cultures are more comfortable with taking risks and exploring new opportunities.

Unit Project

Take another look at the unit's scenario and put yourself in the shoes of a recent graduate preparing for a job interview. Evaluate the corporate culture of a chosen Chinese or Western multinational corporation. Prepare and deliver an introduction for presentation in class. Your introduction should cover the following aspects.

- Analyze the cultural elements, whether high – context or low – context, portrayed in the company's advertisements.
- Assess the company's orientation towards time and activity as demonstrated in speeches or discussions by its leaders and employees.
- Examine the cultural dimensions evident in the company's events, reports, news coverage, and other available information.

Case Analysis

Analyze the following case with the cultural models and theories learned in this unit. Then answer the questions.

Navigating Cultural Differences in a Global Business Meeting

Characters

Alex: A manager from the United States (low-context culture)
Hiroshi: A manager from Japan (high-context culture)
Maria: A project coordinator from Brazil (high-context culture)
Emma: A marketing specialist from Germany (low-context culture)

Alex, Hiroshi, Maria, and Emma are part of an international team working on a new product launch. They are having a virtual meeting to discuss the project timeline, responsibilities, and potential challenges.

Alex: Hi everyone, thanks for joining the call. Let's get started with our agenda for today. First, we need to finalize the project timeline. I'd like to hear everyone's thoughts on our proposed schedule. Emma, could you go first?

Emma: Sure, Alex. Based on our initial plan, I think the timeline looks feasible. We have allocated enough time for market research and product development. However, we need to ensure that all departments stick to the deadlines.

Alex: Great, thanks. Hiroshi, what do you think about the timeline?

Hiroshi: (Pauses for a moment) Yes, I believe the timeline is acceptable. We should be mindful of potential delays, though.

Maria: I agree with Hiroshi. In Brazil, we often encounter unexpected challenges, so it's important to build in some flexibility.

Alex: Good points. We can add a buffer to account for any delays. Now, let's move on to responsibilities. I propose that Emma handles the market research, Hiroshi oversees the product development, Maria coordinates with our suppliers, and I'll manage the overall project. Any objections?

Hiroshi: (Nods) That works for me.

Maria: That sounds good, Alex.

Emma: Agreed.

Alex: Excellent. Lastly, let's discuss potential challenges. Emma, you mentioned earlier that sticking to deadlines might be an issue. Hiroshi, do you foresee any specific challenges in the product development phase?

Hiroshi: In Japan, we prioritize quality over speed. There might be instances where we need extra time to ensure the product meets our standards.

Maria: In Brazil, we might face delays due to supplier issues. It's common for things to take longer than expected here.

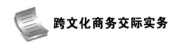
Alex： Understood. We need to communicate these potential delays to the entire team to manage expectations. Let's also schedule regular check-ins to monitor our progress and address any issues promptly. Does that work for everyone?

Emma： Yes, regular check-ins will help us stay on track.

Hiroshi： Agreed.

Maria： Sounds good to me.

Alex： Perfect. Thanks, everyone. Let's make this project a success!

Analysis Questions

Culture and context：

- How do the communication styles of Alex and Hiroshi differ based on their cultural contexts (low-context vs. high-context)?
- What are some potential misunderstandings that could arise from these differences?

Value orientations：

- Discuss how Hiroshi's and Maria's human-nature orientations influence their concerns about potential delays.
- How does Alex's time orientation reflect a typical low-context culture's approach to project management?

Cultural dimensions：

- Examine the power distance evident in the meeting. Does Alex's approach reflect a large or small power distance culture?
- Identify examples of individualism versus collectivism in the team's dynamics.
- Discuss how masculinity versus femininity might influence Hiroshi's focus on quality over speed.
- How does the team's approach to uncertainty avoidance vary, and what strategies do they use to handle it?

Further Reading

1. Understanding Chinese Cultural Patterns

China, with its rich history spanning millennia, embodies a complex tapestry of cultural patterns that shape its society and interactions both domestically and globally. To grasp the essence of Chinese culture is to delve into a world where tradition harmonizes with modernity, where hierarchy intertwines with egalitarianism, and where collectivism coexists with individual aspirations. This exploration will navigate through key aspects that define Chinese cultural identity, providing insights into its values, social structures, and worldview.

2. Historical Roots and Cultural Continuity

China's cultural identity is deeply rooted in its ancient civilization, which spans thousands of years. Key philosophies like Confucianism, Taoism, and Buddhism have profoundly shaped Chinese society, ethics, governance, and worldview.

Confucianism emphasizes hierarchical relationships, filial piety, respect for authority, and the cultivation of virtue. It has historically guided family structures, educational systems, and government administration. Confucian values continue to influence Chinese social norms, emphasizing the importance of family cohesion, loyalty to one's superiors, and the pursuit of moral excellence.

Taoism, with its focus on harmony with nature and the concept of "wu wei" (effortless action), has influenced Chinese attitudes towards life, spirituality, and governance. It encourages a balanced and harmonious approach to living, advocating simplicity, spontaneity, and non-interference.

Buddhism, introduced to China from India, emphasizes compassion, meditation, and the pursuit of enlightenment. It has left a profound imprint on Chinese culture through its temples, artwork, rituals, and moral teachings, fostering spiritual practices and ethical values among its adherents.

3. Social Harmony and Collectivism

Chinese culture places a strong emphasis on social harmony and collective well-being. Unlike Western individualism, which prioritizes personal goals and achievements, Chinese society values the collective good and harmony within relationships.

Familial relationships: Family is considered the cornerstone of Chinese society. Confucian teachings underscore the importance of filial piety (xiao), which involves respect for parents and ancestors, obedience to elders, and the maintenance of family honor. The family unit

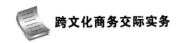

traditionally operates within a hierarchical structure, with elders holding authority and younger members expected to defer to their wisdom and decisions.

Community solidarity: Beyond the family, Chinese culture promotes collective responsibility and solidarity within communities. Concepts like "guanxi" (personal relationships) and "renqing" (favor) emphasize mutual obligations and reciprocity in interpersonal relationships. Building and maintaining harmonious relationships are crucial for social acceptance, career advancement, and personal well-being.

National Identity: Chinese collectivism extends to a strong sense of national identity and pride. Historical narratives, cultural symbols (such as the dragon and phoenix), and shared customs (like Lunar New Year celebrations) reinforce a sense of unity and continuity across diverse regional and ethnic backgrounds.

4. Cultural Symbols and Expressions

Language, art, and symbolism play significant roles in expressing and reinforcing Chinese cultural values, aesthetics, and worldview.

Language: The Chinese language, with its complex system of characters, regional dialects (such as Mandarin, Cantonese, and others), and tonal variations, reflects China's cultural diversity and historical continuity. Written Chinese characters convey rich layers of meaning, historical contexts, and philosophical concepts, shaping both everyday communication and artistic expression.

Art and calligraphy: Chinese art, encompassing painting, calligraphy, sculpture, and ceramics, embodies aesthetic beauty and philosophical depth. Traditional ink wash painting (水墨画) captures the essence of landscapes, nature, and human emotions through minimalist brushstrokes and symbolic imagery. Calligraphy, considered a high art form, not only serves as a means of communication but also as a vehicle for personal expression, moral cultivation, and cultural refinement.

Cultural festivals: Traditional Chinese festivals, such as the Spring Festival (Lunar New Year), Mid-Autumn Festival, Dragon Boat Festival, and others, are vibrant expressions of cultural heritage and community bonding. These festivals feature rituals, performances (like lion dances and dragon parades), culinary delights (like dumplings and mooncakes), and symbolic practices (such as setting off firecrackers to ward off evil spirits), celebrating auspicious occasions and ancestral reverence.

5. Modernization and Cultural Adaptation

China's rapid economic development and urbanization in recent decades have led to significant socio – cultural transformations, blending tradition with modernity and fostering cultural diversity.

Urbanization and lifestyle changes: Urbanization has reshaped social dynamics, lifestyles, and consumption patterns in Chinese cities. Modern urban dwellers often balance traditional values with contemporary aspirations, leading to a hybrid cultural identity. Consumerism, digital technologies, and global trends influence lifestyle choices, leisure activities, and social interactions among urban Chinese youth.

Generational shifts: The younger generations in China, often referred to as the "post–80s" and "post–90s" generations, embody a blend of traditional values and global perspectives. They navigate between familial expectations and personal ambitions, embracing digital connectivity, educational opportunities, and career mobility in a competitive global economy.

Cultural industries: China's cultural industries, including film, music, literature, fashion, and digital entertainment, have flourished amidst economic growth and technological advancement. Chinese cinema, for instance, has gained international recognition for its storytelling, cinematography, and exploration of contemporary social issues. The popularity of Chinese pop music (Mandopop and Cantopop), fashion designers, and digital platforms reflects cultural innovation and global influence.

6. Regional Diversity and Cultural Adaptations

China's vast geographical expanse and diverse ethnic populations contribute to regional variations in cuisine, dialects, customs, and cultural practices.

Culinary diversity: Chinese cuisine is celebrated for its regional diversity, flavors, and cooking techniques. Northern Chinese cuisine, characterized by wheat–based dishes like noodles and dumplings, contrasts with Southern Chinese cuisine, which features rice – based dishes, seafood, and Cantonese dim sum. Each region's cuisine reflects local ingredients, historical influences, and cultural preferences, offering a culinary journey through China's diverse landscapes.

Ethnic minority cultures: China is home to numerous ethnic minority groups, including the Uighurs, Tibetans, Mongols, and others, each with distinct languages, traditions, and religious beliefs. These ethnic communities contribute to China's cultural mosaic, enriching the nation's

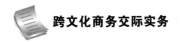

cultural tapestry through traditional crafts, music, dance, and spiritual practices.

Regional customs and festivals: Regional customs and festivals highlight cultural diversity and historical legacies across China. For instance, Tibetan Buddhist rituals during festivals like Losar (Tibetan New Year) emphasize spiritual renewal and community solidarity. These regional customs underscore China's multicultural heritage and adaptive resilience in a globalized world.

7. Global Influence and Soft Power

China's cultural influence extends globally through cultural diplomacy, media, arts, and educational initiatives, promoting international understanding and appreciation of Chinese cultural heritage.

Cultural diplomacy: The Chinese government supports cultural exchange programs, language education initiatives (like Confucius Institutes), and international collaborations in arts and humanities. These initiatives aim to enhance global awareness of Chinese history, language, arts, and philosophy, fostering cross-cultural dialogue and mutual understanding.

Global cultural impact: Chinese cinema, music, literature, and culinary traditions have gained popularity worldwide, contributing to China's soft power and cultural influence. Films by directors like Zhang Yimou and Ang Lee have won international acclaim for their storytelling prowess and visual aesthetics, bridging cultural gaps and promoting cross-cultural dialogue.

Digital media and cultural narratives: The rise of digital technologies and social media platforms has facilitated global access to Chinese cultural content, including digital entertainment, online literature (web novels), gaming, and social networking. Chinese digital platforms like TikTok (Douyin) showcase cultural creativity and youth trends, influencing global popular culture and digital consumption habits.

The cultural patterns of China reflect a dynamic interplay of tradition, adaptation, and resilience shaped by its historical roots, socio-economic transformations, and global interactions. Confucian values of hierarchy, filial piety, and harmony continue to influence social structures and familial relationships. Collectivism underpins Chinese societal norms, emphasizing community solidarity, national identity, and mutual obligations.

Language, art, and symbolism serve as expressions of Chinese cultural identity and collective memory, fostering cultural pride and continuity across diverse regional and ethnic landscapes. China's rapid modernization has brought about socio-cultural changes, blending tradition with innovation and embracing global influences in urban lifestyles, cultural industries, and digital connectivity.

Regional diversity within China enriches its cultural tapestry through culinary traditions, ethnic minority customs, and regional festivals, showcasing cultural heterogeneity and adaptive resilience. China's global influence through cultural diplomacy, media, and soft power initiatives promotes international awareness and appreciation of Chinese cultural heritage, contributing to cross-cultural understanding and global dialogue.

By understanding these nuanced cultural patterns, one gains deeper insights into China's complexities, societal values, and evolving identity in a globalized world, emphasizing continuity with the past and adaptability to future challenges and opportunities.

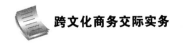

单元小结

1 学习目标

学习完本单元后，你将能够：

- 总结并对比高情境文化和低情境文化的区别特征；
- 解释五个核心价值取向，并评估它们在不同文化中的应用；
- 运用四种文化维度框架评估各种文化；
- 研究一家中国公司和一家外国公司的企业文化，指出它们的相似点和不同点。

2 学习情境

学习完本单元后，根据以下情景完成单元项目：

想象你是一名职业学院的毕业生。你受邀参加一家跨国公司的求职面试，该公司可能位于中国或西方国家。该公司专注于生产尖端技术产品，如智能家居设备、可穿戴技术和虚拟现实设备。在面试过程中，人力资源经理要求你对该公司的企业文化提出见解。

3 文化与语境——高语境文化与低语境文化

3.1 高语境文化

高语境文化中，沟通依赖于物理环境或参与者间的内在理解，言语传达的信息较少。此类文化重视共享的经验、信息网络和传统，文化框架相对稳定，互动时无须详细背景信息。这些文化中，非语言信号（如手势、空间安排和沉默）传达大量信息。

高语境文化的典型例子包括：中国、日本、韩国、非裔美国人、美洲土著人、阿拉伯人、希腊人、拉美、意大利、英国、法国文化。

其共同特点包括：

- 对环境的高度敏感：注意周围环境并利用这些线索来理解和行为。
- 语言沟通次要：主要通过非语言方式传达信息，环境中传递的信息往往比言语重要。
- 轻松掌握语境：由于共享的文化背景和相似的生活经验，交流无须详细解释。
- 重视人际关系：强调建立和维护长期、互信的关系，沟通风格更个人化和间接化。

高语境文化中的沟通动态强调语境、关系和相互理解。例如，中国的传统宴会中，菜肴选择、座次安排和上菜顺序都具有文化意义，反映了对好运、繁荣或长寿的期盼。

3.2 低语境文化

低语境文化中，大部分信息通过言语明确传达。沟通直接、清晰，重视言语和书面表达，非语言信号和语境线索作用较小。这些文化的人口多样化，需要详细的背景信息以确保理解。

低语境文化的典型例子包括：德国、斯堪的纳维亚和美国白人的文化。

其共同特点包括：

- 语言为主要沟通方式：通过言语传达信息，非语言线索和语境提示较少。
- 明确表达规则和意义：通过言语清楚地表达规则、规范和期望，减少误解。
- 言语传达主要信息：信息主要包含在言语中，依赖言语来传递信息。

在低语境文化中，个体期望信息明确、清晰、毫不含糊。含糊不清会让他们不舒服，他们倾向于询问直接、详细的问题以获取清晰的信息。

理解这些差异对于有效的跨文化交流至关重要。低语境文化中的人需要意识到，其偏好的明确沟通可能被视为过于直率或粗鲁，而高语境文化中的人需要认识到其隐含的沟通方式可能会让人困惑或感到挫败。

通过认识和适应这些文化沟通偏好，个体可以跨越不同的沟通风格，实现更有效和谐的跨文化交流。承认两种方法的价值，并努力实现平衡的沟通策略，可以增强多元化和互联世界中的相互理解与合作。

4　价值取向

价值取向代表了复杂的文化框架，为人类行为和认知提供结构和目的。Clyde Kluckhohn 和 Fred Strodtbeck 识别出了所有文化必须解决的五个基本问题，从而揭示了跨社会的基本价值观：

4.1　人性取向

- 人性本恶但可完善：传统西方信仰认为人性本恶，但通过美德行动可以得到救赎。
- 人性善恶并存：人文主义影响下，一些文化认可人性中的善恶并存，需要警惕腐败和不正。
- 人性本善但易受腐蚀：儒家思想认为人性本善，但会受到外界影响，如贪欲或权力的腐蚀，而榜样和道德楷模在维护伦理标准方面至关重要。

4.2　人与自然关系取向

- 征服自然：在现代技术和工业驱动的社会中，强调控制自然，将其视为资源。
- 与自然和谐：强调人类与自然的无缝融合，如澳大利亚土著文化，强调作为土地的守护者。
- 屈从于自然：在对自然世界怀有敬畏的文化中，人类承认自己在自然力量面前的脆弱，选择顺应自然的意愿，如亚马逊部落。

4.3　时间取向

- 过去取向：重视传统和祖先智慧，保持与过去的连续性，如新西兰毛利人的祖先崇拜仪式。

- 现在取向：重视当下的体验，忽视过去或未来，如地中海文化中的"及时行乐"的思维。
- 未来取向：重视进步和创新，展望未来，如硅谷文化，强调技术乐观和创造更美好的未来。

4.4 活动取向

- 做取向：强调有可衡量成果的活动，优先考虑效率和实绩。例如，美国文化重视商业成功和个人成就。
- 存在取向：重视行为本身的内在表达，社会地位和个人关系优先于可衡量的成就。例如，意大利文化重视社交活动和生活享受。
- 成为取向：介于存在和做之间，关注个人成长和自我发展。例如，佛教实践中的冥想和自省。

4.5 人际关系取向

- 个体取向：强调自力更生和独立，个人目标和成就至关重要。例如，美国社会高度重视个人成功和自给自足。
- 群体取向：优先考虑集体目标和身份，决策通过共识做出，忠诚和相互依赖是关键价值。例如，中国文化强调家庭和社区纽带。
- 等级取向：在结构化等级中赋予个人特定角色和责任。例如，印度的传统种姓制度和军事组织都体现了等级取向。

理解这些文化取向可以为我们提供如何在工作伦理和行为模式中体现基本价值观和态度的宝贵见解。然而，这些取向只是理解文化差异的框架，不能预测所有情况下的个人行为。每个人的行为受个人经验、文化背景和具体情况的复杂交互影响。

5 文化维度

文化维度指的是特定文化群体普遍持有的价值观、原则、信仰、态度和伦理。Geert Hofstede 通过对多个国家和地区的广泛研究，确定了六个关键文化维度：权力距离、个人主义与集体主义、男性化与女性化、不确定性规避、长期导向与短期导向以及享乐与克制。以下是其中四个维度的详细介绍：

5.1 权力距离

大权力距离文化：在这种文化中，权力分布不均是被接受和预期的，存在明显的等级制度，决策通常集中在高层，沟通正式，人们尊重长者和上级，接受不平等，社会流动性有限。

- 例子：马来西亚、危地马拉、菲律宾和俄罗斯是大权力距离的文化代表。这些文化拥有更为严格的等级制度，对不平等的权力分配有更大的接受度。
- 影响：在商业领域，管理者需要提供清晰的指示，维持更具权威性的形象；在教育方面，教学方法可能更具指导性；在谈判中，认识到权力距离的差异有助于理解谈判风格和偏好，确保更有效和相互尊重的互动。

小权力距离文化：这种文化追求平等，权力分布更为平均，决策更加分散，鼓励下级参与决策，沟通较为随意，尊重基于个人品质，社会流动性较大，挑战权威较常见。

- 例子：丹麦、以色列、新西兰和奥地利是小权力距离的文化代表。这些文化强调平等和参与性决策，对权威的挑战较为常见。
- 影响：在商业领域，管理者可能更注重团队合作和赋权；在教育方面，教学方法可能更具互动性和参与性；在谈判中，了解权力距离维度有助于理解谈判风格和偏好，确保更有效和尊重的互动。

5.2　个人主义与集体主义

个人主义：强调个人权利、独立和个人成就。个人目标优先于集体目标，强调自主和个人责任，直接沟通，重视隐私和竞争。

- 例子：美国、澳大利亚等个人主义文化，重视个人自由和成就，鼓励个人的独立和竞争。
- 影响：在工作环境中，人们可能更注重个人成就，竞争激烈；领导可能更倾向于自主决策；在冲突处理中，人们更倾向于以较为直接的方式解决冲突。

集体主义：强调群体和集体利益。依赖群体支持，集体目标优先，强调相互依存和共享责任，强调间接沟通，重视社区和家庭关系，鼓励合作。

- 例子：中国、日本等文化，强调家庭和社区的重要性，注重集体利益和共同体的和谐。
- 影响：在工作环境中，人们可能更注重团队合作和群体利益；领导可能更倾向于支持和合作；在冲突处理中，人们更倾向于妥协和保持和谐。

5.3　男性化与女性化

男性化：强调竞争、进取、野心和物质成功。性别角色分明，重视成就和表现，工作中心，直接解决冲突。

- 例子：日本、德国、美国等文化强调竞争和成就，重视工作和成功。
- 影响：在工作环境中，人们可能更强调竞争和成就，工作导向更明显；领导可能更倾向于果断和决断；在性别角色中，可能更强调传统男性特质。

女性化：强调关爱、合作、谦逊和生活质量。性别角色较为模糊，重视人际关系和社会平等，通过妥协解决冲突。

- 例子：瑞典、挪威、荷兰等文化注重平等和人际关系，强调生活质量和合作。
- 影响：在工作环境中，人们可能更注重团队合作和员工福祉，工作与生活平衡更为重要；领导可能更倾向于支持和合作；在性别角色中，更强调男女平等。

5.4　不确定性规避

高不确定性规避：对不确定性和模糊情况容忍度低。规则和结构严格，抗拒变化，规避风险，强调安全感，压力和焦虑较多。

    ● 例子：希腊、葡萄牙、日本和法国等文化注重稳定和安全，对变化和风险较为抗拒。

    ● 影响：在商业领域，管理者可能更倾向于提供明确的指示和维持结构化的环境；在教育中，人们更倾向于规范化的教学方法；在谈判中，人们可能更倾向于保守和规避风险。

低不确定性规避：对不确定性和模糊情况容忍度高。适应灵活，接受风险，重视多样性和创新，压力和焦虑较少，重视成就和创造力。

    ● 例子：丹麦、瑞典、新加坡和美国等文化注重变革和创新，较为开放和适应。

    ● 影响：在商业领域，管理者可能更注重灵活性和创新；在教育中，人们更倾向于鼓励探索性学习方法；在谈判中，人们可能更开放和适应性更强。

理解这些文化维度对于跨文化沟通和管理至关重要，能够帮助改善多元文化环境中的互动和合作。

* 本单元智慧职教线上课程：https：//zyk. icve. com. cn/courseDetailed？ id = obbaaaqvo4doejfjffeicq&openCourse = obbaaaqvw79e5opp1bwbg.

Unit 3　习题参考答案

Unit 4　Intercultural Communication Barriers and Adaptation

Ancient Chinese Wisdom

Explain the following quote and reflect on its contemporary relevance.

Look not at what is contrary to propriety; listen not to what is contrary to propriety; speak not what is contrary to propriety; make no movement which is contrary to propriety. （非礼勿视，非礼勿听，非礼勿言，非礼勿动。）

From *Analects* （《论语》）

Learning Objectives

After learning this unit, you shall be able to:

- Understand the fundamental concepts and importance of intercultural communication.
- Identify and describe various types of cultural barriers in communication.
- Recognize the symptoms and phases of culture shock and apply coping strategies.
- Explain different models and strategies of cultural adaptation.
- Develop skills to enhance intercultural competence and effectively navigate intercultural interactions.

Project Scenario

After learning this unit, finish the unit project on the basis of the following scenario.

Suppose you are going to present a detailed analysis of an intercultural encounter you have had during a workshop. You could use the cultural theories and concepts covered in this unit to analyze it. You may refer to the following steps.

- Step 1: Select an experience that was significant or impactful (it provided insight; it shocked you; it was enjoyable; it posed a challenge, etc.). Then give the experience a title (My Italian Experience, Navigating Cultural Differences in a Business Meeting, A Weekend with a German Family, Miscommunication at the Café, etc.).
- Step 2: Describe the specific intercultural encounter including the time, the place, the event, your reactions and feelings, and the responses of the other people involved.
- Step 3: Reflect on the similarities and differences between your thoughts and feelings about

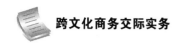

the situation and those of the other individuals involved.

- Step 4: Apply the theories and concepts from this unit to explain your reactions and feelings during the encounter. Consider what you might do differently if you were to face a similar situation in the future.

Lead-in

Watch the movie clips from Green Book and answer the following questions:

- What culture shocks did the main characters, Tony Lip and Dr. Don Shirley, experience in this movie? Why?
- Did Tony and Dr. Shirley adapt to each other's cultures by the end of the movie? How did they deal with the difficulties that they encountered?

Part A   Introduction to Intercultural Communication

1. Importance of Intercultural Communication

In the increasingly interconnected world of today, the significance of intercultural communication cannot be overstated. Effective intercultural communication is crucial for success in local, national, and international business contexts, as well as in educational, social, and personal interactions. Understanding and acknowledging the diversity of voices, cultures, and expertise within any environment are foundational to fostering a collaborative and inclusive atmosphere.

Business Context

In the business world, intercultural communication plays a pivotal role. Companies are no longer confined to their home countries but operate on a global scale. Multinational corporations employ people from diverse cultural backgrounds, necessitating a deep understanding of intercultural dynamics to ensure smooth operations. Misunderstandings or conflicts arising from cultural differences can lead to significant setbacks, including financial losses and damaged reputations. Therefore, businesses prioritize intercultural competence as a key component of their strategies.

For example, a company headquartered in the United States but operating in Japan must navigate the distinct cultural norms of both countries. American communication tends to be more direct, while Japanese communication often relies on context and subtlety. A failure to understand these nuances can result in miscommunication and strained business relationships. Training employees in intercultural communication skills helps mitigate these risks, leading to more effective collaboration and negotiation.

Educational Exchange

Intercultural communication is equally important in educational settings. Universities and colleges host students from around the globe, creating a rich tapestry of cultural diversity. These institutions must foster an environment where students feel understood and respected, regardless of their cultural backgrounds. Intercultural communication skills are essential for educators, administrators, and students to navigate the complexities of a multicultural campus. Consider a scenario where a Chinese student attends a university in the United States. The student may encounter different teaching styles, classroom behaviors, and social norms. If educators are trained in intercultural communication, they can better support the student's adaptation process, enhancing their educational experience and academic success. Conversely, the student can also benefit from understanding and adapting to the cultural norms of their new environment.

Social Interactions

On a social level, intercultural communication enriches personal interactions and relationships. In cosmopolitan cities like Beijing, New York, London, Tokyo, and Paris, people from diverse cultural backgrounds interact daily. These interactions can range from casual conversations to more profound exchanges that foster mutual understanding and respect. For instance, when a foreigner visits China for business, educational exchange, or entertainment, they engage in intercultural communication. Similarly, when Chinese people travel abroad, they also experience intercultural interactions. These experiences broaden perspectives and promote cultural appreciation, which is crucial in today's globalized society.

2. Definitions of Intercultural Communication

The study of intercultural communication involves various terms, often used interchangeably, such as intercultural, international, cross – cultural, and multicultural communication. Understanding these terms and their nuances is essential for a comprehensive grasp of the field.

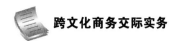

Cultural Studies Perspective

From a cultural studies perspective, intercultural communication examines the political, economic, and lifestyle systems of different countries. This approach focuses on understanding how cultural contexts shape communication behaviors and practices. It involves analyzing how cultural norms and values influence the way people interact, both within and across cultural boundaries.

For example, a study might explore how collectivist cultures (like Japan) prioritize group harmony and consensus in communication, whereas individualist cultures (like the United States) emphasize personal expression and autonomy. Understanding these cultural frameworks helps in interpreting and predicting communication patterns.

Applied Linguistics Perspective

In applied linguistics, the focus is on the relationship between language and culture. This perspective examines how language use reflects cultural values and social norms. It involves studying how linguistic structures and vocabularies are influenced by cultural contexts and how language facilitates cultural transmission.

For instance, certain languages have specific terms for concepts that are culturally significant. The Japanese concept of "wa" (harmony) reflects the cultural importance of group cohesion, while the German word "Gemütlichkeit" captures a sense of coziness and social warmth. These linguistic nuances provide insights into cultural priorities and communication styles.

Expert Definitions

Intercultural communication, as defined by various experts, involves the interaction between individuals who perceive themselves as culturally distinct from one another. According to Collier & Thomas (1998), it is the contact between persons who identify themselves as different in cultural terms. Samovar (2003) expands on this by describing it as communication between people from different cultural backgrounds, emphasizing that it occurs when a member of one culture sends a message intended for a member of another culture. This process is influenced by the distinct cultural perceptions and symbol systems of the participants, which can alter the communication event. Similarly, Zhuang (2004) notes that while the basic components of communication remain the same, what sets intercultural communication apart is the fact that the sources and respondents originate from different cultures.

Historical Context

The term "intercultural communication" was first introduced by Edward T. Hall in 1959. Hall was one of the pioneering researchers who differentiated cultures based on how information is sent and received. He defined intercultural communication as communication between persons of different cultures. His work laid the groundwork for subsequent studies in the field, emphasizing the importance of context in communication. In China, Hu Wenzhong, a prominent professor of intercultural communication, defines it as communication between people of different cultural backgrounds. He highlights the comprehensive nature of the study, which aims to understand all aspects of human cultures and their interactions. This inclusive approach underscores the complexity and richness of intercultural communication.

3. The Relationship Between Culture and Communication

To fully understand intercultural communication, it is essential to study culture and communication together. Culture and communication are intrinsically linked, with each influencing and shaping the other.

Culture

Culture refers to the shared values, beliefs, norms, and practices that characterize a group of people. It encompasses various aspects, including language, traditions, customs, and social behaviors. Culture shapes how individuals perceive the world, interpret experiences, and interact with others.

For example, in high-context cultures (such as Japan), communication relies heavily on non-verbal cues and the context of the interaction. In contrast, low-context cultures (such as the United States) prioritize explicit and direct verbal communication. These cultural differences influence how messages are conveyed and interpreted.

Communication

Communication involves the exchange of information, ideas, and feelings through verbal and non-verbal means. It is the medium through which cultural norms and values are transmitted, negotiated, and reinforced. Effective communication requires understanding the cultural context in which it occurs.

For instance, non-verbal communication, such as gestures, facial expressions, and body language, varies significantly across cultures. A gesture that is considered friendly in one culture might be offensive in another. Understanding these cultural variations is crucial for effective intercultural communication.

Interdependent Relationship

The relationship between culture and communication is interdependent. Culture shapes communication behaviors, and communication practices reflect cultural values. This dynamic interplay means that neither can be fully understood in isolation.

Cultural norms dictate appropriate communication behaviors. For example, in collectivist cultures, indirect communication and maintaining harmony are valued, whereas individualist cultures prioritize directness and self − expression. Meanwhile, Communication practices contribute to the perpetuation and evolution of cultural norms. For instance, the use of social media has transformed communication patterns globally, influencing cultural practices and values.

Understanding this interdependence is essential for navigating intercultural interactions. It enables individuals to adapt their communication styles to different cultural contexts, fostering mutual understanding and respect.

Practical Implications

The practical implications of understanding the relationship between culture and communication are vast. In business, it helps in crafting effective marketing strategies that resonate with diverse cultural audiences. In education, it aids in developing curricula that are inclusive and reflective of global perspectives.

In personal interactions, it enhances empathy and reduces the likelihood of misunderstandings. For example, a marketing campaign targeting a global audience must consider cultural differences in color symbolism, imagery, and messaging. What works in one cultural context may not be effective or even acceptable in another. Similarly, educators must design courses that respect and incorporate diverse cultural perspectives, ensuring that all students feel valued and included.

Challenges and Opportunities

While the relationship between culture and communication presents challenges, it also offers opportunities for growth and learning. Navigating cultural differences requires openness, curiosity, and a willingness to learn from others. It involves recognizing one's own cultural biases and being mindful of how they influence interactions.

On the positive side, intercultural communication enriches personal and professional experiences. It broadens perspectives, fosters creativity, and builds stronger, more resilient relationships. By embracing cultural diversity, individuals and organizations can harness the strengths and insights of a global community.

The importance of intercultural communication in today's world cannot be overstated. It is essential for success in business, education, and personal interactions.

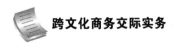

Intercultural Communication
in Business

Understanding the definitions and perspectives of intercultural communication provides a foundation for effective engagement across cultures. The interdependent relationship between culture and communication underscores the need for a holistic approach to studying and practicing intercultural communication. By appreciating and navigating cultural differences, we can build a more inclusive, understanding, and connected world.

Task 1: Understanding the Concepts

1. *Explain why intercultural communication is important in the business context.*
2. *Explain the relationship between culture and communication. How do they influence each other?*

Task 2: Understanding the Concepts

Read each of the following questions and choose the best answer.

1. Which of the following statements best describes intercultural communication?
    A. Communication between people who speak different languages.
    B. Communication between people from different cultural backgrounds.
    C. Communication that occurs within a single culture.
    D. Communication that only happens in business settings.
2. Who first introduced the term "intercultural communication" and in which year?
    A. Edward T. Hall, 1959   B. Samovar, 2003
    C. Collier & Thomas, 1998   D. Zhuang, 2004
3. Which term refers to the shared values, beliefs, norms, and practices that characterize a group of people?
    A. Communication   B. Language
    C. Culture   D. Non-verbal cues

Part B   Understanding Cultural Barriers

Intercultural communication often encounters challenges due to both surface - level and deep-seated cultural differences. These challenges are present in various contexts, such as negotiating contracts with international firms, managing a multicultural team, counseling students from different countries, or working with colleagues who speak different languages. Superficial differences like language, food, dress, and social behaviors can make communication frustrating and occasionally ineffective. However, the deeper aspects of culture, such as values, worldviews, and responses to life events, play a more significant role in shaping

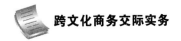

communication.

Effectively navigating intercultural communication requires an understanding and respect for the underlying values and worldviews of different cultures. These cultural structures influence how individuals perceive and interact with their surroundings. Without this understanding, superficial differences can easily escalate into significant communication barriers.

1. Common Barriers in Intercultural Communication

Geert Hofstede identified five major barriers to intercultural communication. Recognizing and addressing these barriers is essential for improving cross-cultural interactions.

Language Differences

Language barriers are not limited to vocabulary and grammar; they also include cultural nuances in communication. Even within the same language, words and phrases can have different meanings depending on the context. For example, in English, the word "table" can refer to a piece of furniture or an act of postponing a discussion, depending on the context. Effective communication requires not only language proficiency but also cultural competence, which involves understanding what to say, how, when, where, and why. To overcome linguistic barriers, communicators need a strong grasp of the foreign language and should seek clarification when confused. For instance, when negotiating a contract, ensure that both parties understand terms like "deadline" or "agreement" in the same way.

Nonverbal Communication

Nonverbal cues, such as gestures, body language, and eye contact, vary significantly across cultures and can lead to misunderstandings. For example, in many Western cultures, direct eye contact is seen as a sign of confidence and honesty, while in some Asian cultures, it may be considered disrespectful or aggressive. Similarly, the "thumbs up" gesture is a positive sign in many countries but can be offensive in others. To navigate nonverbal communication barriers, it's crucial to familiarize oneself with the nonverbal norms of other cultures and to be cautious when using nonverbal cues. For instance, a firm handshake might be interpreted differently in Japan, where a bow is more customary.

Stereotypes

Stereotypes are oversimplified perceptions of people based on limited experience or information, often leading to prejudiced attitudes and behaviors. For example, Western business people might perceive Chinese business people as overly focused on relationships, while Chinese business people might see their Western counterparts as rigid. These stereotypes can hinder effective communication by creating unrealistic expectations. To combat stereotypes, it is essential to educate oneself about other cultures, engage in open-minded discussions, and reflect on personal biases. For example, instead of assuming that all French people are aloof, take the time to get to know individuals personally.

Cultural Biases in Judgments

Cultural biases lead individuals to judge other cultures based on their own cultural norms, often viewing their own culture as superior. For example, Westerners may prefer knives and forks, while Chinese people use chopsticks. Both may believe their method is superior. Reducing cultural biases involves recognizing that different cultures have different but equally valid values and practices. For instance, rather than judging a culture that practices siesta (afternoon rest) as lazy, understand that it is a valuable cultural practice suited to the climate and lifestyle of the region.

High Levels of Stress

Intercultural interactions often involve stress and anxiety due to the unfamiliarity and unpredictability of new cultural contexts. This stress can hinder effective communication by causing discomfort and distraction. Managing stress through preparation, cultural awareness, and tolerance is essential for improving intercultural interactions. For example, learning about the cultural norms and etiquette of a country before visiting can reduce anxiety and make interactions smoother.

2. Emotional and Attitude Barriers

Emotions and attitudes significantly impact intercultural communication. Common emotional barriers include anxiety, uncertainty, and the assumption of similarity. Attitudinal barriers encompass ethnocentrism, prejudice, and racism.

Anxiety and Uncertainty

Anxiety arises from not knowing what is expected in a new cultural context, while uncertainty stems from the inability to predict others' behaviors. Both can impede communication by causing discomfort and distraction. For instance, an employee might feel anxious about presenting to a multicultural team, worrying about potential cultural faux pas. Overcoming these barriers involves preparation, cultural learning, and patience. Practicing mindfulness and stress management techniques can also help.

Assuming Similarity Instead of Difference

Assuming that others from different cultures are more similar to us than they are can lead to miscommunication. For example, assuming that a Japanese colleague shares the same views on punctuality as a German colleague might lead to misunderstandings. Recognizing and respecting

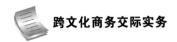

cultural differences is vital for effective intercultural interactions. It's essential to research and understand the specific cultural norms and practices of those you are communicating with, rather than making assumptions based on your own cultural background.

Ethnocentrism

Ethnocentrism is the belief in the superiority of one's own culture, leading to negative judgments about other cultures. This attitude can manifest in various ways, such as expecting others to adopt one's cultural norms or viewing other cultures as inferior. For instance, an American might view a different culture's approach to work - life balance as inefficient without understanding its context. Combating ethnocentrism requires cultural humility and the recognition of the value in diverse perspectives. Engaging in cultural exchange programs or spending time in different cultural environments can help reduce ethnocentric attitudes.

Prejudice

Prejudice involves irrational negative attitudes towards individuals based on their cultural, racial, or ethnic backgrounds, leading to unjust treatment and hindering effective communication. For example, a manager might unfairly assume that a candidate from a particular ethnic group is less competent, despite evidence to the contrary. Reducing prejudice involves education, empathy, and challenging personal biases. Diversity training programs and inclusive policies can help create a more equitable environment.

Racism

Racism is the discrimination or antagonism directed against individuals of different races based on the belief that one's own race is superior. It can manifest in interpersonal interactions or institutional policies. For example, using racial slurs or implementing policies that disproportionately disadvantage certain racial groups are forms of racism. Addressing racism requires active efforts to promote equality and respect for all cultural groups. This can include advocacy, policy changes, and creating platforms for marginalized voices to be heard.

Understanding and overcoming cultural barriers is essential for effective intercultural communication. By recognizing and addressing language differences, nonverbal communication nuances, stereotypes, cultural biases, emotional challenges, and attitudinal problems, we can improve our ability to interact and collaborate across cultures. This requires ongoing learning, self - reflection, and a commitment to cultural

Cultural Barriers
Summary

sensitivity and respect. Whether through formal training, personal experiences, or open dialogue, we can develop the skills needed to navigate the complexities of intercultural communication successfully.

Task 3: Understanding the Concepts

Match each cultural barrier with its corresponding example.

Cultural barriers:

A. Language differences

B. Nonverbal communication

C. Stereotypes

D. Cultural biases in judgments

E. High levels of stress

Examples:

1. A Western traveler feels uncomfortable and stressed in a Middle Eastern market because of the unfamiliar social norms and interactions.

2. During a meeting, a European executive misinterprets a Japanese colleague's lack of eye contact as a sign of dishonesty rather than respect.

3. A French employee finds it challenging to understand an idiomatic expression used by their British coworker.

4. An engineer is perceived as unapproachable because of preconceived notions about their profession's seriousness and lack of humor.

5. A traveler from the United States judges a culture that practices afternoon rest (siesta) as lazy, without understanding the context and benefits of the practice.

Task 4: Deepening Your Understanding

1. Write down three common stereotypes about a culture different from your own. Reflect on where these stereotypes come from and how they might impact your communication with individuals from that culture. Discuss with a partner how these stereotypes can be challenged and overcome.

2. Think of a time when you judged someone from a different culture based on your own cultural standards. Describe the situation and your initial reaction. Reflect on how you could have approached the situation differently to avoid ethnocentric judgment. Share your reflection in a small group discussion.

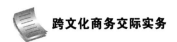

Task 5: Preparing for the Unit Project

Read the following scenarios and answer the following questions.

Scenario 1:

Maria, an American businesswoman, is negotiating a contract with a Japanese company. During the meeting, she notices that her Japanese counterparts avoid direct eye contact and frequently pause before responding to her questions.

Questions:

(1) What nonverbal communication barrier is Maria experiencing?

(2) How should Maria adjust her approach to improve communication?

Scenario 2:

A Chinese student, Li, joins a university in the United States. Li feels anxious and uncertain during group discussions as he is unsure how to express his opinions without offending his American classmates.

Questions:

(1) What emotional and psychological barriers is Li facing?

(2) Suggest two strategies Li can use to overcome these barriers.

Part C   Culture Shock

1. Definition of Culture Shock

Culture shock occurs when individuals are removed from familiar cultural settings and thrust into new, often vastly different environments. This sudden change can lead to feelings of anxiety, confusion, and disorientation, significantly impacting intercultural

Culture Shock vs.
Homesickness

communication if not effectively managed. In our increasingly globalized world, employees and managers frequently find themselves working in unfamiliar territories and cultures, making it essential for both organizations and individuals to comprehend the nature of culture shock, its symptoms, and various manifestations.

Imagine you are a Chinese college student preparing to study abroad in Australia for the summer. Excitement fills you as you anticipate your first overseas trip, especially to an English-speaking country, given your major in English. You believe that language will not pose a significant challenge. However, upon arrival, reality sets in. Despite it being summer back home, it is winter in Australia. You struggle to understand the local dialect and accents, and you find it hard to integrate into the social fabric. Feelings of isolation and loneliness overwhelm you, and you find it difficult to connect with locals, who seem unable to grasp your experience. Nightly tears and a longing for home become part of your routine. What you are experiencing is culture shock.

Culture shock is a common phenomenon among travelers, expatriates, and exchange students. It describes the profound impact of moving from a familiar cultural environment to an unfamiliar one. More precisely, culture shock refers to the often traumatic experience individuals endure when encountering a different culture for the first time.

2. Feelings of Culture Shock

Culture shock, as a concept, was coined to describe the anxiety produced when a person moves to a completely new environment, especially a new country with a distinct cultural backdrop. This term encapsulates the feelings of disorientation, confusion about appropriate behaviors, and uncertainty about social norms and cues.

Typically, the sensation of culture shock begins to manifest a few weeks after arriving in a new place. Initially, individuals may suffer significantly as they experience the following.

Loss of Familiar Signs and Symbols
Culture shock often stems from the anxiety caused by losing all familiar signs and symbols of social interaction. These are the myriad ways we navigate daily life: knowing when to shake hands, what to say upon meeting someone, how to handle tipping, giving orders, making purchases, accepting or declining invitations, and interpreting statements. In one's home country, these activities are second nature, but in a foreign country, individuals may feel lost and uncertain about how to proceed.

Removal of Familiar Cues
Entering a strange culture means all familiar cues are removed, leaving individuals feeling like a fish out of water. Regardless of how open-minded or well-intentioned they may be, the absence of familiar props leads to frustration and anxiety. Initially, individuals might reject the new environment that causes discomfort, perceiving the host country's ways as inferior because they induce sadness.

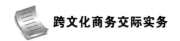

Unfamiliarity and Misunderstanding

Not all cultures operate in the same manner. Many people mistakenly assume that other cultures will behave similarly to their own. When they encounter differences and unpredictability in language, food, or social situations, they experience "shock" or temporary discomfort. However, a positive outcome of living abroad is gaining a better understanding of one's own culture by observing others.

For instance, while American culture may be more direct and clearer in social interactions, Asian cultures often emphasize subtlety and context, which can be confusing to outsiders. In Chinese culture, much goes unsaid but is implicitly understood by locals. For foreigners, this can be perplexing. It's important to remember that despite these differences, humans share similar needs and desires, even if we express them differently.

A practical example involves an American business delegation visiting China to sign a major contract. The Chinese company hosts an elaborate welcome banquet, which the Americans misinterpret as inefficient and overly formal. Consequently, the contract is not signed. Both parties experienced culture shock, misunderstanding each other's intentions based on their cultural norms: the Chinese valued hospitality, while the Americans prioritized business efficiency.

This example underscores the necessity for companies, particularly management, to develop a thorough understanding of foreign cultures. This knowledge is essential to prevent culture shock and ensure successful business interactions with international partners.

3. Symptoms of Culture Shock

Overview of Culture Shock Symptoms

Culture shock manifests in various ways, affecting individuals differently based on their personal experiences and adaptability. Common symptoms include excessive concern about hygiene in drinking water, food, and personal items; a heightened fear of physical contact; feelings of helplessness; dependency on compatriots; irritability over minor frustrations; delays in language acquisition; exaggerated fear of being deceived or harmed; preoccupation with minor health issues; and an overwhelming longing to return to familiar surroundings.

These symptoms can be broadly categorized into physical and psychological aspects. The intensity and duration of these symptoms vary among individuals, with some experiencing mild discomfort while others face severe emotional and physical distress. Not everyone is equally affected by culture shock; some may adapt quickly, while others struggle significantly.

Physical Symptoms of Culture Shock

Physical symptoms of culture shock can be diverse and pervasive, often affecting an individual's overall well – being. These symptoms may include changes in sleep patterns, experiencing insomnia or excessive sleeping; eating habits, developing eating disorders, overeating, or loss of appetite; frequent illnesses, suffering from frequent minor illnesses such as headaches or stomachaches; general discomfort, a persistent feeling of unease without an apparent cause; physical fatigue, feeling constantly tired and lacking energy; and somatic complaints, pain in various parts of the body without a clear medical cause, hair loss, skin eruptions, and new allergies.

Psychological Symptoms of Culture Shock

Psychological symptoms are often more challenging to manage as they affect emotional and mental well – being. These symptoms include loneliness and isolation, feeling detached from both the host culture and one's own; disorientation, experiencing confusion about how to behave or what to expect in social interactions; frustration and irritability, becoming easily annoyed or upset by minor issues; negative stereotyping, developing unfavorable opinions about the host culture; depression and anxiety, feeling sad, anxious, or overwhelmed by the new environment; social withdrawal, avoiding social interactions and isolating oneself; cultural misunderstandings, misinterpreting or miscommunicating during social exchanges, leading to awkward or embarrassing situations.

4. Symptoms of Reverse Culture Shock

Reverse culture shock occurs when individuals return to their home country after spending a significant amount of time abroad. The symptoms can be just as severe as those experienced when first adapting to a new culture. These include disillusionment with home culture, where individuals may find themselves critical of their own culture and idealizing the foreign culture they just left. Frustration and impatience can arise as things that were once familiar and comforting become sources of frustration and impatience. Returnees may experience feelings of being an outsider, despite being in their home country, leading to a sense of being out of place and disconnected from those around them. Changes in relationships can occur as friends and family may have difficulty understanding the experiences of the returnees, resulting in feelings of isolation and frustration. Additionally, returnees may face difficulty readjusting to old routines, struggling to fit back into their old routines and environments and feeling like they have to re−learn how to navigate their home culture.

5. Recognizing Culture Shock

Recognizing culture shock can be challenging because its symptoms often overlap with other forms of stress or illness. Not everyone will experience all symptoms, and the intensity and duration can vary widely among individuals. Here are some key points to remember.

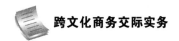

Diverse symptoms can manifest physically and psychologically, from sleep disturbances and increased susceptibility to illnesses to emotional distress and social withdrawal. Physically, individuals may experience changes in appetite, digestive issues, or even headaches due to the stress of adjusting to a new cultural environment. Psychologically, feelings of frustration, confusion, or anxiety are common as individuals navigate unfamiliar social norms and communication styles.

Individual differences significantly shape how people experience culture shock. Background factors such as prior exposure to diverse cultures, language proficiency, and personal resilience all play roles in how quickly or slowly one adapts. Those with more exposure to multicultural environments may find it easier to adjust, while others may face more significant challenges. Adaptation timelines vary widely. While some individuals may acclimate within weeks, others might struggle for months or even years. Factors such as the extent of cultural differences, personal support networks, and the ability to access familiar comforts can influence this adaptation process. In severe cases, returning to a familiar environment may become necessary to alleviate persistent symptoms and regain stability.

By understanding these complexities, both individuals and organizations can better prepare for and manage the challenges of culture shock. Cultivating awareness fosters empathy and patience, essential qualities for providing effective support to those undergoing cultural adjustment. Strategies such as cultural orientation programs, mentorship, and creating inclusive environments can significantly aid in easing the transition and promoting well-being in foreign cultural settings.

Task 6: Understanding the Concepts

Review the symptoms of culture shock. Fill in the two boxes with serial numbers of the following symptoms of culture shock.

(1) Loss of appetite (2) Insomnia (3) Depression (4) Eating disorders
(5) Disorientation (6) Feelings of being an outsider (7) Social withdrawal
(8) Skin eruptions (9) General discomfort (10) Anxiety
(11) Feelings of helplessness (12) Negative stereotyping of the new culture

Physical symptoms: _____

Psychological symptoms: _____

Task 7: Deepening Your Understanding

Decide whether each statement is True (T) or False (F) based on the information about culture shock you've learned in the text.

_____1. Culture shock affects individuals in the same way regardless of their personal experiences and adaptability.

_____2. Physical symptoms of culture shock can include changes in sleep patterns and frequent minor illnesses like headaches.

_____3. Psychological symptoms of culture shock may involve feelings of loneliness, disorientation, and frustration.

_____4. Culture shock only occurs when individuals travel to a foreign country for the first time; it does not apply to returning to one's home country.

_____5. Not everyone will experience all symptoms of culture shock, and the intensity can vary widely among individuals.

_____6. Reverse culture shock is a term used to describe the feelings of disorientation and frustration when returning to one's home country after living abroad.

Part D   Adaptation Processes

1. Understanding Intercultural Adaptation

Intercultural adaptation is the dynamic process through which individuals adjust to and eventually feel at ease in a new cultural environment. It involves not only acclimating to the surface – level differences of the new culture but also reconciling deeper cultural values, norms, and behaviors with those of one's own culture. This

Berry's Model of
Acculturation

adjustment is often a gradual and multifaceted process, influenced by various personal, social, and environmental factors. Whether individuals are voluntary migrants, expatriates, or refugees, their ability to adapt to the host culture shapes their overall well−being and success in the new environment.

2. Models of Intercultural Adaptation

The U−Curve Model
The U−Curve model outlines a typical trajectory of adaptation that individuals undergo when transitioning to a new culture. It consists of several distinct stages.

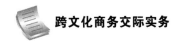

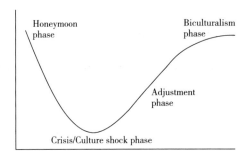

• Honeymoon stage：

Characteristics in this initial phase is marked by excitement and fascination with the new culture. Newcomers are eager to explore their new surroundings, which they find fresh and intriguing. They often feel euphoric about their new experiences and are enthusiastic about the adventure of living in a new culture, often expressing delight in discovering local customs and traditions.

Behaviors during this stage involve actively seeking out new experiences, engaging with locals, and expressing openness to cultural differences. Individuals may overlook or downplay any challenges or differences, focusing instead on the novelty and excitement of the new environment.

Psychological impact includes a sense of adventure and discovery that can create a temporary buffer against the stress of cultural differences. However, this stage is often short-lived as the initial excitement fades and the reality of daily life sets in, revealing the underlying cultural challenges that need to be navigated.

• Crisis stage：

Characteristics in the crisis stage, also known as the culture shock stage, include frustration, confusion, and disillusionment. This period follows the initial excitement and brings challenges such as language barriers, social misunderstandings, and a sense of isolation. Individuals find the new cultural environment difficult to navigate, leading to a decline in the initial euphoria. .

Behaviors commonly observed during this stage include withdrawal, irritability, and anxiety. Individuals might struggle with basic tasks, feel misunderstood, and become critical of the host culture. This phase often brings homesickness and a longing for familiar surroundings, further intensifying negative emotions.

Psychological impact of this stage can be profound with significant emotional distress such as anxiety, anger, and depression. If not managed effectively, it can result in social withdrawal and decreased motivation to adapt to the new environment.

- Adjustment stage:

Characteristics of the adjustment stage include gradually developing strategies to cope with cultural challenges. Individuals start to understand the cultural norms and values of the host culture, leading to a gradual reduction in stress and an increase in comfort. They become more familiar with their surroundings and start to feel a sense of belonging.

Behaviors during this stage involve proactive efforts to learn about the host culture. Individuals seek out social interactions, engage in problem – solving, and start to form meaningful relationships with locals. They participate more actively in the community and adapt to local customs and practices.

Psychological impact represents a turning point in the adaptation process. Individuals regain a sense of agency and control over their environment, leading to a reduction in stress and anxiety. They start to feel more integrated and accepted in the new culture, experiencing a sense of accomplishment and stability. This stage marks the beginning of true adaptation, where the new culture starts to feel like a second home.

- Biculturalism stage:

Characteristics of the final stage include achieving a level of comfort and competence in the new culture. Individuals can function effectively in the host culture while maintaining their original cultural identity. This stage reflects a harmonious balance between understanding and integrating into the new culture while staying true to one's roots.

Behaviors in this stage exhibit a high degree of cultural flexibility. Individuals can switch between cultural contexts with ease and have developed a deep understanding and appreciation for both their home and host cultures. They navigate different cultural settings confidently and fluidly.

Psychological impact in the biculturalism stage is characterized by a sense of belonging and integration. Individuals feel a sense of pride in their ability to navigate multiple cultural contexts and often experience personal growth and increased intercultural competence. This stage signifies a successful blending of cultural identities, leading to enriched perspectives and a more nuanced worldview.

Task 8: Understanding the Concepts

Match each phenomenon (a–f) with the correct stage of intercultural adaptation (1–4).

Stages of Intercultural Adaptation

1. Honeymoon Period
2. Crisis Period
3. Adjustment Period
4. Biculturalism Period

Phenomena

a. John feels a sense of excitement and fascination as he explores the new city and enjoys trying different local cuisines.

b. Maria experiences intense frustration and homesickness as she struggles with language barriers and feels misunderstood by her coworkers.

c. Sarah reaches a point where she can effortlessly switch between cultural contexts, appreciating the positive aspects of both her home and host cultures.

d. Alex starts to develop problem‑solving skills and learns to navigate social norms, gradually feeling more comfortable in the new cultural environment.

e. David feels overwhelmed and isolated as the reality of daily life in a different culture sets in, leading to feelings of anxiety and depression.

f. Emily finds herself enjoying social interactions and forming meaningful relationships with both locals and other expatriates, gaining a deeper understanding of the host culture.

The W‑Curve Model

The W‑Curve model extends the U‑Curve to include the process of re‑adapting to one's home culture after an extended stay abroad.

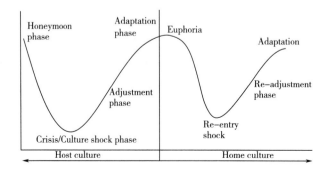

- Initial excitement of return:

Characteristics include excitement and anticipation upon returning home. Individuals look forward to reuniting with family and friends and returning to familiar surroundings. They may also feel a sense of accomplishment for successfully completing their journey abroad.

Behaviors show initial euphoria and relief as returnees are eager to share their experiences and reconnect with their social networks. Additionally, they might engage in activities they missed while away, further enhancing their initial positive emotions.

Psychological impact at this stage is often involves positive emotions and a sense of achievement, as individuals appreciate the comforts and familiarity of home while cherishing memories and lessons learned during their time abroad. However, the initial excitement can quickly give way to challenges as they readjust to their home culture.

- Reverse culture shock:

Characteristics of reverse culture shock, similar to the crisis stage in the U−Curve, involves the challenges of readjusting to one's home culture. Differences that were once taken for granted can now seem strange, leading to feelings of disorientation and frustration, and a sense of being an outsider in familiar surroundings.

Behaviors exhibited by returnees may include feeling out of place in their own culture, experiencing misunderstandings with friends and family, and struggling with the loss of the routines they developed abroad, and grappling with the loss of the routines and social networks they developed in their host country.

Psychological impact it can lead to feelings of isolation, frustration, and disappointment. It can be surprising and disheartening for individuals to realize that their home culture feels foreign and to struggle with integrating back into their previous way of life.

- Gradual readjustment:

Characteristics in the gradual readjustment stage involve individuals beginning to readjust to their home culture. They reestablish routines and reconnect with their social networks, integrating the lessons and experiences gained abroad into their daily lives, which allows them to appreciate their home culture with fresh eyes. This period often involves a gradual easing of the initial cultural shock symptoms as familiarity and routine set in.

Behaviors of returnees in this stage involve actively seeking out familiar activities and reengaging with the community. Individuals may also start to reflect on how their experiences abroad have

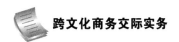

changed them and how they can integrate these changes into their daily life at home. They may seek out opportunities to share their international experiences with others, fostering cross-cultural understanding and appreciation.

<u>Psychological impact</u> of returnees in this stage include individuals adapting to their home culture again, regaining a sense of belonging and stability. They start to feel more comfortable and less conflicted about their dual cultural identities, finding ways to integrate their international experiences into their personal and professional lives.

- Reintegration:

<u>Characteristics</u> in the reintegration stage involve individuals achieving a sense of balance, integrating their new perspectives with their original cultural identity, appreciating both their home culture and the experiences gained abroad. This stage often includes a deeper understanding of cultural nuances and a renewed appreciation for the values and traditions of both cultures.

<u>Behaviors</u> seen in returnees include exhibiting a high level of cultural competence and flexibility, applying the skills and insights gained abroad to their interactions and activities at home. They may also find themselves naturally bridging cultural gaps, facilitating smoother interactions between different cultural groups.

<u>Psychological impact</u> of the reintegration stage is marked by personal growth and a broader worldview. It represents a culmination of the adaptation journey, as individuals embrace their bicultural identity and navigate the complexities of dual cultural belonging with ease and confidence. They may experience a sense of fulfillment and satisfaction in their ability to thrive in diverse cultural environments, recognizing the richness and diversity of human experience.

U-Curve Model & W-Curve Model

Task 9: Understanding the Concepts

Match each phenomenon (a–d) with the correct stage of intercultural adaptation (1–4).

Stages of Intercultural Adaptation

1. Initial Excitement of Return
2. Reverse Culture Shock
3. Gradual Readjustment
4. Reintegration

Phenomena

a. After the initial joy of reuniting with family, John starts feeling out of place in his own country, experiencing frustration and confusion.

b. Emily feels a sense of euphoria and excitement about being back home and reconnecting with old friends and familiar places.

c. Michael begins to reconcile his experiences abroad with his home culture, feeling balanced and comfortable navigating both worlds.

d. Samantha starts reestablishing her routines and gradually feels more at ease with the cultural norms of her home country.

3. Strategies for Effective Adaptation

Coping Mechanisms

Seeking social support is crucial for effective intercultural adaptation. Building a network of friends from both the host culture and among fellow expatriates can provide much–needed emotional support and practical assistance. Having people to share experiences with can make the transition smoother and less isolating.

Maintaining a positive attitude by focusing on the positive aspects of the new culture and the personal growth opportunities it offers can help mitigate feelings of frustration and homesickness. This mindset shift can turn challenges into learning experiences.

Finding ways to bridge cultural gaps by engaging in activities such as language classes or cultural events can facilitate better understanding and integration, helping to create a sense of belonging in the new environment.

Learning and Understanding

Cultural education plays a vital role in intercultural adaptation. Actively seeking out resources for learning about the host culture, like language classes, cultural workshops, and local history tours, can deepen one's understanding and appreciation of cultural differences. This proactive approach can lead to richer, more meaningful interactions with locals. Investing time and effort in learning the local language enhances communication and fosters meaningful connections with members of the host culture. Additionally, observational learning, by paying attention to how locals interact and behave in various situations, provides valuable insights into the cultural norms and expectations, which can guide behavior and help avoid misunderstandings.

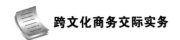

Building Relationships

Forming friendships with locals is essential for a successful adaptation. Developing meaningful relationships with people from the host culture can offer emotional support and help newcomers feel more integrated. These relationships can also provide practical insights into the local way of life.

Engaging in community activities, such as participating in events, volunteer work, and cultural celebrations, fosters a sense of belonging and connection to the local community. This involvement helps build a support network and enhances the sense of community.

Networking with fellow expatriates and members of the international community can also provide a sense of camaraderie and solidarity, offering valuable support and companionship during times of transition and adjustment, and making the adaptation process less daunting.

Personal Reflection

Personal reflection is a powerful tool for intercultural adaptation. Journaling to document thoughts, feelings, and experiences provides a valuable outlet for self-expression and self-discovery, allowing individuals to process their emotions and gain insights into their adaptation journey. This practice can highlight progress and reveal areas needing attention. Self-assessment, reflecting on one's strengths, weaknesses, and areas for growth, helps individuals identify strategies for personal development and self-improvement, fostering a sense of agency and empowerment. Practicing mindfulness and stress management techniques, such as meditation and deep breathing exercises, helps individuals stay grounded and centered amidst the challenges of cultural adaptation, promoting emotional well-being and resilience, and providing tools to handle stress effectively.

Flexibility and Open-mindedness

Flexibility and open-mindedness are essential for successful intercultural adaptation.

Being open to new experiences by embracing curiosity and openness enriches one's adaptation journey, fostering a spirit of exploration, discovery, and personal growth. This attitude can transform initial discomfort into excitement and adventure.

Adapting behavior and expectations is crucial, as individuals learn to adjust their behavior and expectations in response to changing cultural contexts and social dynamics. This adaptability ensures smoother interactions and greater acceptance within the new culture.

Cultivating curiosity and a sense of wonder about the world can inspire individuals to seek out new opportunities for learning, growth, and cultural exchange, fostering a sense of engagement with the world and making the adaptation process more enjoyable and fulfilling.

4. Factors Influencing Adaptation

Personal Factors

Personality traits such as openness, resilience, and emotional stability significantly impact how well an individual adapts to a new culture. Those who are naturally curious and adaptable tend to navigate cultural differences more effectively, finding enjoyment and learning opportunities in new experiences. Additionally, previous experience with different cultures, whether through travel, work, or education, can provide valuable skills and perspectives that facilitate adaptation. These experiences can help individuals recognize and appreciate cultural nuances, reducing the likelihood of culture shock. Furthermore, a person's state of mental health can influence their ability to cope with the stress of cultural adaptation. Individuals possessing strong coping skills and emotional resilience are better equipped to handle the challenges, as they can maintain a positive outlook and manage stress more effectively.

Situational Factors

The level of support from family, friends, and community organizations can greatly influence the adaptation process. Those with a strong support network tend to adapt more easily, as they can rely on others for guidance and assistance. The reason for relocation also plays a significant role, as the motivations behind moving to a new culture, such as work, education, or asylum, can impact the adaptation process. Voluntary moves for positive reasons often result in smoother adaptation, as individuals are more likely to be enthusiastic and open to the new experience. Additionally, the length of stay can affect the level of investment in the adaptation process. Longer stays often necessitate deeper cultural integration, encouraging individuals to learn the language, customs, and social norms of the host culture.

Cultural Factors

The degree of similarity between the home culture and the host culture can impact the ease of adaptation. Cultures with more similarities tend to present fewer challenges, making it easier for individuals to understand and accept new social norms. Moreover, the host cultural openness to foreigners and cultural diversity can influence the adaptation process. More inclusive and welcoming cultures facilitate smoother integration, making it easier for newcomers to feel accepted and understood. When the host culture is open and accepting, it reduces feelings of isolation and encourages positive interactions, enhancing the overall adaptation experience.

Social Support Systems

Having a strong network of family and friends in the host culture can provide emotional support and practical assistance, easing the adaptation process. These close connections can offer a sense of stability and familiarity in an otherwise foreign environment. Community organizations,

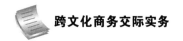
such as cultural centers, religious institutions, and expatriate groups, offer opportunities for social connection, cultural exchange, and support during times of transition and adjustment. These organizations can help individuals build new relationships and find a sense of belonging.

Additionally, <u>support from professional services</u>, such as counseling, coaching, and cultural orientation programs, can provide valuable guidance, resources, and support for individuals navigating the challenges of cultural adaptation and adjustment. These services can help individuals develop strategies for overcoming difficulties and achieving successful integration into the new culture.

Task 10: Deepening Your Understanding

1. *Compare the stages of the U-Curve and W-Curve models. How are the experiences similar or different?*

2. *Reflect on a time when you returned home after an extended period away. Did you experience any stages of reverse culture shock? If so, describe your experience. If not, explain why you think you did not.*

Task 11: Preparing for the Unit Project

Read the following scenarios and answer the questions based on your understanding of the adaptation processes.

Scenario 1:

Sarah, a recent college graduate from the United States, decides to move to Japan to teach English for a year. She is excited about the opportunity to immerse herself in Japanese culture and explore a new country.

(1) Identify which stage of the U-Curve Model Sarah is likely experiencing during her first few weeks in Japan.

(2) Discuss the potential challenges Sarah might face as she transitions from the honeymoon stage to the crisis stage.

(3) Propose two strategies Sarah can use to cope with culture shock during the crisis stage.

Scenario 2:

Carlos, an expatriate from Brazil, has been living in Canada for six months. Initially, he struggled with homesickness and feelings of isolation. However, over time, he has started to feel more comfortable in his new environment and has made friends with both locals and fellow expatriates.

（1）Explain which stage of the U−Curve Model Carlos is likely experiencing at this point in his adaptation process.

（2）Describe how Carlos's behaviors and attitudes might differ between the crisis stage and the adjustment stage.

（3）Discuss the factors that have contributed to Carlos's successful adaptation to his new cultural environment.

Scenario 3：

Mira, a business executive from India, has just returned to her home country after spending five years working in the United States. While she was initially excited to return home and reunite with her family, she finds herself struggling to readjust to Indian culture.

（1）Apply the W−Curve Model to Mira's situation and identify which stage she is likely experiencing upon her return to India.

（2）Explore the potential challenges Mira might face during the reverse culture shock stage.

（3）Suggest two strategies Mira can use to facilitate her readjustment to Indian culture and overcome reverse culture shock.

Assessment

1. *Read each of the following questions and choose the best answer.*

（1）The honeymoon stage in the U−Curve model is characterized by：

    A. Frustration and confusion with the new culture.

    B. Excitement and fascination with the new culture.

    C. A sense of belonging and integration.

    D. Anxiety and depression.

（2）The crisis stage is also known as：

    A. The adjustment stage.

    B. The honeymoon stage.

    C. The biculturalism stage.

    D. The culture shock stage.

（3）During the adjustment stage, individuals typically：

    A. Feel a sense of euphoria about their new experiences.

    B. Struggle with feelings of isolation and homesickness.

    C. Develop strategies to cope with the new cultural environment.

    D. Feel comfortable and competent in both the home and host cultures.

（4）The biculturalism stage is characterized by：

    A. Ongoing feelings of anxiety and frustration.

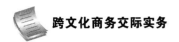

B. A high degree of cultural flexibility and competence.

C. Confusion and disorientation in the host culture.

D. Initial excitement and enthusiasm about the new culture.

(5) In the W–Curve model, the process of adapting back to one's home culture after an extended stay abroad includes:

A. Only positive emotions and a sense of relief.

B. An extended honeymoon stage without any challenges.

C. Reverse culture shock similar to the initial culture shock experienced abroad.

D. Immediate and complete readjustment without any issues.

2. *Decide whether the following statement are true (T) or false (F).*

_____ (1) The honeymoon stage is characterized by frustration and anger as individuals confront the realities of the new culture.

_____ (2) Reverse culture shock is a part of the W–Curve model and occurs when individuals return to their home culture after an extended stay abroad.

_____ (3) During the adjustment stage, individuals begin to develop a positive attitude towards solving problems and understanding the host culture.

_____ (4) Biculturalism involves feeling comfortable in both the old and new cultures, allowing for effective functioning in both contexts.

_____ (5) The crisis stage is marked by a high degree of cultural flexibility and the ability to navigate multiple cultural contexts with ease.

Unit Project

Take another look at a situation from this course. Utilize the theories covered to analyze a particular intercultural interaction you've encountered. Plan your presentation in advance and deliver it during class. When presenting, ensure you address the following aspects:

- Identify any cultural barriers experienced by yourself or others in the communication process.

- Recognize any physical or psychological symptoms of culture shock encountered by you or others, and classify the type of culture shock experienced.

- Utilize either the U–curve or W–curve pattern of intercultural adaptation to elucidate the encounter.

Case Analysis

Analyze the following case with the theories learned in this unit. Then answer the questions.

A Journey of Cultural Exploration in Beijing

John Sullivan, a 35-year-old software engineer from California, had always been fascinated by the idea of experiencing life in a vastly different cultural setting. Having worked for a tech company for over a decade, John had accumulated enough savings and vacation time to finally embark on his long-awaited sabbatical. His destination: China.

Arriving in Beijing on a crisp autumn morning, John was immediately struck by the contrasts between the bustling, modern cityscape and the traditional architecture that peeked through the skyline. Armed with a basic understanding of Mandarin acquired through language courses back home, John felt a mix of excitement and nervousness as he ventured into the heart of the city.

The first few weeks were a whirlwind of exploration and adaptation. John marveled at the historic wonders of the Forbidden City and the serene beauty of the Great Wall. He immersed himself in the local cuisine, sampling everything from Peking duck to spicy Sichuan hotpot, occasionally relying on his limited Mandarin to order meals.

However, as the initial novelty wore off, John began to notice the challenges of daily life in Beijing. Simple tasks, such as navigating the city's labyrinthine subway system or bargaining at local markets, proved more daunting than he had anticipated. Language barriers often left him feeling isolated, and cultural nuances occasionally led to misunderstandings with locals.

One particular incident stood out in John's memory. On a rainy afternoon, he ventured into a small tea house tucked away in a narrow alley. Eager to experience authentic Chinese tea culture, John ordered a pot of fragrant green tea and attempted to engage the elderly tea master in conversation. Despite his best efforts to follow the conversation, John found himself struggling to understand the subtle references to Chinese history and philosophy that peppered their exchange. The tea master, sensing John's confusion, smiled kindly and switched to broken English, patiently explaining the significance of each tea variety and the rituals associated with tea preparation.

Grateful for the tea master's hospitality, John left the tea house with a newfound appreciation for the importance of patience and humility in cross-cultural communication. Over time, he began to invest more effort in improving his Mandarin, enrolling in language classes and practicing with locals whenever possible. His determination to learn the language opened doors to deeper interactions and friendships, gradually easing his sense of isolation.

As weeks turned into months, John's adaptation to life in Beijing progressed in unpredictable ways. He found himself developing a routine that blended Western comforts with Chinese customs. Saturday mornings were reserved for tai chi sessions in the park, where he joined elderly locals in graceful movements under the canopy of ancient gingko trees. Evenings were

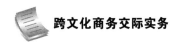

spent exploring Beijing's vibrant arts scene, attending traditional Peking opera performances or modern art exhibitions.

Professionally, John sought opportunities to engage with China's burgeoning tech industry. Through networking events and industry conferences, he forged connections with local entrepreneurs and innovators, exchanging ideas and perspectives on software development and emerging technologies. His background in Silicon Valley proved to be a valuable asset, enabling him to offer insights into global trends while learning from China's unique approach to technology and innovation.

Yet, amidst the excitement and professional growth, John faced moments of doubt and homesickness. Occasional phone calls with family and friends back home served as reminders of the distance that separated him from his familiar life in California. He missed the casual camaraderie of weekend barbecues and hiking trips in the Sierra Nevada mountains, moments that now felt like distant memories from another lifetime.

One evening, while strolling through Beijing's historic hutongs, John stumbled upon a small neighborhood eatery renowned for its dumplings. Enticed by the savory aroma wafting from the kitchen, he decided to step inside and sample the local delicacies. Seated at a communal table, he struck up a conversation with a group of young professionals who shared his love for travel and adventure. Over plates of steaming dumplings and glasses of baijiu, friendships blossomed, bridging cultural divides with laughter and shared experiences.

Reflecting on his journey as his sabbatical drew to a close, John realized how profoundly his time in China had transformed him. He had learned to navigate the complexities of a foreign culture with grace and humility, embracing both the challenges and rewards of cross-cultural living. His Mandarin had improved significantly, allowing him to engage in meaningful conversations and forge lasting connections. More importantly, he had gained a deeper understanding of China's rich history, diverse traditions, and dynamic society.

As John boarded the flight back to California, he carried with him not only memories of his adventures in China but also a newfound appreciation for the interconnectedness of our global community. He knew that his experiences abroad would continue to influence his personal and professional growth, shaping his perspectives and enriching his interactions with colleagues and friends around the world.

With a sense of gratitude and anticipation, John looked forward to sharing his stories of China's beauty and complexity, inspiring others to embrace the transformative power of cultural exploration and cross–cultural understanding in an increasingly interconnected world.

Questions

1. How did John experience the stages of intercultural adaptation during his time in China?

2. What were the key challenges John faced in adapting to life in Beijing, and how did he overcome them?

3. What coping mechanisms did John employ to overcome the challenges of cultural adaptation?

4. In what ways did John's professional background contribute to his adaptation process in China?

5. How did John's journey in China contribute to his personal and professional development?

Further Reading

The Impact of Artificial Intelligence on Intercultural Communication

Enhanced Language Translation and Understanding

Artificial Intelligence (AI) has revolutionized language translation and understanding, significantly impacting intercultural communication. AI–powered translation tools, such as Google Translate and Microsoft Translator, utilize machine learning algorithms to provide real–time translations across multiple languages. These advancements have reduced language barriers, enabling individuals from diverse cultural backgrounds to communicate more effectively.

AI translation algorithms employ neural networks to improve accuracy by analyzing vast datasets of translated texts. Unlike traditional rule–based translation systems, which rely on predefined linguistic rules, AI models can recognize and understand contextual nuances and idiomatic expressions. This capability allows for more natural and accurate translations, enhancing cross–cultural communication and collaboration.

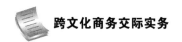

Moreover, AI‐driven translation tools continue to evolve through continuous learning and feedback mechanisms. As users interact with these systems, they provide valuable data that helps improve translation quality over time. This iterative process ensures that AI translations become increasingly nuanced and culturally sensitive, addressing the diverse linguistic needs of global audiences.

Cultural Sensitivity in AI Development

Developing AI systems that are culturally sensitive is essential for fostering effective intercultural communication. Cultural nuances, norms, and sensitivities vary widely across different communities, and AI algorithms must account for these differences to avoid misinterpretations or unintended offenses.

Researchers are exploring ways to integrate cultural context into AI models by incorporating cultural data and feedback loops during the development process. This involves training AI systems on diverse datasets that reflect the linguistic and cultural diversity of the target audience. By exposing AI models to a wide range of cultural contexts, developers can ensure that these systems learn to recognize and respect cultural differences.

Furthermore, ongoing efforts are focused on designing AI interfaces that are adaptable and customizable to accommodate diverse cultural preferences and communication styles. This includes incorporating features such as multilingual interfaces, culturally appropriate imagery, and localized content to enhance user experience and engagement across cultures.

Facilitation of Cross‐Cultural Collaboration

AI technologies facilitate cross‐cultural collaboration by providing virtual environments where individuals from different cultural backgrounds can interact and collaborate in real‐time. Virtual reality (VR) and augmented reality (AR) platforms create immersive experiences that simulate face‐to‐face interactions, regardless of geographical distances.

These virtual environments enable users to engage in cross‐cultural communication, teamwork, and problem‐solving exercises, fostering empathy and understanding across cultural divides. By experiencing different cultural contexts firsthand, individuals can develop a deeper appreciation for cultural diversity and overcome stereotypes and prejudices.

Moreover, AI‐powered collaboration tools, such as collaborative document editing platforms and project management software, streamline communication and coordination among multicultural teams. These tools leverage AI algorithms to automate repetitive tasks, facilitate information sharing, and optimize workflow efficiency, enhancing productivity and innovation in cross-cultural settings.

AI-Driven Cultural Analysis and Insights

AI's data analytics capabilities empower organizations to gather and analyze vast amounts of cultural data, providing valuable insights into consumer behavior, preferences, and trends. By leveraging AI-driven analytics tools, companies can identify cultural patterns and dynamics that influence consumer decision-making and communication preferences.

For example, social media platforms use AI algorithms to analyze user interactions, content consumption patterns, and sentiment analysis to tailor content and advertisements to diverse cultural audiences. By understanding cultural nuances and preferences, companies can create more relevant and engaging marketing campaigns that resonate with their target demographics.

Moreover, AI-driven cultural analysis enables organizations to adapt their products and services to meet the specific needs and preferences of diverse cultural markets. By incorporating cultural insights into product design, branding, and messaging, companies can enhance their competitive advantage and build stronger connections with global audiences.

Ethical Considerations and Bias Mitigation

Despite its potential benefits, the integration of AI in intercultural communication raises ethical concerns, particularly regarding bias and fairness. AI algorithms can inadvertently perpetuate stereotypes or cultural biases if not properly trained or validated with diverse datasets.

Researchers and developers are actively working on bias mitigation techniques to ensure that AI systems uphold ethical standards and promote unbiased intercultural interactions. This includes implementing fairness testing procedures, diversity audits, and algorithmic transparency measures to identify and mitigate biases in AI models.

Furthermore, promoting diversity and inclusion in AI development teams is essential for mitigating cultural biases and ensuring that AI systems reflect the perspectives and values of diverse communities. By fostering collaboration and diversity in AI research and development, organizations can create more culturally sensitive and inclusive technologies that benefit all users.

Challenges of AI-Powered Communication

While AI enhances intercultural communication in many ways, challenges persist in leveraging technology for cross-cultural interactions. For example, reliance on AI translation may hinder language learning and proficiency development, as users may become overly dependent on automated translation tools.

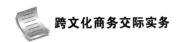

Moreover, AI-mediated interactions may lack the spontaneity and authenticity of face-to-face communication, potentially affecting relationship-building and trust across cultures. Balancing the convenience of AI with the need for genuine human connection remains a critical consideration in leveraging technology for intercultural dialogue.

Furthermore, ensuring the accessibility and affordability of AI technologies in diverse cultural contexts is essential for promoting equitable access to communication tools and resources. Bridging the digital divide and addressing disparities in technology access requires collaborative efforts from governments, businesses, and civil society organizations.

Education and Training in AI for Intercultural Competence

As AI becomes integral to intercultural communication, there is a growing need for education and training in AI literacy and intercultural competence. Educators and professionals must understand how AI influences communication dynamics and equip individuals with the skills to navigate and leverage AI tools effectively in diverse cultural contexts.

This includes fostering critical thinking about AI's role in shaping cultural interactions and preparing individuals to adapt to evolving technological landscapes. Incorporating AI literacy and intercultural communication skills into educational curricula and professional development programs can empower individuals to navigate the complexities of intercultural communication in an AI-driven world.

Future Directions and Innovations

Looking ahead, the integration of AI with other emerging technologies holds promise for further enhancing intercultural communication. Innovations in natural language processing, emotional intelligence recognition, and affective computing could revolutionize cross-cultural communication by providing personalized, culturally sensitive interactions.

Moreover, ongoing research into AI's ethical implications and regulatory frameworks will shape its responsible deployment in intercultural contexts. By addressing ethical concerns and promoting diversity and inclusion in AI development, stakeholders can harness the transformative potential of AI to bridge cultural divides and build more inclusive societies.

AI is reshaping intercultural communication by breaking down linguistic barriers, fostering cross-cultural understanding, and enabling personalized interactions. While challenges like bias and authenticity remain, the transformative potential of AI in promoting global dialogue and collaboration is undeniable. By embracing AI responsibly and cultivating intercultural competencies, individuals and organizations can harness technology to bridge cultural divides and build more inclusive societies.

单元小结

1 学习目标

学习完本单元后，你将能够：

- 理解跨文化交际的基本概念及其重要性；
- 识别并描述沟通中的各种文化障碍类型；
- 认识文化冲击的症状和阶段，并应用应对策略；
- 解释不同的文化适应模型和策略；
- 提升跨文化交际能力，能够有效地进行跨文化互动。

2 学习情境

学习本单元后，根据以下场景完成单元项目：

假设你将在研讨会期间对你经历的一次跨文化交流进行详细分析。你可以使用本单元中介绍的文化理论和概念进行分析，并可以参考以下步骤。

步骤1：选择一个对你有重要意义或影响深远的经历（它让你有了新的见解；让你震惊；让你感到愉快；带来了挑战；等等）。然后给这个经历起一个标题（我的意大利经历；在商务会议中应对文化差异；与德国家庭共度的周末；在咖啡馆的误会；等等）。

步骤2：描述这次具体的跨文化交流，包括时间、地点、事件、你的反应和感受，以及其他相关人员的反应。

步骤3：反思你对这个情境的想法和感受与其他相关人员的想法和感受之间的相似点和不同点。

步骤4：运用本单元的理论和概念解释你在交流中的反应和感受。考虑如果再次遇到类似情况，你可能会有什么不同的做法？

3 跨文化交流

3.1 跨文化交流的重要性

在全球化时代，跨文化交流在商业、教育、社会和个人互动中都至关重要。理解和尊重多元文化是促进合作和包容的基础。

3.2 商业环境中的跨文化交流

在商业世界中，跨文化交流起着至关重要的作用。跨国公司雇用拥有不同文化背景的员工，因此需要深入理解跨文化动态，以确保公司的顺利运营。文化差异引发的误解或冲突可能导致重大损失和声誉受损。

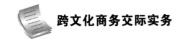

3.3 教育交流中的跨文化交流

在教育环境中，跨文化交流同样重要。大学和学院接待来自全球各地的学生，创造出丰富的文化多样性。教育工作者、管理者和学生需要具备跨文化交流技能，以应对多元文化校园的复杂性。

3.4 社会互动中的跨文化交流

在社会层面，跨文化交流丰富了个人互动和关系。在像北京、纽约、伦敦、东京和巴黎这样的国际大都市中，拥有不同文化背景的人们每天都在互动。这些互动可以促进相互理解和尊重。

4 跨文化交流的定义

跨文化交流涉及不同文化背景的人之间的接触与交流。理解这一领域的相关术语及其细微差别至关重要。

4.1 文化研究视角

从文化研究的角度来看，跨文化交流考察不同国家的政治、经济和生活方式系统。这种方法强调关注文化背景以及如何塑造成员的交流行为。

4.2 应用语言学视角

在应用语言学中，重点是语言与文化之间的关系，研究语言使用如何反映文化价值和社会规范。

4.3 专家定义

Collier & Thomas（1998）：跨文化交流是指在文化上自我认同为不同的人之间的接触。

Samovar（2003）：跨文化交流是指拥有不同文化背景的人之间的交流。

Zhuang（2004）：跨文化交流的特点在于交流的双方来自不同的文化环境。

4.4 历史背景

"跨文化交流"一词由 Edward T. Hall 在 1959 年首次提出。他的工作奠定了该领域的基础，强调了交流中语境的重要性。在中国，胡文仲教授定义跨文化交流为不同文化背景的人之间的交流。

5 文化与交流的关系

理解跨文化交流需要同时研究文化和交流。文化和交流是相互影响的，任何一方都塑造并反映着另一方。文化塑造交流行为，而交流实践反映文化价值。

5.1　实际意义

理解文化与交流之间的关系，在商业、教育和个人互动中具有广泛的实际意义。

5.2　挑战与机遇

虽然文化与交流之间的关系带来了挑战，但也提供了成长和学习的机会。应对文化差异需要开放、好奇和愿意向他人学习的态度。跨文化交流可以丰富个人和职业经历，拓宽视野，提升创造力，建立更强大、更有韧性的关系。

总之，跨文化交流在当今世界中至关重要。理解其定义和视角为有效互动提供了基础，通过处理文化差异，我们可以建立一个更包容、更相互理解的世界。

6　文化障碍

跨文化交流由于表层文化和深层文化的差异而面临挑战。表层文化差异包括语言、食物、服饰和社会行为，而深层文化差异包括价值观、世界观和对生活事件的反应，对交流影响更大。

6.1　主要文化差异

有效的跨文化交流需要建立基于理解、尊重不同文化的世界观和价值观。这些文化结构影响着个人对周围环境的感知和互动。

Geert Hofstede 提出了五个主要的跨文化交流障碍：

- 语言差异：语言障碍不仅限于词汇和语法，还包括沟通中的文化细微差别。同一语言中，词语和短语在不同语境下可能有不同的含义。克服语言障碍需要对外语有深入理解，并在困惑时寻求澄清。
- 非语言交流：非语言线索（如手势、肢体语言和眼神交流）在不同文化中差异显著，容易导致误解。了解其他文化的非语言规范并谨慎使用非语言线索是关键。
- 刻板印象：基于有限经验或信息对人的简化看法，通常导致偏见。克服刻板印象需要了解其他文化、进行开放讨论并保持反思个人的偏见。
- 文化偏见：文化偏见使人根据自己的文化标准来判断其他文化，通常认为自己的文化优越。减少文化偏见需要认识到不同文化虽有不同，但同样具有其独特的价值和实践。
- 高压力水平：跨文化互动由于陌生性和不可预测性常引起压力和焦虑，阻碍有效沟通。通过准备、文化意识和容忍来管理压力是改善跨文化互动的关键。

6.2　情感和态度障碍

情感和态度显著影响跨文化交流。常见的情感障碍包括焦虑和不确定性，态度障碍包括假设相似而非差异、民族中心主义、偏见和种族主义。

- 焦虑和不确定性：焦虑源于在新文化背景下不知道期望，不确定性来自无法预测他人行为。克服这些障碍需要提前做好准备、学习和耐心。

● 假设相似而非差异：假设来自不同文化环境的人与我们相似，可能导致误解。认识并尊重文化差异对有效的跨文化互动至关重要。

● 民族中心主义：民族中心主义表现为认为自己的文化优越，对其他文化做出负面判断。克服民族中心主义需要文化谦逊的态度和认识到多元视角的价值。

● 偏见：偏见是基于文化、种族或民族背景对个人的非理性负面态度而产生的不公正待遇，会阻碍有效交流。减少偏见需要教育、同理心和挑战个人偏见。

● 种族主义：种族主义是基于种族优越感对不同种族的歧视或敌意。克服种族主义需要积极努力促进平等和尊重所有文化群体。

理解和克服文化障碍对有效的跨文化交流至关重要。通过识别和解决语言差异、非语言沟通细微差别、刻板印象、文化偏见、情感挑战和态度问题，我们可以提高跨文化互动和合作的能力。

7 文化冲击

7.1 文化冲击的定义

文化冲击是指个人从熟悉的文化环境进入一个全新的、不同的环境时产生的焦虑、困惑和迷失感。这种现象会严重影响跨文化交流。

7.2 文化冲击的感觉

文化冲击通常在人到达新环境几周后开始显现，包括：

● 失去熟悉的标志和符号：日常社交行为、购物、接受邀请、理解言辞等。

● 失去熟悉的提示：在陌生文化中，所有熟悉的提示消失，使人们感到迷茫和焦虑。

● 不熟悉和误解：不同文化的运作方式各异，容易导致暂时的不适和困惑。

7.3 文化冲击的症状

7.3.1 生理症状
● 睡眠模式的改变：失眠或过度睡眠。

● 饮食习惯的变化：饮食失调、暴饮暴食或食欲不振。

● 频繁的疾病：头痛或胃痛等。

● 一般不适感：持续不安。

● 身体疲劳：持续疲倦和缺乏精力。

● 躯体投诉：身体疼痛、脱发、皮肤疾患、过敏症等。

7.3.2 心理症状
● 孤独和隔离感：感到与周围环境脱节。

● 迷失感：社交中的迷茫。

● 挫折和易怒：对小事烦躁。

- 负面刻板印象：对主流文化形成不利看法。
- 抑郁和焦虑：感到悲伤和焦虑。
- 社交退缩：避免社交。
- 文化误解：社交中的误解导致尴尬。

7.4　反向文化冲击的症状

反向文化冲击是个人在国外生活后回到自己的国家时出现的症状，包括对家乡文化的幻灭感、挫折感、不耐烦、局外人感觉、关系变化以及重新适应旧习惯的困难。

7.5　识别文化冲击

识别文化冲击可能会遇到困难，因为其症状与其他压力或疾病重叠。要点包括：
- 多样的症状：从睡眠问题到情绪困扰。
- 个人差异：每个人的文化冲击体验都有其独特性。
- 适应时间：适应新文化的时间因人而异。

8　文化适应过程

8.1　文化适应的定义

文化适应是个体在新的文化环境中逐渐调整并最终感到自在的动态过程，涉及表层文化差异的适应以及深层文化价值观、规范和行为的协调。无论是自愿移民、外派人员还是难民，适应能力都会影响其整体的福祉。

8.2　文化适应模型

8.2.1　U 形曲线模型
- 蜜月阶段：在初期感到兴奋与新奇，积极探索新文化，暂时忽视文化差异带来的压力。
- 危机阶段：在文化冲击期感到挫折、困惑和失望，可能出现社交退缩和思乡情绪。
- 调整阶段：逐步适应文化规范，压力减轻，舒适感和归属感增加。
- 双文化阶段：能有效在新文化中生活，同时保持自身文化认同，展现出高度的文化灵活性。

8.2.2　W 形曲线模型
- 回归初期兴奋：回家后初期的兴奋和期待。
- 逆向文化冲击：重新适应原文化的挑战，感到迷失和挫折。
- 逐步重新适应：逐渐重新进入日常生活和社会关系，融合国外经历。
- 再整合阶段：达到文化平衡，欣赏并整合双文化身份，展现文化适应能力。

8.3 有效适应策略

- 应对机制：寻求社会支持，保持积极态度，参与文化交流活动。
- 学习和理解：学习当地文化和语言，观察当地人行为。
- 建立关系：结交本地朋友，参与社区活动，与外派人员联网。
- 个人反思：写日记，自我评估，练习正念和压力管理。
- 灵活和开放：接受新体验，调整行为和期望，培养好奇心。

8.4 影响适应因素

- 个人因素：性格特质，先前经验，心理健康。
- 情境因素：支持水平，搬迁原因，逗留时间。
- 文化因素：文化相似度，东道主文化开放性。
- 社会支持系统：家庭和朋友，社区组织，专业服务。

＊本单元智慧职教线上课程：https：//zyk.icve.com.cn/courseDetailed? id＝obbaaaqvo4doejfjffeicq&openCourse＝obbaaaqvw79e5opp1bwbg.

Unit 4 习题参考答案

Unit 5　Verbal Intercultural Business Communication

Ancient Chinese Wisdom

The Master says, "How can one refuse to follow the sound advice that conform to rituals? But it is commendable only if one can amend his erroneous ways of behavior according to the advice. How can one not feel happy to hear words pleasant to the ear? But it is commendable only if one makes efforts to find out the real intention or the real implications. If one feels happy only with honeyed words without finding out the intentions and implications or claims to take the advice without amending his erroneous ways of behavior, I simply can do nothing about him. " （子曰：" 法语之言，能无从乎？改之为贵。巽与之言，能无说乎？绎之为贵。说而不绎，从而不改，吾末如之何也已矣。）

From *Analects* （《论语》）

Learning Objectives

After learning this unit, you shall be able to：

- Understand and identify different verbal communication styles.
- Identify the varieties of language.
- Illustrate the language differences and deal with translation problems.
- Analyze the norms from different cultural contexts and learn to communicate with people from different background in business interaction.

Project scenario

After learning this unit, finish the unit project on the basis of the following scenario.

Suppose you work as a director of Human Resources in a joint-venture company, which is one of the largest auto manufactures in South China. You are going to inform a senior sales manager from Ireland that he would be fired. And you need to find a suitable way to soften this bad news.

Lead-in

Watch a video clip about marketing across cultures and figure out

What is Marketing

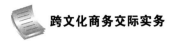

how did the verbal expressions work out in this scene.

Part A   Verbal Communication

1. Definition of Verbal Communication

Verbal communication (VC) refers to the communication that is carried out either in oral or in written form with the use of words. People are chatting with their friends, discussing an issue in a group, or making a public speech. University students are composing an article, finishing a professor's assignment on campus, the employees are writing a report to their managers in a company by email.

Verbal communication can express all kinds of ideas we want to express. It can be clear and more efficient than other ways. It is also able to keep and disseminate information. In addition, cultural factors need to be considered in verbal communication. Lions in English culture are the symbols of courage, danger, and power, which are considered as the king of animals. But lions do not enjoy such a connotative meaning in Chinese culture.

2. Cultural Factors in Verbal Communication

A word may have rich culturally created connotative meanings in one language, while it is seldom used with the same meanings in another. As what has been explained above, verbal communication can be conducted both in spoken form and written form. It has cultural features sometimes. Therefore, people from different cultural backgrounds have different ways of verbal communication. In the following study we will show how differently the Easterners and the Westerners communicate.

Task 1: Understanding the Concepts

Compare the following translations according to cultural factors involved, then make more examples together with your partners.

1. 拦路虎: a lion in the way (or path)   2. 虎穴取子: beard the lion in his den

3. 虎头蛇尾: in like a lion, out like a lamb   4. 挥金如土: spend money like water

5. 胆小如鼠: as timid as rabbit   6. 拍马屁: kiss the ass of someone

7. 像热锅上的蚂蚁: like a cat on hot bricks   8. 招惹是非: wake a sleeping dog

---

Task 2: Furthering Your Understanding

With the help AI technology, work out the following cultural associations of colors, then make more examples together with your partners.

1. Red in China means joy, power and celebration; what about in Europe?
2. Yellow in China implies the meaning of honor and royalty, what about in Europe?

3. Attributes of Verbal Communication

Verbal communication can express all kinds of ideas we want to express; it can both keep and disseminate information and be more clarified and efficient than other ways. But ways of VC between Easters and Westerners are greatly different. Easterners are generally more polite, vague, and often beating about the bush with a lot of conversational greetings and concern for others; while Westerners are generally more direct and rude, they often get down to business or come to the point directly with their personal opinions first.

When talking, Easterners tend, often superficially, to yield to the other party's views without making any open protest. Westerners, however, are usually direct in presenting their different ideas or protest.

In the languages by Easterners there are quite a few honorific forms which Westerners think are redundant. Westerners do have polite expressions, but for each meeting the phrase for exchanging these expressions is usually very short. To Easterners, Westerners appear rude.

When it comes to a position, Easterners tend to state the reasons first. Westerners, on the contrary, usually state their position first, then the reasons.
When it comes to conversational greetings and get down to business, Before discussion Easterners tend to spend a lot of time talking about unimportant things, preparing for the serious discussion. Westerners don't do so.

Easterners often show a lot of concern for others, which Westerners consider as bothering other people's business. Easterners tend to be vague when talking, which often bring unhappiness to Westerners as it is against their habit.

When debating in the West, two parties usually take several turns of arguments, while in the East the two sides express their respective views at most once, then both sides either yield to

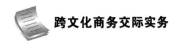
each other, or just keep silent.

4. Language and Culture

Semantics is a system that associates words to meaning, and the study of the meaning of words. We use words to communicate with the outside world, to share the past, to exercise some control over the present, to form images of the future as well.

We use the words to persuade, to exchange ideas, to express views, to seek information, and to express feelings. Language is important; it has the significant influence on human behaviors.

Task 3: Understanding the Concepts

We name the same object differently and words are different in various languages. Make more examples according to the example below.

1. Fangzi In Chinese, 房子
2. in English, House
3. in Spanish, Case
4. in Thai, ban
5. in German, Haus
6. in French, Maison
7. in Irish Gaelic, Tigh

Task 4: Furthering Your Understanding

Discussing the following jokes with your partner and answer the questions below.

1. An Irish old lady went to an American hotel for her holiday. She called the receptionist to arrange a morning call. "would you please do me a favor to wake me up at 8 o'clock tomorrow morning?" "Sure, I will knock you up then", the receptionist replied. The old lady ran into rage and shouted "I beg your pardon?"

Question1: Why did the woman take such a reaction?

2. Three Japanese, who knew some Chinese, were one day at Guangzhou subway station. They saw a warning sign which read: XIAO XIN DI HUA! （小心地滑）. They were extremely surprised to see that nobody around them skating, though the floor was really very smooth.

Question2: Why were the three Japanese surprised ?

3. In a hotel laundry in London, when a young man saw the sign "when light flashes, remove clothes", he took off all his clothes.

Question3: Why did the man take off all his clothes?

Part B   Pragmatics in Intercultural Communication

<u>Pragmatics</u> is the study of the effect that language has on human perceptions and behaviors. The aim of the study is focused on how speakers use the language to reach successful communication. It will help us understand how to communicate properly in cultural context.

Pragmatics focuses on the contextual meaning; while the semantics focuses on the meaning from linguistic knowledge. By understanding words or sentences semantically, we will commit pragmatic failure unconsciously.

Instead of searching for what "words mean", we should look for what "people mean". Instead of "words are containers of meaning"; it is assumed that "people are containers of meaning".

1. Pragmatic Communicative Competence

Task 5: Furthering Your Understanding

Compare each pair of the following expressions, which one do you think it's appropriate and effective. Or are they properly communicated between the speaker and listener in the given context?

1. Dogs are the best friends of human beings.
2. I ate dog meat.
3. Chinese dragons are great.
4. Chinese dragons are ferocious.
5. This is a present for you. It is not so good.
6. This is a present for you. Hope you like it.
7. I don't think your idea is good.
8. From my point of view, your idea is not good enough.
9. Bottom up. Take this cup of alcohol. If you don't. Me either.
10. Help yourself, please. I made all these by myself. Please enjoy them.

Cognitive Components
- Knowledge about others (culture–and country–specific knowledge)
- Theoretical knowledge of cultures (knowledge about the way cultures work, cultural differences and their implications)
- Self-awareness

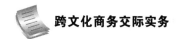

2. Analysis of Pragmatic Failure

In English, when people want to express gratitude for the help provided by others, the commonly used English phrase is "Thank you." The speech act of "Thank you" is used to express appreciation. The most frequently used English response phrase is "You're welcome." However, for Chinese-speaking English learners, when they hear someone expressing gratitude towards them, they might immediately respond with "Never mind," clearly intending to convey the meaning of "It doesn't matter" or "You're welcome," but leaving the listener quite surprised. This is because "Never mind" is often used in situations where one person apologizes and the other person wants to indicate that they do not mind, implying a form of "consolation" for the other person. Clearly, this misuse of expression leads to pragmatic or language use errors.

Traditional language teaching often overlooks the communicative value of language. In other words, while teachers focus on developing students' linguistic abilities, they may not pay enough attention to fostering their communicative competence, that is, how to speak, when to speak, and why to say what is being said. This can lead to misunderstandings between the interlocutors, affecting the effectiveness of communication and even preventing the achievement of the intended communicative goals.

Pragmatics in Intercultural Communication

The following analysis will be based on the examples.

Example 1
A: Your dress looks really good.
B: Oh, no. Just so-so.

Analysis:
From the conversation, it can be seen that responding modestly to someone's compliment is a reaction pattern influenced by traditional Chinese values. Due to the impact of Chinese pragmatic habits, the complimented party might not respond with "Thank you" which aligns with English expression conventions. In English-speaking countries, people tend to accept compliments, whereas in China, people tend not to accept them directly or at all.

Example 2
A. I'm afraid you must have a tired journey. (您一路辛苦了。)
B. ...

Analysis:

When Chinese hosts welcome foreign guests at the airport, saying, and translate it into English as "I'm afraid you must have a tired journey. " Grammatically, this is correct English. However, it may sound unnatural to people from English – speaking countries. Clearly, sometimes direct translation of Chinese into English isn't appropriate; even though it conforms to English grammar and semantic rules, it might not align with the cultural background of English. In such situations, the common English greetings would be "Did you have a good trip/flight?" / "Did you enjoy your trip?" / "How was the trip?", etc.

Task 6: Cross-culture Comparison

Match the following Chinese expressions with their English equivalence.

Zone	Description in Chinese culture	Description in English culture
1	红糖	Supercilious look
2	红茶	Green-eyed, Jealous
3	眼红	Innocent
4	红白喜事	Hackers
5	清白	Weddings & Funerals
6	白眼	Black tea
7	黑客	Brown sugar

Part C Oral Communication

Language facilitates group interaction and allows information and knowledge to be transferred from individual to individual, from place to place, and from generation to generation. Speaking effectively is extremely important for successful business work places. Talking over phones, informal colleague chatting, conducting conferences, making sales promotion presentations, are only a small part of oral communication skills. It involves expressing and sharing ideas and information as well as influencing others through verbal and nonverbal symbols.

Making an effective oral presentation requires careful planning and preparation. Here are some steps and tips to help you make a successful presentation.

A poor Listening and Good Listener

Understand your audience. Before starting your presentation, understand who your audience is, their level of knowledge on the topic, and what they expect from your presentation. This will help you tailor your content and delivery to meet their needs. For example, German businessmen tend to get down to business at the beginning of their presentation while American business people often start their presentation by telling a joke.

Choose a clear and focused topic. Select a topic that is relevant and interesting to your audience. Make sure it is not too broad or too narrow. A focused topic will help you stay on track and keep your audience engaged. Try to focus on the idea you want your listeners to take away with them. Usually, people will be bored by the residue message. Most of European business people prefer coming to the point to *beating around the bush.*

Research & design your topic. Gather information from reliable sources and organize it in a logical manner. Use facts, statistics, and examples to support your points and make your presentation more convincing. You can achieve this by designing your introduction, establishing credibility, restricting your main points to three, organizing your business presentation by a clear and attractive outline of major points.

Practice your delivery confidently. Practice your presentation several times before the actual event. This will help you become more confident and comfortable with your material. Pay attention to your pace, tone, and body language.

Use visual aids. Incorporate visual aids such as slides, charts, and images to enhance your presentation. Make sure they are relevant, easy to read, and do not distract from your message.

Engage your audience. Keep your audience engaged by using interactive techniques such as asking questions, encouraging discussion, and incorporating stories or real-life examples.

Be prepared for questions. Anticipate possible questions from your audience and prepare responses in advance. This will show that you have a deep understanding of your topic and are willing to engage in a dialogue with your audience.

End with a strong conclusion. Summarize your main points and reiterate your key message in a memorable way. This will help reinforce your message and leave a lasting impression on your audience. Finally, conclude the business presentation with a call to action.

Evaluate your performance. After your presentation, take time to reflect on your performance. Identify areas where you did well and areas where you can improve. This will help you become a better presenter in the future.

Task 7: Understanding the Concepts

Read each of the following questions and choose the best answer.

1. When you meet someone for the first time in an American context, which of the following greetings is most appropriate?

 A. "Where are you from?"

 B. "How much money do you make?"

 C. "What is your favorite hobby?"

 D. "May I know your age?"

2. In a Japanese business meeting, what behavior is considered respectful?

 A. Interrupting while others are speaking

 B. Directly expressing disagreement with a senior colleague

 C. Bowing slightly when greeting colleagues

 D. Leaving the meeting room without excusing oneself

3. In an Indian cultural setting, which gesture should be avoided as it may be considered offensive?

 A. Nodding the head up and down

 B. Waving goodbye with an open palm

 C. Placing the hand on the heart when expressing sincerity

 D. Using a thumbs-up sign to indicate approval

4. In Arab culture, which of the following is considered a polite way to refuse an offer?

 A. Saying "No, thank you" directly and firmly

 B. Offering an explanation for why you cannot accept the offer

 C. Repeatedly declining the offer after the first refusal

 D. Accepting the offer and then returning it later

5. When visiting a Chinese family's home, which action shows respect for the host?

 A. Refusing food or drink that is offered

 B. Finishing all the food on your plate to show you enjoyed it

 C. Criticizing the taste or quality of the food

 D. Leaving immediately after finishing your meal

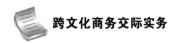

6. When entering a foreign country, what is the most appropriate way to greet someone in a formal setting?

    A. Shaking hands   B. Bowing deeply   C. Winking   D. Embracing

7. During a business meeting in an international context, which of the following behaviors might be considered rude?

    A. Direct eye contact

    B. Interrupting the speaker

    C. Keeping your hands visible

    D. Offering a firm handshake

8. In many English-speaking cultures, how do people typically respond when someone compliments them?

    A. By denying the compliment

    B. By accepting the compliment and saying "thank you"

    C. By offering a compliment in return

    D. By ignoring the compliment

9. What is the best approach to address someone with a higher level of authority in an English-speaking professional environment?

    A. Using their first name only

    B. Using their title (Mr., Mrs., Ms.) followed by their surname

    C. Asking them how they prefer to be addressed

    D. Addressing them informally without any title

10. In cross-cultural communication, what does it mean if someone from a Western cultural background says "It's good to see you" upon meeting someone after a short time apart?

    A. They are genuinely happy to see the person

    B. They are just being polite and don't really care about the person

    C. They are implying that they have not seen the person for a very long time

    D. They are suggesting that the previous meetings were not good

Part D   Written Communication

Written communication is the communication by means of written symbols. The cave dwellers that inhabited the earth millennia ago had a simple solution when it came to the challenge of communicating in written form across cultures. They used pictographs（古代石壁画）— carved or drawn pictures describing a simple concept or event. No words, no alphabet, no chance of lost subtleties and confused meanings.

Gradually, over the years, the pictures became symbols, and the symbols became <u>letters</u> to represent sounds. The Egyptians used <u>hieroglyphic（象形文字）</u> — a combination of pictographs, <u>ideographs（表意文字）</u> and phonograms — and later became the first to use pictures to represent sound in addition to ideas and objects.

Letters, memorandums, and reports are the major forms of written communication in business. Without these written information exchanges, sales contracts couldn't be fulfilled, goods would not be delivered or shipped, letter of credit would not be established and new techniques would not be devises. Therefore, writing skills are supposed to be a basic requirement for business employees.

Whether you're following up on a job interview or a sales pitch, knowing how to write a business letter is a great skill to have. Most business letters follow an established, easy-to-follow format you can adapt for any situation.

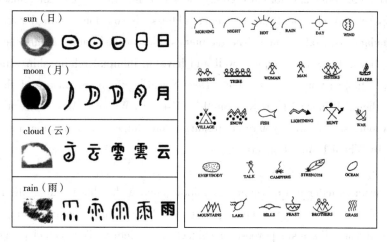

Chinese pictographs   Western pictographs

The following are some guilds for beginners. Please translate them into Chinese to ensure your total understanding.

<u>A typed business letter</u> has a top margin of 2 inches, while the other 3 margins are the standard 1 inch. Change the margins in your word processor by selecting "Page Layout", "Margins", and then "Custom Margins".

<u>There are 3 types of business letter formats</u>: full block, modified block, and semi-block. Full block format is the most traditional and widely used amongst companies, making it perfectly modifiable for any context.

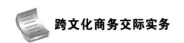
List your company's name and address in the top left corner. This allows the recipient to know exactly where the letter is coming from and where they should send their follow-up letter.

Put the date 2 lines underneath the address. Writing out the full date is the most professional choice and lets the recipient know when you mailed the letter. Keep a left indent for this line as well. For example, rather than writing "10/15/12", write the full date as "October 15, 2012" or "15 October 2012". Putting the date before the month is standard in European countries. If you are writing your letter over several days, date it with the day when it was finished.

Address the letter to a specific individual rather than a full company, so it gets to the right person. If you don't know the name of the person you're sending the letter to, contact the company to see who you should reach out to for your specific demands.

The salutation is an important indicator of respect and indicates professional familiarity. It officially starts your letter and formally greets the recipient. Keep your salutation left-aligned with a line space between it and the recipient's address. If you don't know the recipient well, "Dear Sir/Madam" is a safe choice. The recipient's title and last name can also be used "Dear Dr. Smith". If you know the recipient well and have an informal relationship with them, you may consider a first-name address, like "Dear Susan". If you're unsure of the recipient's gender, type their full name "Dear Kris Smith". Use "To Whom It May Concern" only if you don't know whom, specifically, you're addressing. Don't forget a comma after a salutation or a colon after "To Whom It May Concern".

Typically, a business letter has a beginning, middle, and end. This is called the body of your letter and is where you state your purpose or reason for writing. The first paragraph is your introduction and states the main purpose or subject of the letter. The second paragraph details specific information about your purpose or subject. Put statistics, data, or first-hand accounts in this paragraph. Your second paragraph could consist of more than one small paragraph, as long as it stays on a single page. The third paragraph is your conclusion and restates your purpose.

Time is money, as the saying goes, so the tone of your letter should be brief and professional. Make your letter a quick read by diving straight into the matter and keeping your comments brief in the first paragraph. For instance, you can always start with "I am writing to you regarding..." and go from there. Don't concern yourself with flowery transitions, big words, or lengthy, meandering sentences. Your intent should be to communicate what needs to be said as quickly, clearly, and cleanly as possible.

Be persuasive in your letter and state your needs or wants in a way that makes the recipient want to help you.

Be aware if you're writing the letter on an organization's behalf. If you're stating the company's perspective, you should use "we" so the reader knows that the company stands behind your statement.

In the last paragraph or conclusion, summarize your points and clearly outline your planned course of action or what you expect from the recipient. Note that the recipient may contact you with questions or concerns and say thank you for their attention to the matter at hand.

Your call to action could be as simple as, "Please read the attached document and send your feedback," or as detailed as, "Let's work together to fight climate change by integrating eco-friendly transportation and shipping into our company. "

The closing, like the salutation, is an indicator of respect and formality. "Sincerely" or "Best regards" are common professional closings. Place this complimentary close 2 lines below the last line of the body of your letter with a comma after it.

Task 8: Understanding the Concepts

Read each of the following questions and choose the best answer.

1. In a business email, which phrase is most appropriate for closing when you want to encourage future contact?

    A. "I hope this message finds you well. "

    B. "Please feel free to contact me if you have any questions. "

    C. "Best wishes for your success. "

    D. "Thank you for your time and consideration. "

2. Which of the following is the correct format for a business letter heading?

    A. Your Name, Your Company, Your Address

    B. Your Company, Your Address, Your Name

    C. Your Address, Your Company, Your Name

    D. Your Name, Your Address, Your Company

3. What is the most professional way to start a formal business proposal?

    A. "Hello, I'm writing to propose..."

    B. "Dear Mr. /Ms. [Last name], I would like to propose... "

    C. "To whom it may concern, I am writing to suggest... "

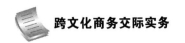
D. "Hi there, I think we should consider..."

4. When addressing an envelope in a business context, what order should you write the recipient's information in?

    A. Name, Street Address, City, State, ZIP Code

    B. Street Address, City, State, ZIP Code, Name

    C. City, State, ZIP Code, Street Address, Name

    D. State, City, Street Address, ZIP Code, Name

5. Which phrase best conveys urgency in a business email without being impolite?

    A. "I urgently request your immediate attention to this matter. "

    B. "Kindly respond as soon as possible. "

    C. "It would be great if you could reply quickly. "

    D. "A prompt response will be highly appreciated. "

Task 9: Furthering Your Understanding

The following questions are based on your understanding of cultural differences, Choose the most suitable answer to each of the questions.

1. Shirley travelled to Boston in the United States. After checking in the hotel, she took the elevator and found that the hotel didn't have the 13th floor. How would you explain this phenomenon?

    A. Americans avoid using the number 13 because of religious reason.

    B. Americans avoid using the number 13 because of they are superstitious.

    C. Americans avoid using the number 13 because of the initial 13 colonies of America.

    D. Americans avoid using the number 13 because of political factors.

2. Professor Zhao attended the B. A. thesis defense of her department last weekend. During the thesis defense conference, he found a male Pakistan student wearing slippers. How do you think of the Pakistan student's behavior?

    A. He wanted to be cool and attract other's attention.

    B. He wore slippers to show for religious reasons.

    C. He used to wear slippers in his country.

    D. He didn't take the thesis defense seriously.

3. Zhou Xiao was seeking her MBA in Rio, Brazil. On New Year's Eve, he and his Chinese classmates went to the beach to celebrate the New Year. When they got there, they found that most of Brazilian people wear white clothing. How do you think of their white clothing?

A. They wore white clothing to wish for peace and happiness.

B. They wore white clothing in memory of a historical character.

C. They wore white clothing to express their love for white color.

D. They wore white clothing to say good bye to the past.

Task 10: Preparing for the Unit Project

Program Problem: Let us look at how we have to take different cultures into consideration in business communication.

As a assistant to the chief executive, You are told to prepare an outline programme for the second day of a visit by a group of eight people from European companies that your organization supplies with products. They arrived at different times during the previous evening. Experience show that a typical programme might be something like the following.

7: 30 a. m.	Wake-up call at hotel, followed by breakfast
8: 00 a. m.	Bus leaves hotel
9: 45 a. m.	Bus arrives at head office
10: 00 a. m.	Tour of main factory
11: 00 a. m.	Tour of research facility
11: 30 a. m.	Tour of product development facility
12: 30 a. m.	Lunch
1: 30 p. m.	Introduction to our chairman
2: 00 p. m.	Meeting about new product lines to be introduced next year
4: 00 p. m.	End of meeting
4: 10 p. m.	Board bus
4: 30 p. m.	Arrives at Scenic Mountain site. Visit that site
6: 00 p. m.	Cocktail party at Garden Hotel
7: 00 p. m.	Board bus
7: 30 p. m.	Return to hotel
8: 00 p. m.	Dinner at Golden Palace Restaurant
10: 00 p. m.	Visit night market
11: 30 p. m.	Karaoke

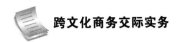

Now design a more realistic schedule for the visitors using the same scenario as above. Try not to put too much into the program. Note how your program covers all the essentials but leaves time for the guests to relax. In addition, you need to pay close attention to the visitor's migration background, in case some of whom may be of Jewish American origin.

Part E Language Diversity and Translation Problems

1. Language Diversity and Translation

Language diversity is a reality that we face every day, with an estimated 7,000 languages spoken across the globe. However, this diversity also brings about significant challenges when it comes to translation and communication.

One of the biggest problems in translation is the lack of direct equivalents between languages. Words and phrases that are common in one language may not exist in another or may have different meanings altogether. This can lead to confusion and misunderstandings, particularly in technical or specialized fields where precision is essential.

Another issue is the nuances of language, such as idioms, colloquialisms, and cultural references, which do not translate directly into other languages. Translators must find ways to convey these nuances accurately while maintaining the intended meaning of the original text.

Moreover, translation requires a deep understanding of both the source and target languages, as well as the cultures they represent. A translator must be able to identify cultural differences and adapt their translation accordingly to avoid cultural insensitivity or misinterpretation.

Finally, there is the challenge of keeping up with the ever-evolving nature of language. New words and phrases are constantly being introduced, and languages continue to evolve over time. Translators must stay up-to-date with these changes to ensure their translations remain accurate and relevant while language diversity presents significant challenges for translation It is essential to recognize and address these issues to facilitate effective communication across linguistic and cultural barriers.

2. Pidgins and Lingua Francas

Pidgins and lingua francas are both types of simplified languages that emerge in multilingual settings, but they differ in their origins, structures, and functions.

Language Diversity

Pidgins are contact languages that develop when groups of people with different native languages need to communicate with each other. Pidgins typically have a limited vocabulary, simplified grammar, and pronunciation, and they often rely heavily on context and gestures for meaning. Pidgins are usually not the first language of any speaker, but rather a second or third language used for specific purposes such as trade or communication with colonizers.

Lingua francas, on the other hand, are common languages that are used as a means of communication between speakers of different native languages. Unlike pidgins, lingua francas are usually standardized languages with a more complex grammar and vocabulary. They are often used as official languages in international organizations or as a medium of instruction in schools. Lingua francas can also be used as a means of cultural exchange and diplomacy.

In summary, while both pidgins and lingua francas are simplified languages used for communication between speakers of different native languages, pidgins are typically more rudimentary and less standardized, while lingua francas are more complex and serve as official languages in various contexts.

*注释：洋泾浜语与世界语都是出现在多语言环境中的简化语言类型，但它们在起源、结构和功能上有所不同。洋泾浜语与世界语是接触语言，当拥有不同母语的人群需要相互交流时，洋泾浜语便产生了。洋泾浜语通常词汇量有限，语法和发音简化，它们往往严重依赖上下文和手势来传达意义。洋泾浜语通常不是任何人的母语，而作为第二或第三语言用于特定目的，例如贸易或与殖民者沟通。另一方面，世界语是作为不同母语者之间沟通手段的共同语言。与洋泾浜语不同，世界语通常是标准化的语言，具有更复杂的语法和词汇。它们经常被用作国际组织的官方语言或学校的教学媒介。世界语也可以作为文化交流和外交的手段。总之，虽然洋泾浜语与世界语都是用于不同母语者之间沟通的简化语言，但洋泾浜语通常更为简单且不太规范，而世界语更为复杂，并在各种情境中充当官方语言。

3. Taboos and Euphemisms

Taboos and euphemisms are cultural and linguistic phenomena that reflect societal values, beliefs, and norms. They exist in all cultures, including Chinese and English-speaking ones, though the specific topics that are considered taboo may vary.

Taboos are subjects or words that are deemed inappropriate or forbidden to discuss in certain contexts due to their sensitive or offensive nature. These can include topics related to death, sex, bodily functions, and other personal matters that are considered private or uncomfortable in a given culture. For example, in many Asian cultures, it is considered rude to discuss someone's age, especially if they are older, as this can be seen as disrespectful. In

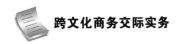

English-speaking cultures, discussing one's salary or financial situation can be considered impolite or intrusive.

Euphemisms are polite or indirect expressions used to de-emphasize an unpleasant topic or to avoid using a direct, potentially offensive term. They are often used as a substitute for taboo words or phrases. For instance, instead of saying "die", euphemisms like "passed away" or "lost" might be used. Similarly, instead of saying "disabled", one might use "differently abled" to be more inclusive and respectful.

In cross-cultural communication, understanding the nuances of taboos and euphemisms is crucial to avoid pragmatic errors and to foster effective dialogue. This includes:

Recognizing cultural differences: Knowing which topics are sensitive in different cultures can help avoid unintentional offense.

Using euphemisms appropriately: Applying euphemisms correctly can demonstrate respect and tactfulness in conversation.

Contextual awareness: Being aware of the context in which certain words or phrases are used can guide the choice of language to ensure it is appropriate for the situation.

Language sensitivity: Being sensitive to the language preferences of others, especially when discussing personal or sensitive topics, can enhance mutual respect and understanding.

Learning and adaptation: Continuously learning about the ever-evolving aspects of taboos and euphemisms in various cultures can aid in adapting to diverse social environments.

In conclusion, mastering the art of using euphemisms and being aware of taboos is essential for effective intercultural communication. It not only helps in avoiding misunderstandings but also shows respect for the cultural diversity of the people we interact with. As English learners, understanding the similarities and differences between Chinese and English taboos is vital to improve cross-cultural communication skills.

Assessment

Read each of the following questions and choose the best answer.

1. What is the primary goal of intercultural business communication?

    A. To speak fluently in another language

    B. To understand and respect cultural differences

    C. To sell products internationally

    D. To travel to different countries

2. Which of the following is an example of high-context culture?

    A. United States　　　B. Germany　　　C. Japan　　　D. Australia

3. In which country would you most likely use a first name basis when addressing someone?

    A. China   B. Brazil   C. United Kingdom   D. India

4. What is the importance of active listening in intercultural communication?

    A. It helps to avoid misunderstandings

    B. It allows for more speaking time

    C. It ensures that the speaker feels heard

    D. All of the above

5. How should you respond if a business associate from a high-power distance culture praises your work?

    A. Criticize their own work

    B. Humble acceptance

    C. Boast about your achievements

    D. Ask for a raise

6. In which culture is it considered impolite to say "no" directly?

    A. American   B. Russian   C. Japanese   D. French

7. What is the best way to show respect in a hierarchical society?

    A. Address people by their first name

    B. Use informal language

    C. Follow the chain of command

    D. Interrupt conversations frequently

8. Why is it important to be aware of cultural differences in nonverbal communication?

    A. It can prevent misunderstandings

    B. It can help you learn a new language

    C. It can improve your travel experiences

    D. All of the above

9. Which of the following is not an example of effective intercultural communication?

    A. Using humor to break the ice

    B. Avoiding eye contact during negotiations

    C. Dressing appropriately for the occasion

    D. Speaking slowly and clearly in a foreign language

10. How should you approach negotiating with someone from a collectivist culture?

    A. Focus on individual goals and achievements

    B. Emphasize group harmony and consensus

    C. Use aggressive tactics to get what you want

    D. Avoid making any concessions or compromises

Unit Project

Review the scenario of this unit and play the role of the director of sales department.

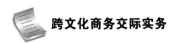

To deliver a business presentation on your new product to your international partners. Be aware of the methods to cope with the aspects of cross – culture communication to guarantee the communication is effective in the process of your presentation. Complete your checking list of essential elements you have done. Take the elements into consideration.

Case Analysis

Read the following case carefully and analyze the case by providing the answers for the following questions.

Q1：Please describe the cross‑cultural conflicts in the case.

Q2：What are the possible solutions to these conflicts?

Q3：Please evaluate this case with cross‑cultural theories.

Richard (American) was director of Oneal Inc. The Arab company in Saudi Arabia reached out to her company for collaboration. Therefore, she was designated to meet with their Arab counterparts in Riyadh, Saudi Arabia for further progress.

Three days later, Richard arrived at Riyadh and was arranged to meet Mohamed (manager of the Arab company) at 2 p. m. in the Arab company.

Richard came to the Arab company at 2 p. m. However, Mohamed didn't show up on time. Richard waited in the meeting room, checking her watch from time to time and paced the floor restlessly. Finally, Mohamed arrived at 2：45 p. m.

Mohamed：I am manager of the Arab company of Mohamed Aramco. Nice to meet you.

Richard：Nice to meet you, too. I'm Richard Huge. Thank you for meeting with me.

Mohamed：How was your trip?

Richard：Great.

Mohamed：Where are you staying while you're here?

Richard：At the hotel near the park.

Mohamed：I've never stayed there, but I've heard nice things about it. It's very handy for the conference venue.

. . .

Mohamed：Is this the first time that you have come to Saudi Arabia?

Richard：I came here three years ago.

Mohamed：Do you like Riyadh?

Richard：Yes, it's a beautiful city. (*feeling a bit impatient*)

. . .

So much talking (one hour later)

Richard: Let's start our business.

Mohamed: Oh, okay.

. . .

During the meeting, Mohamed's assistant knocked on the door.

The assistant: Excuse me! Boss you have an incoming call.

Mohamed (*answered the phone*) : Hello?. . .

Richard looked at her watch again.

. . .

Further Reading

How to Make a Business Presentation in English

Could you imagine you have to give an important presentation in English tomorrow, how would you feel about it? This reading text will help you learn useful phrases and techniques to introduce yourself and your topic, keep your ideas organized, deal with problems and respond to questions from audience members.

Imagine you are standing in front of your colleagues, you need to introduce yourself and what your presentation is about. What are some words and phrases you could use?

Part One　How to Introduce Yourself and Your Topic

If some people in the audience don't know who you are, you should introduce yourself and your position as well. In a more formal setting, you could say something like this, "Good morning, everyone. For those who don't know me, my name is Richard, and I work in the marketing department. " or "Hello everybody. Before we begin, let me introduce myself briefly. I'm

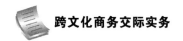

Reese, and I'm the head of HR. " If you work in a informal company, you could say, "Hi guys, if you don't know me, I'm Sylvia and I work in digital marketing. " or you could also say, "Hello! I see some new faces, so I'll introduce myself first: I'm Julia and I'm one of our customer service team. "

Next you need introduce your topic. If your presentation topic is simple, you could say just one sentence like this, "Today, I'm going to be talking about our new HR policies and how they affect you. " or "I'd like to talk to you about quality control and why are all responsible for quality control whichever department you work in. " If your topic is more complex, you might add more details to break your ideas into stages. For example, "I'll begin by outlining polices, and then I'll go on highlighting what they mean for you and your working habit. Finally I'll discuss why we feel these polices are necessary and beneficial for us all. " Here are examples which you could use as templates to begin your presentation.

You could start by saying that "I'll begin by .... then I'll ... finally, I'll..." or you could also say "First of all, I'll... I'll continue by... To finish, I'll...".

Part Two   How to Make a Strong Start

In our life, there are good speakers and bad speakers. Good speakers grab your attention and don't let go and you want to hear what they want to say. You feel interested and energized by listening to them. Bad speakers are the opposite. Even if you try to make yourself listen, you find that your attention drifts away. Your eyelids feel heavy and you have to struggle to stay awake. So here is a question: what's the differences between good speakers and bad speakers? And how can you make sure you speak effectively when you make your presentation in English? Here is one way to think about it: bad speakers don't think they have to earn your attention while good speakers understand that no one has to listen to them, so they work hard to make you want to pay attention. What does this mean to you and your presentation? Getting people's attention starts from the beginning. You need to make it clear what people should expect from your presentation, and why they should care about what you have to say. Sounds like a nice idea, but how do you do this?

Here are three techniques you can use.

One is to establish a problem which many people in your audience have. Then establish that you have a solution to their problem. For example, Have you ever felt unfairly treated at work, or felt that the work you do isn't appreciated? We've been working to design new HR policies that will make sure all staff get fair recognition for their contribution to the company. In this way you take a boring-sounding topic like HR policies, and you make it more relevant to your audience by connecting it with their experiences and feelings.

The second technique is to mention an interesting fact or surprising statistics to get people's attention. For example, you could start by a question like this: "Did you know that the average office worker spends eight hours a day at work, but only does four hours of productive, useful work? I'm here to tell you about quality control, and how you can use this idea to make better use of your time?"

Finally, you can engage people by telling a short story and connecting it to your topic. Stories are powerful, and they can add an emotional dimension to your topic if you do it well. For example, "I once met a young salesman — I won't mention his name. He spent several weeks building a relationship with a potential client. He worked overtime, and he was working so hard that he was under severe stress which started to affect his personal life. In the end, he didn't close the deal. The client signed with another firm. Today, I'm going to talk about confidence as a sales tool, and how you can avoid the traps that this young man fell into".

Part Three   Using Signposting Language

There's a famous quote about making presentation: "Tell the audience what you're going to say, say it, and then tell them what you've said." This comes from Dale Carnegie, a very successful American salesman and writer. He lived a long time ago, but his advice is still relevant today. The point is that having interesting or relevant information is not enough. How you structure and organize your information is equally important. Using signposting language means using words and phrases to show the audience where your points begin and end, to show what's coming next, and to remind them about things you talked about before. You can use signposting language to move from one point to the next.

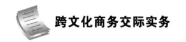
单元小结

1 学习目标

完成本单元学习后，你将能够：

- 理解并识别不同的口头交流风格
- 识别语言的多样性
- 说明语言差异并处理翻译问题
- 分析不同文化背景下的规范，并学会在商业互动中与不同背景的人沟通

2 情景模拟

假设你是一家位于华南地区最大的汽车制造合资企业的人力资源总监。你需要通知一位来自爱尔兰的高级销售经理，他将被解雇。你需要找到一种合适的方式，来委婉地传达这个坏消息。

3 言语交流

3.1 言语交流的定义

言语交流是指使用词语进行的口头或书面形式的交流。例如，人们与朋友聊天，小组讨论问题，进行公开演讲，撰写文章，完成教授布置的作业，员工通过电子邮件向公司经理写报告。

言语交流可以表达我们想要表达的各种想法。它比其他方式更清晰、更高效。它还能保存和传播信息。此外，在言语交流中需要考虑文化因素。在英语文化中，狮子是勇气、危险和力量的象征，被认为是动物之王。但在中国文化中，狮子并不享有这样的内涵意义。

3.2 言语交流中的文化因素

一个词可能在一种语言中有丰富的文化创造的内涵意义，而在另一种语言中很少具有相同的含义。它有时具有文化特征。因此，不同文化背景的人有不同的口头交流方式。下面我们就展示东方人和西方人交流的不同之处。

言语交流可以表达我们想要表达的各种想法；它既能保存信息也能传播信息，并且比其他方式更清晰、更高效。但是东方人和西方人之间的交流方式大不相同。东方人通常更有礼貌、更含糊，经常"拐弯抹角"地交谈，有很多寒暄和对他人的关心；而西方人通常更直接，他们常常直接进入正题或首先提出个人观点。

当谈话时，东方人往往表面上顺从对方的观点，而不作任何公开抗议。然而，西方人通常会直接提出他们的不同意见或抗议。在东方人的语言中有许多敬语形式，西方人认为这些是多余的。西方人确实有礼貌的表达，但每次会面交换这些表达的时间通常很短。对东方人来说，西方人显得粗鲁。当谈到立场时，东方人倾向于先陈述理由。相反，西方人通常先表明立场，然后才是理由。

当涉及寒暄和进入正题时，东方人在讨论之前倾向于花很多时间谈论不重要的事情，为严肃的讨论做准备。西方人不这样做。东方人经常表现出对他人的大量关心，西方人认为这是干涉别人事务的行为。东方人在谈话时往往含糊其词，这常常给西方人带来不快，因为这不符合他们的习惯。在西方辩论时，双方通常会有几轮争论，而在东方，双方最多只表达一次各自的观点，然后要么互相让步，要么保持沉默。

3.3　语言与文化

语义学是一个将单词与意义关联起来的系统，是对单词意义的研究。我们用单词与外部世界交流，分享过去，对现在施加一些控制，形成对未来的形象。

我们用词语来说服、交换想法、表达观点、寻求信息和表达感情。语言很重要；它对人类行为有重大影响。

4　跨文化交流中的语用学

语用学是研究语言对人类感知和行为的影响。该研究的目的是关注说话者如何使用语言以实现成功的交流。它将帮助我们理解如何在文化语境中恰当地交流。

语用学关注语境意义，而语义学则关注来自语言学知识的意义。通过语义上理解单词或句子，我们会无意识地产生语用失误。

我们应该寻找"人们意味着什么"，而不是"单词意味着什么"。假设"人是意义的容器"，而不是"单词是意义的容器"。

5　语言多样性与翻译

我们每天都面临着语言多样性的现实，全球估计有 7 000 种语言在使用。然而，这种多样性也给翻译和沟通带来了重大挑战。

翻译中最大的问题之一是语言之间缺乏完全对等的词汇。一种语言中常见的词语或短语在另一种语言中可能不存在，或者意义完全不同。这可能导致混淆和误解，特别在技术或专业领域，精确性至关重要。

另一个问题是语言的细微差别，如习语、口语表达和文化参考，这些不能直接翻译成其他语言。翻译者必须找到准确传达这些细微差别的方法，同时保持原文的意义。

此外，翻译需要对源语言和目标语言以及它们代表的文化有深刻理解。翻译者必须能够识别文化差异，并相应地调整他们的翻译，以避免文化不敏感或误解。

最后，还有跟上不断发展的语言的挑战。新的单词和短语不断被引入，语言随着时间的推移继续演变。翻译者必须跟上这些变化，以确保他们的翻译保持准确和相关。尽管语言多样性给翻译带来重大挑战，但认识到并解决这些问题对于促进跨语言和文化障碍的有效沟通至关重要。

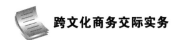

　　＊本单元智慧职教线上课程：https：//zyk．icve．com．cn/courseDetailed？id＝obbaaaqvo4doejfjffeicq&openCourse＝obbaaaqvw79e5opp1bwbg.

Unit 5　习题参考答案

Unit 6 Nonverbal Intercultural Business Communication

Ancient Chinese Wisdom

The master said, "When walking along with two others, I can always learn from those I am with. I would single out their good qualities and follow them, then notice their bad qualities and avoid them". (子曰："三人行，必有我师焉，择其善者而从之，其不善者而改之。")

From *Analects* （《论语》）

Learning Objectives

After learning this unit, you shall be able to:

- Get to know what is nonverbal communication.
- Describe the different types of nonverbal communication.
- Enhance the intercultural awareness and sensitivity.
- Understand and appropriately utilize nonverbal communication techniques across various cultures.

Project Scenario

After learning this unit, finish the unit project on the basis of the following scenario.

Suppose you are a Chinese business professional leading a delegation to negotiate a joint venture with a American company. The meeting will take place in the United States, and you are aware that you can infer the inner thoughts through facial expression and gestures during negotiations. In order to handle the process of the negotiation, you need to prepare yourself and your team for effective nonverbal communication during the meeting.

Lead-in

Watch the video clip from Friends about nonverbal communication and answer the following questions.

- What meanings do you think the nonverbal behavior in the video clip conveyed?
- What do you think of the importance of the nonverbal communication?

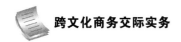

Part A   Nonverbal Communication

Good communication mixes words and silent signs. It is said that only 7% of our message comes from the words we say. A huge 93% comes from nonverbal signs. This shows how important nonverbal communication is in the context of cross−cultural business interactions. It's about sending messages without talking or writing, particularly crucial when verbal communication is limited by language barriers or cultural differences. Being good at this can help you a lot with making friends, engaging with them, and building strong bonds, especially with people from different cultures.

This part of the book focuses on nonverbal communication in the cross−cultural business setting. It explains what nonverbal communication is, highlights its significance in cross−cultural business interactions, discusses its various functions, and delves into the diverse forms it takes, especially focusing on the application of different types of nonverbal communication in the context of international business.

1. Definition of Nonverbal Communication

Non−verbal intercultural communication refers to the process of exchanging information and meaning between individuals from different cultural backgrounds without using spoken or written language. It involves the use of body language, gestures, facial expressions, eye contact, posture, and other non−verbal cues that can convey emotions, attitudes, and intentions across cultural boundaries. Understanding and interpreting non−verbal cues is crucial in intercultural communication as it helps to avoid misunderstandings and foster mutual understanding and respect.

The study of nonverbal communication really took off in the 1950s. In 1952, Ray Birdwhistell released *An Introduction to Kinesics*, which was key in exploring how we use our bodies to communicate. Then, in 1959, Edward T. Hall wrote *The Silent Language*, looking at how people use their bodies and the space around them to send messages. Hall said that nonverbal communication involves using all our senses except hearing.

Paul Ekman also studied facial expressions and emotions, finding that certain facial expressions are linked to specific feelings across different cultures. This meant that our faces show emotions in a way that everyone can understand, no matter what language they speak.

Over time, researchers have discovered more about body language, personal space, and other nonverbal ways of communicating. Technology has helped us see these interactions more clearly.

Nowadays, understanding nonverbal communication is super important, especially in the business world where people from different cultures meet. Getting this right helps build strong relationships and avoid misunderstandings. As we learn more, we get better at interacting with each other globally.

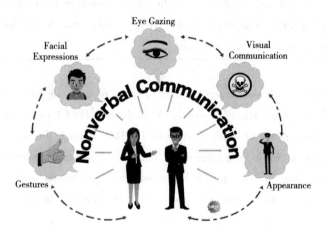

Task 1: Cross-cultural Comparison

Compare and contrast a characteristic nonverbal behavior commonly observed in Chinese individuals during everyday interactions with that of Americans.

2. Importance of Nonverbal Communication

Nonverbal behavior is a key component of communication studies. As previously discussed, nonverbal communication includes "everything except the actual words". A significant portion of the information and emotion we gather from conversations is not conveyed through the actual words spoken but rather through nonverbal cues.

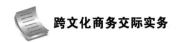

These cues include facial expressions, body language, gestures, eye contact, and even the tone of voice. In essence, it means that what is not said verbally often carries substantial weight in how we interpret and understand communication. The following three reasons can help us better understand the importance of nonverbal communication:

Firstly, nonverbal behavior <u>makes up a large part of the meaning we get from conversations</u>. One level of meaning is the openly stated messages, which is the cognitive content. This is the part we consciously interpret. Another level, affective content, involves emotions, attitudes, and behaviors.

Dialogue 1

Tom: Good morning, John. How's it going?

John: Oh, hey. I'm good, just the usual workload.

Later Tom noticed John's facial tension and the pile of documents on his desk. It became clear that "managing fine" was his way of saying he was drowning under the pressure of upcoming deadlines and project complexities.

The cognitive content of this encounter consists of what is said out loud, while the affective content involves the transmission of feelings. Mehrabian (1981) suggests that 93% of the meaning in a conversation is conveyed nonverbally — 38% through the voice and 55% through facial expressions. Thus, while communicating, only 7% of our messages are conveyed through words, 38% through our voice, and 55% through our expressions and actions. Nonverbal behavior is important because it represents most of the emotion expressed in conversations.

Secondly, nonverbal behavior is important because it <u>naturally mirrors the speaker's subconscious</u>. We usually try to control the words we speak. Sometimes we may slip up and reveal too much. However, with nonverbal behavior, our true emotions may be revealed. Even skilled deceivers can be uncovered by subtle nonverbal cues they unintentionally display. Nonverbal behavior isn't easily manipulated; we tend to trust it, even when verbal statements contradict it. It occurs instinctively, without conscious thought. We often overlook these nonverbal signals, but they greatly influence communication.

Dialogue 2

Officer (calmly): We're investigating a case and need you to account for your whereabouts last night.

Suspect (with hand under the chin, eyes darting side to side): Oh, no problem. I was at home watching a movie by myself last night.

> **Officer** (looking directly at the suspect): Can you tell me what movie you watched?
>
> **Suspect** (touching his nose, slightly hesitant): It was a sci-fi film, something like *Interstellar Exploration.*
>
> **Officer** (nodding gently): I see. Do you have any receipts from buying the movie ticket or any online viewing records at home?
>
> **Suspect** (starting to fidget with his fingers, avoiding eye contact): Uh, I mean, I might have remembered it wrong; I was actually reading a book at home.
>
> **Officer** (evenly): What's the name of the book?
>
> **Suspect** (visibly nervous, looking around): It's just a novel, *Door to the Dark Night.*
>
> **Officer** (calmly): So you said the title was "Door to the Dark Night", right? We'll continue to verify that.

In this dialogue, the suspect exhibited several typical nonverbal signs of deception when answering the officer's questions. His shifting eye contact, nose touching, and finger fidgeting were signs of nervousness and discomfort. When asked about specific details, he became increasingly tense and changed his initial story. These nonverbal behaviors indicated that the suspect was likely lying.

A third reason for the importance of nonverbal communication is that <u>nonverbal communication follows us everywhere, even when we don't say a word</u>. It's like another language our bodies and faces speak. We send messages with our actions, like nodding, smiling, or crossing our arms. Our body movements and the way we use space can also tell others how we feel. For instance, if we are happy, we might move our body more freely; if we are nervous, we might fidget or avoid eye contact.

These nonverbal signals help us understand each other better. They can show if someone is happy, sad, angry, or scared without them needing to explain. Understanding these silent cues is especially important when words aren't enough or when someone might be feeling unsure. For example, think about a job interview. The way you sit, shake hands firmly, and make eye contact can show you're confident. Or, in a friendship, if someone leans in when you talk, it can mean they're really listening and care about what you're saying.

Paying attention to these nonverbal signs can greatly improve how people connect with others. It helps people be better friends, coworkers, and family members, avoid misunderstandings and build stronger, more understanding relationships.

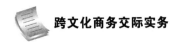
Task 2: Understanding the Concepts

Present some examples concerning the differences between verbal communication and nonverbal communication.

Verbal Communication	Nonverbal Communication
Conscious	Subconscious
Discontinuous	Continuous
Acquired	Natural

3. Functions of Nonverbal Communication

Nonverbal communication performs several key functions. They underline the close link between gestures and words. For instance, a teacher might use their hands to highlight a crucial point (emphasizing) or maintain eye contact to encourage student participation (controlling). These functions are accenting, complementing, contradicting, regulating, repeating and substituting.

Accenting: Nonverbal communication can be used to emphasize or highlight specific words or phrases spoken during conversation. For example, a speaker might raise their voice or use gestures to underscore a key point, drawing the listener's attention to it and ensuring its importance is understood.

Complementing: Nonverbal cues often complement the verbal message by adding context or emotional nuance. For instance, a warm smile or a nod can reinforce positive feedback, while folded arms might suggest defensiveness or disagreement, thus enriching the message with additional layers of meaning.

Contradicting: Sometimes nonverbal signals can contradict the spoken words, sending a mixed message. For example, saying "I'm fine" in a monotone voice while frowning might indicate that the person is actually not okay, showing that nonverbal cues can reveal true feelings that spoken words seek to conceal.

Regulating: Nonverbal communication helps regulate the flow of conversation by signaling turn-taking, pauses, and transitions between topics. Raised eyebrows or a head nod can invite a person to speak, while looking away or crossing arms might signal that it's time to end the conversation or change the subject.

Repeating: Nonverbal actions can be used to repeat or reinforce a verbal message, enhancing clarity and understanding. For example, pointing to an object while mentioning it or using a gesture to illustrate a concept can help solidify the message in the listener's mind.

Substituting: In situations where speaking might be inappropriate or not possible, nonverbal communication can substitute for verbal messages. A thumbs-up or a OK sign can stand in for actual words, conveying agreement or approval without making a sound. This can be particularly useful in environments where speaking would disrupt or in situations of speech impairment.

Nonverbal communication in business contexts encompasses various types that supplement or replace spoken language, including body language, para-language, time language and special language etc.

Task 3: Understanding the Concepts

Work in groups. Conduct online research to identify examples from intercultural business communication that specifically illustrate each of the seven functions of nonverbal communication.

Functions	Examples
Accenting	
Complementing	
Contradicting	
Regulating	
Repeating	
Substituting	

Part B   Body Language

Body language is a significant component of nonverbal communication, conveying meanings through physical behavior, movements, and postures. It includes various cues such as gestures, facial expressions, eye contact, and body postures. These nonverbal signals can indicate emotions, attitudes, and intentions, often reinforcing or contradicting the spoken words.

1. Gestures

Gestures are a key part of nonverbal communication. Some gestures have common meanings, but many differ from one culture to another. Here are examples of how the same gesture can

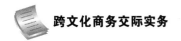

have different interpretations across cultures.

<u>Nodding</u>: In many cultures, nodding means agreement or affirmation. However, in Bulgaria and neighboring regions, a head nod similar to the affirmative gesture in Western cultures actually indicates disagreement or negation. Conversely, a head shake, which in many countries means "no", is used to express agreement. This can lead to considerable confusion during cross-cultural interactions if the gesture's true meaning is not understood.

<u>Thumbs-up</u>: In many Western cultures, thumbs-up indicates approval or a job well done. Conversely, in the Middle East, specifically in Iran and Afghanistan, the thumbs-up gesture should be used with caution as it can carry an obscene connotation similar to the extended middle finger in Western cultures. It is often considered rude or offensive, especially if the gesture is directed at someone.

<u>Tapping your fingers</u>: Tapping your fingers on the table or any surface may convey impatience in the United States. Someone observing this behavior might infer that the person is ready to move on or is becoming impatient with the current pace of events. In Japan, however, this same gesture is more likely to be interpreted as a signal of urgency or a polite way of indicating that someone should speed up their actions, without carrying the negative connotation of impatience.

<u>OK sign</u>: The OK sign, formed by connecting the thumb and forefinger into a circle, means everything is okay in most Western contexts. However, in Brazil, making the circle with your fingers and pointing it towards someone is a serious insult equivalent to an aggressive and offensive hand gesture in the United States. In Japan, the same hand gesture is associated with money; small businesses or street vendors might use it while discussing prices, signaling "about this much" or "that is the price".

<u>Peace sign</u>: The peace sign gesture is made by extending the index finger and middle finger while keeping the other fingers folded down. The two extended fingers are then parted to form a "V" shape, and the palm typically faces outward. This gesture is widely recognized as symbolizing peace in many Western countries due to its association with the victory sign during World War II. However, its cultural meaning can vary significantly.

In many European and American contexts, the peace sign simply denotes peace or victory. It's often used in positive contexts, such as photographs or when promoting harmony.

In South American countries like Brazil and Venezuela, the same peace sign (two fingers up, palm facing out) is considered extremely rude and offensive. The gesture there is similar to flipping the bird (the middle finger) in many Western cultures. Using this gesture publicly could provoke serious social disapproval or even physical confrontation.

In some Asian countries, especially in Japan and South Korea, the peace sign gesture might not carry the same connotation of peace as it does in the West. Instead, it's sometimes used in playful or cute poses, often by young people or during photo-taking. However, it doesn't have the strong obscene connotation as in Brazil.

In some Middle Eastern countries, the peace sign may not have a universally understood meaning and could be viewed simply as a neutral gesture. However, given the vast diversity across Middle Eastern cultures, it's advisable to use non-verbal communication cautiously and observe how locals interact before using any hand gesture.

The peace sign serves as a vivid example of how the same gesture can have completely opposite meanings in different cultures. What is a symbol of peace and positivity in one culture can be deeply offensive in another. This underscores the importance of understanding cultural nuances when engaging in international business or when traveling abroad. Being aware of these differences can help individuals navigate cross-cultural interactions with respect and sensitivity, avoiding unintentional offense that could harm personal or professional relationships.

These examples illustrate how important it is to understand the cultural context when interpreting nonverbal gestures in international business communication.

Case Analysis

> During an international business meeting between American and Brazilian teams, an American manager attempted to signal agreement using the OK sign gesture. This action, while commonly accepted in the US as a sign of approval or agreement, was deeply offensive to the Brazilian team.
>
> The misunderstanding led to a tense meeting atmosphere and nearly jeopardized the potential business deal.

The root cause of the conflict was the vast difference in cultural interpretations of the OK sign gesture. In the US, forming a circle with the thumb and forefinger is a positive affirmation. However, in Brazil, this hand gesture is obscene and should be avoided in professional settings. The American manager's use of this gesture was therefore perceived as unprofessional and disrespectful by the Brazilian team.

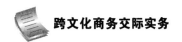

The misuse of the gesture created an immediate sense of discomfort and offense among the Brazilian executives, making it difficult for them to continue the meeting constructively. This not only strained the relationship but also threatened to derail the business negotiations.

After realizing the error, the American manager apologized sincerely for the unintended offense. To manage the situation and prevent future similar incidents, both parties agreed to participate in a session on cross-cultural communication. These sessions aimed to educate everyone on the differences in nonverbal cues and appropriate behaviors in each other's cultures.

Additional steps showed as follows.

Cultural sensitivity training: Organizing regular training sessions to educate staff on cultural differences, focusing on both verbal and nonverbal communication.

Clear communication guidelines: Establishing clear guidelines for appropriate behavior during international meetings, including a list of avoidable gestures and their potential consequences.

Open dialogue: Encouraging open dialogue between teams from different cultures to discuss potential areas of misunderstanding and how to avoid them.

Continuous learning: Promoting a culture of learning within the organization, where employees are encouraged to share their own cultural insights and learn from others.

Relationship mentoring: Assigning cultural mentors to international projects, who can guide and advise on cultural matters in real-time.

2. Postures

In the realm of non-verbal communication, postures serve as a powerful tool for expressing emotions, intentions, and attitudes. An individual's posture can convey a wide range of information, from confidence and openness to defensiveness and withdrawal. In many cultures, an open posture, such as leaning forward with uncrossed arms and legs, can signal interest, receptivity, and a willingness to engage. This posture is often well-received in business and negotiation settings as it suggests a collaborative and friendly approach.

Conversely, a closed posture, characterized by crossed arms and legs, can indicate defensiveness, disinterest, or discomfort. This posture may create barriers in cross-cultural interactions, as it can be perceived as standoffish or unapproachable. Posture can also reflect status and power dynamics. For example, individuals in positions of authority may adopt more expansive postures, taking up more physical space, while those who are less confident or of lower status may adopt more constricted postures.

It's essential to recognize that the interpretation of postures can vary significantly across cultures. What is considered a friendly or open posture in one culture might be seen as aggressive or disrespectful in another. For instance, in some Asian cultures, pointing one's feet towards another person or a sacred object can be highly offensive, whereas this gesture might go unnoticed or have a different connotation in Western cultures.

Before engaging in cross-cultural interactions, observe the postures commonly used by your interlocutors. This can provide insight into cultural norms and preferences. Where appropriate, mirroring the postures of your counterparts can foster a sense of rapport and mutual understanding. Be mindful of your postures and make adjustments according to the context and cultural norms. For example, if you are in a culture that values formality, maintain a more composed and less expansive posture during meetings. During interactions, be responsive to feedback. If your posture is misinterpreted or seems to cause discomfort, adjust accordingly. This flexibility not only avoids conflict but also demonstrates respect and cultural sensitivity.

In conclusion, postures play a vital role in non-verbal communication, especially in the context of cross-cultural interactions. By being aware of and adapting your posture, you can enhance communication effectiveness and build stronger, more respectful international relationships.

3. Eye Contact

In the realm of business communications, eye contact is a potent non-verbal signal that can convey confidence, interest, respect, or dominance. However, the rules and meanings associated with eye contact vary significantly across cultures. Here's an exploration of cultural differences in eye contact and their implications for cross-cultural business interactions.

In many Western societies, including the United States, steady eye contact is generally seen as a sign of honesty, confidence, and attentiveness. During business conversations, maintaining moderate to strong eye contact suggests sincerity and engagement. However, excessive eye contact may be perceived as aggressive or challenging.

In many East and Southeast Asian cultures, such as Japan and Korea, intense eye contact can be viewed as rude or confrontational. Modesty and respect often dictate less frequent or softer eye contact, especially when speaking with superiors or in formal settings. In these cultures, indirect eye contact or looking away periodically can show politeness and deference.

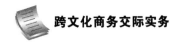

In the <u>Middle East</u>, intense eye contact is common and expected during conversations, reflecting attentiveness and interest. However, it is important to note that during conversations with the opposite sex, especially in conservative societies, prolonged eye contact may be considered inappropriate or flirtatious.

In many <u>Latin American countries</u>, lively and expressive communication styles are prevalent, and eye contact is an integral part of the interaction. It signals interest and connection. However, similar to Middle Eastern cultures, there may be specific circumstances where reduced eye contact is preferred, especially in mixed−gender formal settings.

In many <u>African societies</u>, eye contact is an essential aspect of communication and can indicate respect and attentiveness. However, the duration and intensity of eye contact can vary based on context and relationship dynamics. For instance, in some tribes, intense eye contact can signify a challenge or confrontation, whereas in others, it might be a way to demonstrate sincerity.

In conclusion, while eye contact is a universal aspect of human communication, its execution and interpretation are deeply influenced by culture. By understanding and adapting to cultural norms regarding eye contact, you can improve the effectiveness of your cross−cultural business communications and build stronger, more respectful professional relationships.

4. Facial Expressions

Facial expressions play a critical role in business communication as they are key in conveying emotions and attitudes, transcending language barriers to directly express an individual's reactions and feelings. However, the interpretation and use of facial expressions vary across cultures, which is crucial for effective cross−cultural business communication. Here, we will explore the cultural differences in facial expressions and their significance in non−verbal business communications.

In many <u>Western societies</u>, facial expressions tend to be more open and expressive, with a wider range of emotions shown. For instance, Americans may display enthusiasm, surprise, or disappointment openly through facial expressions during business discussions. This openness helps to build rapport and show sincerity.

In contrast, many <u>Asian cultures</u> value subtlety and restraint in emotional expression, particularly in formal or business settings. For example, Japanese and Chinese individuals might control facial expressions to maintain composure and avoid causing discomfort or losing face. Smiling can be used ambiguously, sometimes to conceal true feelings or ease social tension.

In Middle Eastern societies, facial expressions are an integral part of communication but can be misinterpreted by those unfamiliar with the culture. For instance, Arab individuals might use intense facial expressions to negotiate or discuss business matters, which can be seen as aggressive or overly emotional by Western standards.

Latin American cultures are known for their expressiveness, including facial expressions that can be vibrant and emotive. In business interactions, this expressiveness can create a warm and engaging atmosphere but may also require careful management to ensure professionalism and clarity in message delivery.

In African societies, facial expressions often reflect the communal and relationship–oriented nature of communication. Smiles and nods are commonly used to encourage dialogue and show agreement, even when disagreements exist, reflecting a focus on harmony and respect.

In conclusion, facial expressions are a rich and complex aspect of non–verbal communication that varies significantly across cultures. By developing an awareness of these differences and adapting your communication style accordingly, you can improve the effectiveness of your cross–cultural business interactions and foster stronger, more respectful professional relationships.

5. Body Touch

In the realm of business communication, body touch, also known as haptics or tactile communication, can play a significant role in establishing rapport, trust, and understanding. However, the use and interpretation of body touch vary greatly across cultures, impacting how individuals from different backgrounds interact in professional settings. Here's an exploration of cultural differences in body touch and their significance for non–verbal business communications.

In many Western societies, including the United States and Canada, the use of body touch in business settings is generally limited and cautious. A handshake is a common and accepted form of physical contact, symbolizing agreement or greeting. However, more extensive or frequent physical contact might be considered unprofessional or inappropriate.

In many Asian countries, physical contact is typically more restricted than in Western cultures, especially between genders and in formal contexts. For instance, in Japan, bowing is a common form of respectful greeting that replaces physical contact. In India, the traditional Namaste gesture (hands together, slight bow) serves a similar purpose.

In many <u>Middle Eastern societies</u>, body touch is more common and can include hugging, holding hands, or touching arms during conversations. These gestures are expressions of warmth and friendship. However, it's essential to be aware that such interactions might be strictly regulated by cultural norms regarding gender and social status.

<u>Latin American cultures</u> are known for their warm and tactile style of communication. Physical contact, such as light touches on the arm or back, might be used frequently and can indicate friendship and camaraderie. However, as with Middle Eastern cultures, the degree of physical contact can depend on the relationship and the context.

In <u>African societies</u>, the use of body touch varies widely but often plays a significant role in communication. Handshakes, embraces, and other forms of physical contact can be ways to show respect, acknowledgement, or solidarity. The meaning and appropriateness of these gestures can depend on the ethnic group, region, and specific social context.

Examples of Kinetics

In conclusion, body touch is a complex aspect of non-verbal communication that requires careful navigation in cross-cultural business settings. By understanding and respecting the diverse norms surrounding physical contact, you can foster positive relationships and ensure successful interactions across cultures.

Task 4: Preparing for the Unit Project

1. Applying the Concepts

Work in groups. Do some research and make a note of the information on body language *dos* and *don'ts* in business settings for a specific culture.

2. Critical Thinking

Analyze the potential challenges and strategies for adapting to these nonverbal norms in international business interactions.

Part C Para-Language

Para-language refers to the non-verbal aspects of speech that accompany the actual words spoken, including vocal qualities such as volume, pitch, pace, and tone. These elements can modify the meaning or emphasize the emotions behind the words, often conveying subtleties that transcend the literal interpretation of the spoken text.

Para – language may also include the intentional use of silence, as well as other vocal expressions like laughter, crying, and sighs, which add an additional layer of emotional depth and context to communication. It is an integral part of both verbal and non – verbal communication, influencing how messages are received and understood by listeners.

Imagine the music embedded in your voice. It's not the words you say, but the melody with which you sing them. Consider the volume that can either swell or diminish, the pitch that can soar or descend, the pace that may hurry or dawdle, and the tone that adds a distinct color to your voice. These elements possess the capacity to alter the meaning of your spoken words or to underscore the feelings concealed within them.

And in the realm of para–language, let us not overlook the significance of silence — a potent tool in its own right, capable of communicating just as much as sound itself. Silence can be an intentional withholding of speech, a nonverbal expression of emotion, or a strategic pause that speaks volumes.

Silence, viewed as a facet of para – language, can articulate a vast array of emotions and implications, such as careful consideration, empathy, wrath, strain, contemplation, expectation, deference, restraint, comfort, and secrecy. The way we interpret silence often hinges on the context in which it occurs and the individuals participating in the conversation.

1. Stress and Intonation

Stress and intonation in para–language play a crucial role in conveying meaning and emotion in verbal communication.

Stress refers to the emphasis or force given to a particular word or syllable within a sentence. It can dramatically alter the meaning of a sentence or phrase. By stressing a specific word, a speaker can emphasize its importance in the context of the message. For instance, "I said I was sorry" can convey different levels of sincerity or frustration depending on which word is stressed. Sometimes stress can distinguish between words that are spelled the same but have different meanings based on syllable emphasis, such as "permit" (permission) versus "permit" (to allow). Stress can also clarify the speaker's intention or emotional state, indicating excitement, anger, surprise, or other feelings.

Intonation involves the variation in pitch or tone used when speaking. It can influence how a statement is perceived, indicating questions, commands, or varying degrees of uncertainty or confidence.

- Rising intonation: Often used in yes or no questions or indicating uncertainty, curiosity, or encouragement for the listener to continue speaking.

- Falling intonation: Typically found in declarative statements or commands, indicating certainty or finality.
- Level intonation: A steady pitch that can sometimes be associated with boredom or disinterest.

Understanding and adapting to these para – language elements is essential for effective intercultural communication, as misinterpretations can lead to confusion or offense. Practice and awareness can help individuals improve their ability to use and interpret stress and intonation appropriately in diverse cultural contexts.

Task 5: Understanding the Concepts

Work in pairs. Each student should take a turn reading one of the following sentences out loud, focusing on placing stress on different words each time to change the meaning.

1. I need the report tomorrow.
2. Can you help me with this?
3. We're meeting at 3 p. m.
4. That's a good idea.
5. I didn't say that.
6. Let's discuss this further.
7. I have a meeting now.
8. Could you send me the updates?
9. It's been a pleasure working with you.
10. I think we should reconsider this approach.

---

2. Speech Rate

Speech rate refers to the pace at which an individual speaks, usually measured in words per minute (WPM) or syllables per second. It can vary depending on the speaker's emotional state, level of engagement with the topic, cultural background, and more.

Speaking rapidly can make it challenging for the audience to absorb the information and track the speaker's line of reasoning, potentially giving off an impression of irritability, impatience, or unreliability. Conversely, a slower speaking tempo often conveys confidence, carefulness, and prudence, helping the speaker seem more relaxed and making a positive impact on their audience. Nevertheless, if one speaks too slowly, the interaction can become dull, causing the listeners to lose interest and focus. Thus, maintaining an appropriate speech speed is crucial.

A moderate speech rate is generally clearer and easier to understand. Too fast, and listeners may miss information; too slow, and they may lose interest or become impatient. Fast speech can be perceived as eager, excited, or even anxious, while slow speech can come across as confident, thoughtful, or disinterested. And a dynamic speech rate can make conversations more engaging, helping to emphasize important points and maintain the listener's interest.

3. Volume

Volume refers to the relative loudness or softness of a speaker's voice during verbal communication. It can vary from whisper-quiet to almost shouting and is an important aspect of how speech is delivered and interpreted.

Several factors can influence the volume at which someone speaks. Normally, frustration, anger, or excitement can lead to increased volume, while sadness, introspection, or uncertainty might result in a softer voice. Besides, public speaking or noisy environments necessitate a louder volume, whereas intimate conversations or quiet settings allow for softer speech. Some cultures are more comfortable with expressive, loud speech, while others value a softer, more restrained vocal expression. Extroverted or assertive individuals might speak more loudly, while introverted or cautious speakers might naturally have a softer volume.

In intercultural business settings, adjusting your volume appropriately can help ensure your message is received as intended.

- Be aware: Pay attention to the volume of your conversation partners and the environmental noise level to gauge the appropriate volume for your speech.
- Modulate: Vary your volume to emphasize key points, but do so in a culturally sensitive manner.
- Avoid extremes: Unless necessary, avoid speaking too loudly or too softly to prevent misinterpretation or discomfort.

Task 6: Furthering Your Understanding

1. *Read the following passage aloud at your normal volume. Have someone else listen and provide feedback on your usual speaking volume.*

Communication is the key to success in the global marketplace. It allows us to build relationships, understand diverse perspectives, and collaborate effectively. By mastering the nuances of intercultural communication, we can navigate the complexities of international business with confidence and grace.

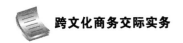
> **2.** *Read the passage again, intentionally changing your volume. Soften your voice on less important words and emphasize key points with increased volume. Consider how different volumes made you feel and how they might affect your messages in various contexts.*

Task 7: Preparing for the Unit Project

1. Applying the Concepts

Initiate an online exploration to uncover details about the para-language frequently employed in corporate deals. Following this, collaborate in quartets to deliberate and devise a concise workshop for the negotiation squad. Formulate precise recommendations regarding the employment of para-language to bolster the impending talks with the American firm.

2. Critical Thinking

In the context of intercultural business interactions, how is "silence" perceived? Can it be categorized under a specific type of para-language? Collaboratively examine these queries with your peers and subsequently share your insights with the larger audience.

Part D   Time Language

1. Chronemics in Cross-Cultural Business Communication

Time language, also known as Chronemics, plays a critical role in cross-cultural business communication. Different cultures have different rhythms when it comes to time, showing us a lot about their values and norms. It involves understanding and respecting different cultural perspectives on time, which can significantly impact business interactions. This chapter will delve into the importance of Chronemics, its variations across cultures, and practical strategies for effectively adapting to these variations in a business context.

Cross-culture
Time Differences

Chronemics refers to the study of time in communication, exploring how individuals perceive, structure, and utilize time within their interactions. It focuses on various aspects of time management and perception.

2. Punctuality and Deadlines

Cultures vary widely in their attitudes towards punctuality and deadlines. For instance, in North

America and Northern Europe, being on time is generally seen as a sign of respect and professionalism. In these cultures, deadlines are firm and lateness is often perceived as a lack of commitment or organizational skill. These cultures typically follow a monochronic approach to time, where schedules are strictly planned and each task or appointment is allocated a specific block of time.

On the other hand, some Mediterranean and Latin American cultures have a more flexible approach to time. While punctuality is still valued in these regions, there may be a greater tolerance for delays, especially in social settings. These tend to favor a polychronic approach, where time is seen as less rigid and people may handle multiple tasks or interactions simultaneously.

3. Pacing of Interactions

The pacing of interactions also varies among cultures. In Western societies, there is often a preference for direct, fast-paced communication, reflective of a goal-oriented mindset where efficiency is highly valued. This style aligns with the monochronic tendency to compartmentalize time and focus on one thing at a time. In contrast, Eastern cultures, such as those in Asia, may favor a slower, more deliberate pace in communication. This reflects a polychronic preference for building relationships and ensuring harmony, allowing for more simultaneous interactions and a less linear approach to task completion.

4. Timing of Interactions

The appropriate timing of interactions is another crucial aspect of Chronemics. For example, in the United States, it is common to schedule meetings well in advance and to stick closely to the planned agenda, reflecting a monochronic culture's preference for planning and structure. However, in some African and Middle Eastern cultures, a more spontaneous approach to scheduling may be the norm, with meetings and discussions often occurring in a more flexible, organic manner that can be characterized as polychronic.

5. Adapting to Chronemics Differences

To effectively navigate Chronemics differences in cross-cultural business communication, consider the following strategies.

Research and preparation: Before engaging in business with an unfamiliar culture, research their customs regarding time. This knowledge can help you adapt your behavior to suit their expectations.

Flexibility and patience: Be prepared to adjust your own time preferences and show patience

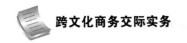

when dealing with cultures that have different rhythms.

Clear communication: When scheduling meetings or setting deadlines, make sure to communicate clearly about expectations and, if necessary, confirm understanding in writing.

Building relationships: In some cultures, taking time to build relationships before diving into business discussions is essential. Reflect on the value this can add to long – term collaborations.

Cultural sensitivity: Show sensitivity to the fact that your approach to time may not be the same as your interlocutor's. Acknowledge and respect their cultural norms, even if it means adapting your own behavior.

In conclusion, Time language or Chronemics plays a fundamental role in cross-cultural business communication. By understanding and respecting the diverse ways in which different cultures perceive and use time, business professionals can enhance their effectiveness and build stronger, more respectful international relationships.

Part E Spatial Language

1. Spatial Language: Definition and Cultural Variability

Spatial language, a crucial form of non-verbal communication, involves using space, including distance, orientation, and territoriality, to convey messages and emotions. It plays an integral role in cross-cultural business interactions where differences in spatial perceptions and usage can lead to misunderstandings or misinterpretations. Understanding spatial language helps individuals adapt their behaviors, fostering effective communication and building trust among international colleagues and clients.

Cultures significantly vary in how space is perceived and used. For instance, cultures such as those in Northern Europe and North America tend to value personal space and prefer larger physical distances during interactions. In contrast, Latin American and Mediterranean cultures typically have a more flexible approach to personal space, often allowing for closer interaction distances.

2. Four Types of Spatial Distances

Anthropologist Edward T. Hall identified four types of spatial distances in everyday human interactions.

Intimate distance (up to 18 inches / 45 cm) — Typically reserved for intimate relationships, it involves physical contact and comfort with close proximity. Examples include embracing, kissing, and comforting.

Personal distance (1. 5 to 4 feet / 45 to 120 cm) — This distance is used for interactions among friends and family, suggesting a level of familiarity. It allows for ease in conversation without the sense of crowding.

Social distance (4 to 12 feet / 1. 2 to 3. 6 meters) — Common in social and professional settings, this distance reduces physical involvement and personal warmth, facilitating more formal or consultative interactions. It is the standard distance maintained in most business meetings and casual social gatherings.

Public distance (over 12 feet / 3. 6 meters) — Used for public speaking and performances, this distance is intended to enhance the speaker's authority and visibility while reducing individual engagement. It is appropriate in large lectures, presentations, and ceremonies.

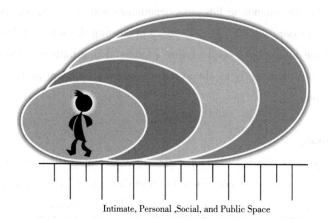

Intimate, Personal ,Social, and Public Space

These categories illustrate how spatial language varies across different contexts and relationships, reflecting cultural norms and expectations. Misunderstanding these unspoken rules can lead to discomfort or offense. For instance, standing too close during a professional meeting in a culture that values personal space might be perceived as aggressive or disrespectful, whereas maintaining a larger distance in a more contact-oriented culture could be seen as aloof or unfriendly.

Understanding these nuances is essential for navigating cross-cultural interactions effectively. By recognizing and respecting these differences, individuals can avoid unintentional gaffes and build stronger, more respectful professional relationships.

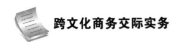

Task 8: Cross-culture Comparison

In Chinese culture, interaction is divided into four distinct zones. These zones are influenced by various factors such as age, gender, and regional background. After examining these zones in Chinese culture, we will contrast them with their American counterparts to highlight the cultural disparities.

Zone	Descriptions in Chinese Culture	Cultural Differences
Intimate zone		
Personal zone		
Social zone		
Public zone		

Task 9: Preparing for the Unit Project

1. Applying the Concepts

Plan an itinerary for the upcoming business negotiation with a U. S. company, taking into consideration all necessary details. This includes organizing the setup of the meeting room to ensure a professional atmosphere conducive to successful negotiations. After finalizing these plans, document them thoroughly to obtain your manager's approval and lay the groundwork for a positive outcome.

2. Critical Thinking

Various cultures possess distinct characteristics in their interaction zones. Investigate the underlying cultural elements that contribute to these disparities. This exploration will provide greater understanding of the diverse ways in which cultures interact.

Assessment

1. *Read each of the following questions and choose the best answer.*

(1) In Japanese business culture, deep bows are commonly used to show respect. What is an appropriate nonverbal response for a Western businessperson upon receiving a deep bow?

    A. Look away to avoid distraction.

    B. Offer a similarly deep bow in return.

    C. Give a firm handshake while maintaining eye contact.

    D. Nod slightly with a small smile.

(2) In many Latin American cultures, business communication is typically:

    A. Brief and direct to the point.

B. Formal with minimal facial expression.

C. Informal and accompanied by touch on the arm or back.

D. Conducted at a distance with little eye contact.

(3) In Arab cultures, individuals often stand closer to each other during conversation than is common in Western cultures. This proximity is intended to express:

A. Dominance.

B. Discomfort.

C. Intimacy and trust.

D. Impatience.

(4) During a meeting in Thailand, a participant consistently avoids direct eye contact with the speaker. This behavior is generally seen as:

A. Disrespectful.

B. A sign of deception.

C. An expression of respect.

D. An indication of boredom.

(5) In German business culture, punctuality is highly valued. If a German businessperson arrives exactly on time for a meeting, it is generally considered:

A. Acceptable, but arriving slightly early is preferable.

B. Impolite, as it shows lack of regard for the other party's time.

C. Perfectly normal and expected.

D. Late, as they typically expect everyone to be early.

(6) In Indian culture, the gesture of patting a child's head is generally considered:

A. A sign of affection and care.

B. An insult to the child's dignity.

C. A way to bless the child.

D. An appropriate form of discipline.

(7) During negotiations in Russian culture, it is common for individuals to sit close to each other, occasionally touching the other person's arm or knee. This behavior is intended to:

A. Show dominance.

B. Indicate personal space invasion.

C. Express friendliness and build rapport.

D. Intimidate the other party.

(8) In Brazilian business settings, an individual who is animated and uses broad gestures while speaking is typically perceived as:

A. Dishonest.

B. Emotional and unstable.

C. Enthusiastic and engaging.

D. Aggressive and confrontational.

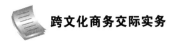

（9）In Chinese business culture, the color red is often associated with:

    A. Bad luck.

    B. Death and mourning.

    C. Good fortune and prosperity.

    D. Mediocrity and average.

（10）In Swedish business culture, direct and factual communication is valued over more expressive or emotional dialogue. This communication style is known as:

    A. High-context.

    B. Low-context.

    C. Indirect.

    D. Ambiguous.

2. Decide whether the following statements are true (T) or false (F).

_____ （1）A firm handshake is often seen as a sign of confidence and sincerity in many Western cultures. However, it's important to be aware that cultural norms vary, and what is considered appropriate in one culture might not be in another.

_____ （2）While direct eye contact is generally seen as a sign of respect and engagement in many Western societies, it can be viewed as confrontational or disrespectful in some Asian cultures. It's crucial to understand the cultural context when engaging in nonverbal communication.

_____ （3）Nonverbal cues such as gestures can significantly impact the atmosphere of a business meeting. Using appropriate gestures can demonstrate openness and engagement, helping to establish a positive environment conducive to collaboration.

_____ （4）The use of personal space, also known as "proxemics", plays a significant role in conveying intentions and attitudes during business interactions. Cultural norms regarding personal space can vary widely, and understanding these differences can help avoid misunderstandings and build rapport.

_____ （5）While face-to-face interactions may have more immediate consequences from nonverbal misunderstandings, mitigating misunderstandings caused by nonverbal cues is still important in written communication. This includes aspects like tone, emoticons, and the use of capital letters, which can all convey nonverbal signals in written form.

Unit Project

Re-examine the scenario of this unit. Prepare and present a poster to introduce important nonverbal communication factors in business negotiations to your colleagues who are to participate in the negotiation. Pay attention to the following points:

• Create a mind map that outlines the definition and roles of nonverbal communication. Introduce the logistics for the business negotiation, encompassing the itinerary and setup of the meeting room.

- Analyze the para–language frequently utilized by Americans in business negotiations.
- Decode the meanings of gestures and facial expressions typically employed by Americans during business negotiations.
- Prepare for instances where emojis might be appropriate to use.

Case Analysis

Analyze the following case with the cultural models and theories learned in this unit.

Intercultural Nonverbal Communication in Business
This case study examines a scenario where a Chinese company, Jiangsu Imports & Exports Co. (JIEC), negotiated a deal with a American corporation, Universal Electronics Inc. (UEI).

JIEC wanted to export high–quality electronic components to the U. S. market and had identified UEI as a potential distributor. Negotiations were scheduled to take place in Los Angeles, California. During the negotiations, the Chinese team used minimal gestures and maintained a reserved demeanor, which the American team misinterpreted as lack of interest or confidence. The American team, on the other hand, used broad gestures and maintained eye contact, which the Chinese team found aggressive and uncomfortable.

To overcome these challenges, both parties had to adapt their nonverbal communication styles. The Chinese team started using more gestures and maintained steady eye contact to show engagement, while the American team toned down their gestures and allowed for periods of silence to accommodate the Chinese negotiators' communication style.

This case study highlights the importance of understanding and adapting to different cultural norms in nonverbal communication. By acknowledging and respecting each other's communication styles, JIEC and UEI were able to build rapport and ultimately reach a successful agreement.

Further Reading

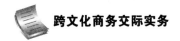

Nonverbal Intercultural Business Communication

A Primer for Global Professionals

In the realm of international business, effective communication transcends mere words. Nonverbal cues play a pivotal role in conveying intent, establishing rapport, and fostering mutual understanding across cultural boundaries. As global professionals navigate the intricate landscape of intercultural interactions, mastering nonverbal communication becomes indispensable.

The Silent Language of Business

Consider the silent language of business: the nod that seals a deal, the handshake that initiates a partnership, or the subtle frown that signals concern. These nonverbal cues, often unconsciously deployed, carry profound implications. Yet, their interpretation is not universal. What signifies confidence in one culture may denote arrogance in another. Thus, understanding the nuances of nonverbal communication is essential for global success.

Posture and Presence

Posture, a key component of nonverbal communication, reflects attitude and influences perception. A confident posture — shoulders back, head held high — conveys authority and preparation. Conversely, a hunched stance may suggest insecurity or lack of readiness. In negotiations, a dominant posture can reinforce one's arguments, while a more reserved demeanor may facilitate active listening and empathy.

Gestural Diversity

Gestures, another vital nonverbal element, vary widely across cultures. The thumbs – up gesture, seen as positive in Western cultures, may be offensive in Middle Eastern countries. Over–reliance on gestures in cultures that value understated expressions can appear theatrical or unprofessional. Recognizing and adapting to cultural gestural norms foster seamless business interactions and prevent misunderstandings.

The Dance of the Eyes

Eye contact, a powerful nonverbal tool, also varies culturally. In Western societies, direct eye contact typically indicates attentiveness and sincerity. However, in some Asian cultures, excessive direct eye contact can be disrespectful. Being attuned to these differences can ensure that your gaze communicates respect rather than discord.

Personal Space: The Territory of Trust

Personal space, the invisible bubble surrounding individuals, dictates comfort during conversations. Cultures with close proximity preferences, like those in Latin America or the Middle East, value a smaller personal space, facilitating closer interactions. In contrast, cultures like Northern Europe and North America prioritize a larger personal space, reflecting individualism and privacy. Respecting the other's personal space demonstrates sensitivity and professionalism.

Embracing Nonverbal Nuance

As the global business landscape becomes increasingly interconnected, embracing nonverbal nuance is no longer optional — it's imperative. By attuning to the silent symphony of intercultural communication, global professionals can harmonize relationships, bridge cultural divides, and achieve business objectives with finesse and efficacy.

Remember, mastering nonverbal intercultural business communication is not about memorizing gestures or adopting a specific demeanor. It's about being observant, respectful, and adaptable. It's about understanding that communication transcends words and that true connection lies in the spaces between them.

Furthering Your Understanding

To deepen your knowledge of nonverbal intercultural business communication, consider exploring resources like Erving Goffman's *Behavior in Public Places*, which delves into the sociology of human behavior, or Allan and Barbara Pease's *The Definitive Book of Body Language*, offering insights into the science behind nonverbal cues. Additionally, attending workshops, engaging in cultural exchanges, and practicing mindfulness can enhance your nonverbal fluency and intercultural competence.

In conclusion, as you venture into the global arena, let your nonverbal prowess speak volumes, fostering connections that transcend the spoken word. Remember, effective intercultural communication is an art form, with nonverbal cues as its brushstrokes and cultural awareness as its canvas.

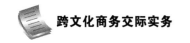

单元小结

1 学习目标

学习了这个单元之后，你将能够：

- 了解什么是非语言交流；
- 描述不同类型的非语言交流；
- 增强跨文化意识和敏感性；
- 了解并恰当运用不同文化中的非语言沟通技巧。

2 学习情境

在完成这个单元后，根据以下情景完成该单元项目：

假设你是一名中国商务专家，率领一个代表团与一家美国公司就合资企业进行谈判。会议将在美国举行，你知道在谈判过程中可以通过面部表情和手势来推断对方的内心想法。为了处理好谈判过程，你需要为自己和团队在会议期间进行有效的非语言沟通做好准备。

3 非言语交流

良好的沟通融合了语言和无声的手势。据说，我们的信息中只有7%来自我们所说的话，93%来自非语言符号。由此可见，在跨文化商务互动中，非语言沟通多么重要。非言语交流是指不通过说话或书写来传递信息，这在语言沟通受到语言障碍或文化差异限制时尤为重要。善于非语言沟通可以帮助你结交朋友、与他们打交道并建立牢固的纽带，尤其是与拥有不同文化背景的人。

3.1 非言语交流的定义

非语言跨文化交际，是指拥有不同文化背景的个人之间在不使用口头或书面语言的情况下交流信息和意义的过程。它涉及肢体语言、手势、面部表情、眼神交流、姿势和其他非语言线索的使用，可以跨越文化界限传递情感、态度和意图。理解和解释非语言暗示在跨文化交际中至关重要，因为它有助于避免误解，促进相互理解和尊重。

如今，理解非语言沟通是非常重要的，尤其在拥有不同文化背景的人相遇的商业世界里。正确理解这一点有助于建立牢固的关系，避免误解。随着我们学习得越来越多，我们在全球范围内的互动也会越来越好。

3.2 非言语交流的意义

意义的一个层面是公开陈述的信息，也就是认知内容。这是我们有意识解读的部分。另一个层面是情感内容，涉及情绪、态度和行为。非语言交流之所以重要，是因为它自然而然地反映了说话者的潜意识。即使我们一言不发，非语言交流也无处不在。我们用行动传递信息，比如点头、微笑或交叉双臂。我们的肢体动作和利用空间的方式也能告诉别人我们的感受。

3.3　非言语交流的功能

非语言交流具有几种关键功能。它们强调了手势与语言之间的密切联系。

● 强调：非语言交流可以用来强调或突出谈话中的特定词语或短语。例如，说话者可能会提高声音或使用手势来强调某个关键点，以引起听者的注意并确保其重要性得到理解。

● 补充：非语言暗示通常通过增加语境或情感细微差别来补充语言信息。例如，一个温暖的微笑或点头可以强化积极的反馈，而双手合十则可能暗示着防卫或不同意，从而使信息的含义更加丰富。

● 自相矛盾：有时，非语言信号会与口头语言相矛盾，传递出一种混合信息。例如，皱着眉头用单调的声音说"我很好"，可能表示对方实际上不好，这说明非语言暗示可以揭示谈话者一方试图掩盖的真实感受。

● 调节：非语言交流通过表示轮流发言、停顿和话题转换来帮助调节谈话流程。扬眉或点头可以邀请对方发言，而双手交叉于头后方或交叉双臂则表示该结束谈话或转换话题了。

● 重复：非语言动作可以用来重复或强化语言信息，从而提高信息的清晰度。例如，在提到一个物体时用手指着它，或用手势来说明一个概念，都有助于在听者的脑海中巩固信息。

● 替代：在说话不合适或不可能说话的情况下，非语言交流可以替代语言交流。一个竖起的大拇指或一个 OK 的手势可以代替实际的语言，在不发出声音的情况下传达同意或批准的意思。在说话会造成干扰或有语言障碍的环境中，这种方法尤其有用。

4　肢体语言

肢体语言是非语言交流的重要组成部分，它通过肢体行为、动作和姿势传达意义，包括手势、面部表情、眼神交流和身体姿势等各种暗示。这些非语言信号可以传达情绪、态度和意图，通常可以强化或反驳口语。

4.1　手势

手势是非语言交流的重要组成部分。有些手势有共同的含义，但许多手势因文化而异，包括点头、竖大拇指、敲击手指、OK 手势、和平手势等。

在许多欧美文化中，和平手势仅仅表示和平或胜利。在巴西和委内瑞拉等南美国家，同样的和平手势（竖起两根手指，掌心朝外）被认为是极其粗鲁和具有冒犯性的。在那里，这个手势类似于许多西方文化中的翻转鸟（竖中指）。公开使用这个手势会引起他人的严重反感，甚至引发肢体冲突。在一些亚洲国家，尤其是日本和韩国，和平手势可能不像在西方那样具有和平的含义；相反，和平手势在这些地方有时会以俏皮或可爱的姿势出现，通常由年轻人在拍照时使用。在一些中东国家，和平手势可能并不具有

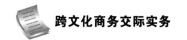

普遍理解的含义，可能只被视为一种中性手势。

4.2 姿势

在非语言交流领域，姿势是表达情绪、意图和态度的有力工具。一个人的姿势可以传递从自信和开放到防卫和退缩等各种信息。

在许多文化中，开放的姿势，如身体前倾、手脚不交叉，可以表示有兴趣、乐于接受和愿意参与。在商务和谈判场合，这种姿势通常很受欢迎，因为它表示一种合作和友好的态度。相反，以交叉双臂和双腿为特征的封闭姿势则可能表示防卫、不感兴趣或不舒服。这种姿势可能会在跨文化交流中造成障碍，因为它可能被视为冷漠或难以接近。姿势还能反映地位和权力动态。例如，处于权威地位的人可能会采取更开阔的姿势，占据更多的物理空间，而那些不太自信或地位较低的人可能会采取更拘谨的姿势。

4.3 眼神交流

在商务沟通领域，眼神交流是一种有效的非语言信号，可以传达自信、兴趣、尊重或主导地位。然而，与眼神交流相关的规则和含义在不同文化中存在很大差异。

在包括美国在内的许多西方社会，稳定的目光接触通常被视为诚实、自信和专注的标志。在商务交谈中，保持适度甚至直率的目光接触表明真诚和投入；然而，过度的目光接触可能会被视为具有攻击性或挑战性。

在许多东亚文化和东南亚文化中，如日本和韩国，强烈的目光接触会被视为粗鲁或对抗。谦虚和尊重往往要求目光接触时不要太频繁或太柔和，尤其是在与上级领导交谈或正式场合中。在这些文化中，间接的目光接触或不时地将目光移开，可以显示礼貌和尊重。

在中东，交谈时眼神接触是很常见的，也是人们所期望的，这反映了人们的专注和兴趣；但需要注意的是，在与异性交谈时，尤其在保守的社会中，长时间的眼神交流可能会被认为不恰当甚至具有调情意味。

在许多拉美国家，活泼、善于表达的交流方式非常普遍，眼神交流是互动中不可或缺的一部分。它意味着兴趣和联系。不过，与中东文化类似，在一些特殊情况下，人们可能更喜欢减少目光接触，尤其在男女混杂的正式场合。

在许多非洲社会中，目光接触是交流的一个重要方面，可以表示尊重和关注。然而，眼神交流的持续时间和强度会因环境和关系动态而有所不同。例如，在一些部落中，强烈的眼神接触可能意味着挑战或对抗，而在其他部落中，眼神接触可能是一种表达诚意的方式。

4.4 面部表情

面部表情在商务交流中起着至关重要的作用，因为它是传达情感和态度的关键，可以跨越语言障碍，直接表达个人的反应和感受。

在许多西方社会，面部表情往往更加开放和富有表现力，所表现的情绪范围也更广。例如，美国人在商业讨论中可能会通过面部表情公开表现出热情、惊讶或失望。这种开放性有助于建立融洽的关系并显示出诚意。

许多亚洲文化重视情绪表达的含蓄和克制，尤其在正式或商务场合。例如，日本人和中国人可能会主动控制面部表情，保持镇定，避免引起不适或尴尬。微笑可以模棱两可地使用，有时是为了掩饰真实情感或缓和紧张气氛。

在中东社会，面部表情是交流不可或缺的一部分，但可能会被不熟悉该文化的人误解。例如，阿拉伯人在谈判或讨论商业问题时可能会使用强烈的面部表情，而按照西方标准，这可能会被视为咄咄逼人或过于情绪化。

拉美文化以善于表达而著称，其中包括充满活力和情感的面部表情。在商务交往中，这种表现力可以营造一种热情洋溢的氛围，但需要精心管理，以确保信息传递的专业性和清晰度。

在非洲社会，面部表情通常反映出沟通的公共性和关系导向性。微笑和点头通常用于鼓励对话和表示同意，即使存在分歧也不例外，这反映了当地文化对和谐与尊重的重视。

4.5   肢体接触

在商务交流领域，肢体接触（又称触觉或触觉交流）在建立融洽关系、信任和理解方面发挥着重要作用。然而，拥有不同文化背景的人对身体接触的使用和理解大相径庭，这影响了不同背景的人在职业环境中的互动方式。

在包括美国和加拿大在内的许多西方社会，商务场合中身体接触较为有限和谨慎。握手是一种常见且被接受的身体接触形式，象征着同意或问候；然而，更广泛或频繁的身体接触可能会被认为是不专业或不恰当的。

在许多亚洲国家，身体接触通常比西方文化更受限制，尤其在两性之间和正式场合。

在中东，肢体接触更为常见，包括拥抱、牵手或在交谈中接触手臂。这些手势表达了热情和友谊。不过，必须注意的是，这种互动可能会受到性别因素和社会地位因素等文化规范的约束。

拉美文化以热情和触觉敏锐的交流方式著称。肢体接触，如轻触手臂或后背，可能会经常使用，并能表示友谊。

在非洲社会中，身体接触的应用差别很大。握手、拥抱和其他形式的身体接触可以是表示尊重、认可或团结的方式。这些手势的含义和恰当性取决于不同的族群、地区和具体的社会环境。

5   副语言

副语言指的是伴随实际话语而出现的非语言方面的言语，包括音量、音调、节奏和语气等声音特质。这些因素可以改变言语的含义或强调言语背后的情感，往往传达出超越口语字面解释的微妙意含。副语言还可能包括有意使用沉默，以及其他声音表达方式（如笑声、哭声和叹息声），这些都为交流增加了一层情感深度和语境。副语言是言语和非言语交际不可分割的一部分，影响着听众对信息的接收和理解。

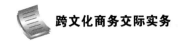

5.1 重音和语调

重音是指在句子中对特定单词或音节的强调或力度。它可以极大地改变句子或短语的意思。语调是指说话时音调或音色的变化。它可以影响人们对语句的理解，表示疑问、命令或不同程度的不确定或自信。

5.2 语速

语速是指一个人说话的速度，通常以每分钟字数（WPM）或每秒音节数来衡量。它可能因说话者的情绪状态、对话题的投入程度、文化背景等因素而出现差异。

适度的语速一般比较清晰易懂。语速过快，听众可能会错过信息；语速过慢，听众可能会失去兴趣或变得不耐烦。语速过快会让人觉得急切、兴奋甚至焦虑，而语速过慢则会让人觉得自信、深思熟虑或不感兴趣。动态的语速可以使谈话更有吸引力，有助于强调重要观点并保持听众的兴趣。

5.3 音量

音量是指语言交流时说话者声音的相对响亮或柔和程度。音量可以从低声细语到近乎喊叫不等，是语言表达和理解的一个重要方面。在跨文化商务环境中，适当调整音量有助于确保你的信息被如实接收：

- 注意交谈伙伴的音量和环境噪声水平，以判断讲话时的适当音量。
- 可以通过改变音量以突出重点，但要注意保持对不同文化的敏感性。
- 除非必要，避免说话声音过大或过小，以免引起误解或不适。

6 时间语言

不同的文化有不同的时间节奏，向我们展示了它们的价值观和规范。这就需要理解和尊重不同文化对时间的看法，这可能会对商务互动产生重大影响。本单元深入探讨计时学的重要性、其在不同文化中的差异，以及在商业环境中有效适应这些差异的实用策略。

时间学（Chronemics）指的是对交流中时间的研究，探讨个人如何在互动中感知、安排和利用时间。它侧重于时间管理和感知的各个方面。

6.1 守时和截止时间

不同文化对守时和截止日期的态度大相径庭。例如，在北美和北欧，守时通常被视为尊重和专业的标志。在这些文化中，最后期限是很严格的，迟到通常被视为缺乏承诺或组织能力。在这些文化中，人们通常采用单时制的时间观念，严格规划时间表，为每项任务或约会分配特定的时间。而某些地中海和拉美文化圈对时间的态度则更为灵活。虽然这些地区仍然重视守时，但对延误的容忍度也更高，尤其在社交场合。这些地区倾向于采用多时间方法，时间观念不那么死板，人们可以同时处理多项任务或互动。

6.2　互动的节奏

在西方社会，人们往往喜欢直接、快节奏的交流，这反映出一种以目标为导向的思维方式，即高度重视效率。这种风格与单时倾向一致，即把时间分割开来，一次只专注于一件事。与此相反，东方文化（如亚洲）可能更倾向于缓慢、深思熟虑的沟通节奏。这反映出多时倾向于建立关系和确保和谐，允许更多同时进行的互动和较少线性的任务完成方式。

6.3　互动的时机

在美国，人们通常会提前安排好会议，并严格遵守计划议程，这反映了单时制文化对计划和结构的偏好。然而，在非洲和中东的一些文化中，更自发的日程安排方式可能是常态，会议和讨论往往以一种更灵活、更有机的方式进行，这可以被称为多时态文化。

7　空间语言

空间语言是一种重要的非语言交流形式，该概念涉及利用空间（包括距离、方位和地域性）来传递信息和情感。空间语言在跨文化商务互动中发挥着不可或缺的作用，因为空间认知和使用上的差异会导致误解或曲解。了解空间语言有助于个人调整行为，促进有效沟通，并在国际同事和客户之间建立信任。

人类学家爱德华·霍尔（Edward T. Hall）指出了人类日常交往中的四种空间距离。

● 亲密距离：通常是指亲密关系中的身体接触和近距离的舒适感，例如拥抱、亲吻和安慰。

● 个人距离：用于朋友和家人之间的互动，表示一定程度的熟悉。这样可以轻松交谈，不会产生拥挤感。

● 社交距离：常见于社交和职业场合，可以减少身体上的接触和个人的热情，有利于更正式的或咨询性的互动。该距离是大多数商务会议和休闲社交聚会中保持的标准距离。

● 公众距离：用于公开演讲和表演，目的是增强演讲者的权威性和可见度，同时减少个人参与。该距离适用于大型演讲、演示和仪式。

* 本单元智慧职教线上课程：https://zyk.icve.com.cn/courseDetailed? id = obbaaaqvo4doejfjffeicq&openCourse = obbaaaqvw79e5opp1bwbg.

Unit 6　习题参考答案

Unit 7 Intercultural Management

Ancient Chinese Wisdom

If the people are led by laws, and uniformity sought to be given them by punishments, they will try to avoid the punishment, but have no sense of shame. If they are led by virtue, and uniformity sought to be given them by the rules of propriety, they will have the sense of shame, and moreover will become good. ("导之以政，齐之以刑，民免而无耻。道之以德，齐之以礼，有耻且格。)

From *Analects* (《论语》)

Learning Objectives

After learning this unit, you shall be able to:

- Explain the relationship between cultural values and intercultural management.
- Understand the characteristics of multicultural team management.
- Clarify the concepts of business ethics and social responsibility.
- Apply intercultural management theories to specific overseas projects.

Project Scenario

After learning this unit, finish the unit project on the basis of the following scenario.

Suppose you work in a Chinese multinational company, which is focusing on networking and telecommunications, featuring professional equipment and service supply in the domestic and overseas markets. You and several colleagues are dispatched to a country located in South America to establish relevant projects and explore the network with a number of local institutions. You are the secretary of the team, and you are trying to help your Chinese colleagues to adapt to the new cultural environment and to build an effective multicultural team with the local employees. You and your team should ensure sustainable development, meet local requirements, and maintain a long-term cooperative relationship with the locals.

Lead-in

Watch the video clip about the a case of multinational company management and answer the following questions.

- What were the challenges and how were they solved?

• As the participant in the scenario, what will you do for the corporate management?

Part A　The Effect of Culture on Management

1. Management

Management refers to the processes and activities involved in overseeing and coordinating the work of individuals or groups to achieve organizational goals effectively and efficiently. Effective management is crucial for any business or organization, as it directly impacts productivity, employee satisfaction, and overall success.

Case Study in Intercultural Management

2. Intercultural Management

In today's globalized economy, intercultural management has become a critical component of business success. As companies expand their operations across borders, they must learn to navigate the complexities of diverse cultural norms, values, and practices. This requires a deep understanding of how culture influences communication, decision – making, and leadership styles, as well as an ability to adapt to changing circumstances and build effective relationships with people from different backgrounds.

At its core, intercultural management involves recognizing and respecting cultural differences while fostering a sense of shared purpose and common goals among employees, clients, and stakeholders. It requires leaders to be open–minded, flexible, and sensitive to the needs and expectations of others, even when they differ significantly from their own. By embracing diversity as a source of strength rather than a liability, companies can create more inclusive and innovative workplaces that drive growth and competitiveness.

One key aspect of intercultural management is developing cross–cultural communication skills. This involves learning to listen actively, ask questions, and seek clarification when necessary, as well as being aware of potential misunderstandings or conflicts that may arise due to language barriers or cultural nuances. It also means being able to adapt one's communication style to suit different audiences and contexts, whether it's presenting a proposal to a group of investors or negotiating a deal with a supplier from another country.

3. Work in Multicultural Organizations

Value orientations and cultural dimensions serve as fundamental frameworks for reference in international business and cross – cultural management. They are commonly employed to interpret the diverse differences encountered during global engagements.

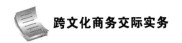
When you work with people from different backgrounds, it's important to be open and ready to learn about their ways of thinking and doing things. Don't guess or criticize how they do things differently from you. Staying loyal to what you believe in can get tricky when you're dealing with others who have different priorities and values.

Take time to learn about the customs, beliefs, and ways of the people you'll work with. Understand their past, words, celebrations, and manners. Knowing these helps stop mix-ups and see things on their way. Always think about these following three questions.

Religion: are there rules for eating, resting, clothes, or actions I should know to not upset anyone?

Gender: should I act or talk differently because of this? Age and rank — does age or being high up matter in their culture? How much do they matter, and should I show more respect?

Age and seniority: does this person's culture give particular importance to age or seniority? How important are they, and do I need to appear more respectful?

Talking with people from different places can be tricky because they talk differently. Pay attention to how they talk and match their style. Speak clearly and simply, stay away from words or phrases that might confuse them, and watch out for gestures or looks that could be misunderstood. When you're with people from other cultures, really listen to them. Let them share their thoughts without cutting in or telling them what you think. Be interested in what they say and ask questions to make sure you understand them right.

Task 1: Understanding the Concepts

Watch a video and learn about high context and low context communication.

High-Context Versus Low-Context Communication

Task 2: Furthering Your Understanding

According to what you've learned about cultural values in previous units, fill in the blanks with the serial numbers of the following words.

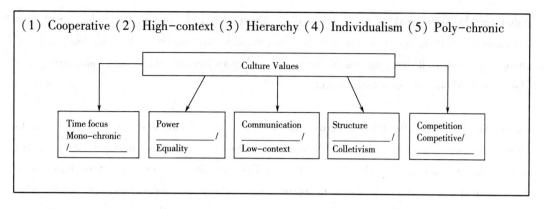

4. The Effect of Cultural Values on the Functions of Management

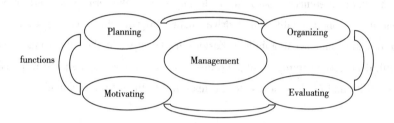

Planning

In the realm of planning and management, cultural differences between Eastern and Western philosophies manifest themselves profoundly, reflecting centuries – old traditions, societal values, and strategic approaches. The East, heavily influenced by Confucianism, Taoism, and collectivist principles, emphasizes harmony, long – term perspectives, and consensus – driven decision – making. In contrast, the West, shaped by Aristotelian logic, individualism, and capitalist ideals, favors short-term goals, direct communication, and data-driven strategies.

Eastern cultures, particularly in China but also evident in Japan and Korea, often adopt a holistic approach to planning. This is characterized by considering the broader societal impacts and future implications of decisions. For instance, Chinese companies might focus on establishing relationships and trust before entering business negotiations, which can be perceived as a slower process but is intended to ensure long – term cooperation and minimal conflict. Additionally, the concept of "face" plays a crucial role in Eastern management styles; maintaining respect and hierarchy is vital, and open criticism is usually avoided to preserve group harmony.

The Western approach is typically more linear and results – oriented. In the U. S. and many parts of Europe, businesses prioritize efficiency, innovation, and individual achievement. Managers are often measured by their ability to meet quarterly targets and stock performance

185

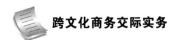

indicators. Decision-making tends to be more direct and based on empirical data, with less emphasis on relationship-building and more on explicit goal setting. This can lead to rapid changes in strategy if data suggests it's necessary, whereas Eastern firms might persevere with a plan to uphold stability and commitments.

Communication styles also differ markedly. In the West, open debate is encouraged as a mean to identify the best course of action. Problems are addressed head-on, and managers are expected to take decisive actions quickly. Conversely, in Eastern cultures, communication tends to be more indirect to avoid conflict and maintain group cohesion. Subtle cues and non-verbal communication play significant roles in understanding intent and reaching consensus.

Another aspect where differences arise is in leadership styles. Western leaders are often lauded for their charisma and visionary qualities that drive change from the top down. They are expected to provide clear direction and accountability. Eastern leadership, on the other hand, may be more collective, with decisions emerging from group discussions and a sense of shared responsibility. This style values humility and credits success to the team rather than the individual.

However, it's important to note that globalization has led to a convergence of management practices. Many Eastern companies have adopted Western practices to become more competitive internationally, while some Western firms have begun to integrate Eastern philosophies to foster more collaborative and sustainable business models. The reality lies in a blend of strategies that combine the strengths of both worldviews to navigate an increasingly complex global marketplace.

In conclusion, while stark differences exist between Eastern and Western approaches to planning and management, these distinctions offer valuable insights into creating versatile and culturally sensitive organizations. As the world becomes more interconnected, the ability to understand and adapt to these cultural nuances will be a key competency for any global manager.

Task 3: Understanding the Concepts

Fill in the blanks with two prominent views of time. Then fill in the two boxes with the serial numbers of the following phrases.

(1) focus more on relationships

M _____ time

(2) focus more on tasks

P _____ time

Organizing

Organizing encompasses the formulation of the organizational framework, as well as the structuring of job roles and the workflow hierarchy. At times, managers must also provide targeted training to equip employees with the requisite knowledge and skills for success. In organizations adopting a hierarchical perspective on power, the structure is typically stringently regulated, with authority and accountability being centralized. With the equality view of power, the structure fosters individual independence and self-governance.

The practices of organizing and management reflect the cultural underpinnings of a society, drawing inspiration from its history, social mores, and philosophical roots. These cultural attributes significantly influence organizational strategies, leadership styles, and employee engagement in the East versus the West.

In Eastern cultures, particularly influenced by Confucianism as seen in China, Japan, and Korea, organizing and management emphasize collective harmony, long-term stability, and an indirect communication style. For instance, decision – making often involves a careful consideration of collective interests and future implications, rather than just short-term gains. There is a tendency towards hierarchical structures where seniority and social ranking play critical roles. This respect for hierarchy maintains order and harmony within the organization but may also slow down decision processes as it requires consensus from various levels.

Western organizing and management, notably in the United States and Europe, value individualism, direct communication, and results-oriented strategies. Organizations are often structured with clear lines of authority and responsibility, encouraging swift decision-making and accountability at all management levels. Leaders are expected to take charge, delegate effectively, and motivate their teams to achieve concrete objectives. The focus on individual achievement and innovation fosters a competitive environment that rewards performance.

Task 4: Understanding the Concepts

Fill in the blanks with two prominent views of time. Then fill in the two boxes with the serial numbers of the following phrases.

(1) Tightly controlled and centralized   (2) autonomous and decentralized

E _____   H _____

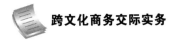

Motivating

Motivation is the driving force that propels employees to achieve organizational goals, and its practices are deeply influenced by cultural contexts. Significant disparities exist between Eastern and Western cultures in their motivational approaches, stemming from their respective value systems and philosophical foundations.

In Eastern cultures, particularly in Confucian-influenced societies like China, motivation is often intrinsically linked to group harmony and collective success. Businesses emphasize the well-being of the company as a whole, which fosters a sense of belonging and loyalty among employees. This collective orientation encourages individuals to work hard for the sake of the team and the long-term prosperity of the organization. Additionally, respect for hierarchy means that recognition from senior figures can be a powerful motivator, while concerns over "saving face" can drive employees to avoid mistakes and perform at a high standard.

On the other hand, the Western culture places considerable value on individual achievements and personal accountability. Motivation in the West is frequently tied to performance metrics, competition, and personal recognition. Incentives such as bonuses, promotions, and accolades are common methods used to motivate employees. There's also a preference for setting clear, achievable targets that align with an employee's personal career development, thereby empowering them to take ownership of their roles and responsibilities.

Managers are catalysts for employee motivation, ensuring their presence and productivity. This encompasses the sharing of a collective vision, the encouragement of strength development, and the inspiration for consistent top performance. Mastery of effective communication is indispensable in this role.

Cultural individualism reflects the degree to which a society prioritizes the individual's role above that of the collective. In contrast, cultural collectivism underscores the primacy of the group's interests. Within collectivist societies, individuals are encouraged to comply with norms and act in the best interest of the collective.

Communication of expectations also varies between the two cultures. In the West, direct communication is favored to ensure clarity and transparency about what is expected from employees. In the East, expectations may be conveyed more subtly, allowing employees to intuit and respond to unspoken cues, which maintains harmony and avoids confrontation.

Leadership styles further highlight this divide. In the West, transformational leadership that inspires followers through vision and charisma is prevalent. Leaders are encouraged to motivate by setting clear visions, empowering others, and recognizing individual contributions. Conversely, in the East, paternalistic leadership that prioritizes care and concern for followers is more common. This style relies on nurturing loyalty and a strong sense of community, which in turn motivates employees to contribute to the collective's welfare.

In conclusion, while Eastern and Western motivational practices differ significantly, they each reflect deeper cultural values regarding the relationship between the individual and the collective, and the means of achieving success. As the global business environment continues to integrate diverse cultures, companies are increasingly exploring hybrid motivational strategies that balance individual aspirations with collective goals to harness the full potential of their multicultural work forces. Understanding these differences is crucial for global organizations to design effective motivational systems that resonate across cultural boundaries.

Task 5: Understanding the Concepts

Fill in the blanks with two prominent views of time. Then fill in the two boxes with the serial numbers of the following phrases.

(1) Anticipate that employees will fulfil or enhance their duties.
(2) Anticipate that employees will adhere to or prioritize the welfare of the group.

| I _____ | | C _____ |

Evaluating

The processes of evaluation within organizations offer insightful perspectives on cultural differences between the East and the West. These differences reflect historical, philosophical, and social values that shape how individuals and teams are assessed and how their performances are interpreted.

In Eastern cultures, particularly those influenced by Confucian principles, evaluation tends to be holistic and relationship-oriented. Here, an individual's performance is often considered in the context of their contributions to the group's harmony and long-term goals. Loyalty, seniority, and commitment to the collective well-being are highly valued and can play a significant role in assessment outcomes. This approach emphasizes the importance of non-verbal communication and subtle cues, where understanding unwritten rules and indirect expressions is

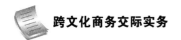

crucial for success.

Eastern evaluation practices also tend to be less explicit about performance feedback. To preserve "face" and social hierarchy, criticisms may be delivered privately or wrapped in nuanced language, if at all. This indirectness can make it challenging for outsiders to interpret individual standings within a group. Moreover, the emphasis on collective achievement can sometimes overshadow individual recognition, with credit often given to the team rather than the individual.

Conversely, in the West, evaluation practices are typically more direct, objective, and based on individual performance. Companies in the U. S. and Europe often use concrete metrics and targets to measure employee performance. Goals are usually specific, measurable, and aligned with the company's strategic objectives. The feedback process is explicit, encouraging open dialogue about strengths and areas for improvement. This transparent approach is intended to promote clarity, growth, and accountability within the organization.

Western evaluations also place considerable weight on innovation, risk-taking, and individual initiative, which are seen as drivers of personal and organizational success. Leaders and managers are expected to provide constructive feedback that motivates employees to exceed their personal bests continually. Furthermore, face-to-face interactions during evaluations are standard, allowing for immediate clarification and understanding between evaluator and evaluate.

Managers invest time in gauging the efficacy of their teams and their goal achievement. The more they discern what succeeds and what falters, the better they are equipped for future decision-making. Managers must assimilate and recalibrate strategies to align with corporate objectives.

In low-context corporate cultures, evaluating is inclined to be task-driven in accordance with monitoring. In high-context corporate cultures, evaluating tends to be process-driven.

In conclusion, while Eastern evaluation practices underscore relationships and group dynamics, their Western counterparts focus on individual achievements and measurable outcomes. Globalization is leading to the emergence of hybrid models that combine elements of both approaches, aiming to maintain cultural sensitivities while promoting clear and consistent performance metrics. As cross-cultural collaboration becomes increasingly common, companies are tasked with creating evaluation systems that are fair, transparent, and culturally adaptable to engage diverse workforces effectively.

Task 6: Understanding the Concepts

Fill in the blanks with two prominent views of time. Then fill in the two boxes with the serial numbers of the following phrases.

(1) task-driven to ensure performance objectives
(2) process-driven in cultural context

| H _____ cultures | L _____ cultures |

Part B   Multicultural Team Management

1. Definitions of a Global Team

A global team typically epitomizes a multicultural assembly, comprising individuals from diverse cultural backgrounds. These team members could be drawn from two or more distinct corporations.

They must delineate their respective domains of accountability and arrange their constituents accordingly. Furthermore, they must cultivate effective group dynamics to promote collaborative strides toward objective realization.

2. Cultural Variations in Team Management

The way teams are managed offers a rich tapestry of contrasting philosophies between Eastern and Western cultures. These differences not only reflect historical legacies and social values but also influence the style and effectiveness of teamwork within organizations.

In many Eastern cultures, the concept of team management is deeply influenced by Confucian ideals, emphasizing collective responsibility and group harmony. Hierarchy plays a crucial role in this dynamic, with each member understanding their place and contributing to the team's success while maintaining interpersonal balance. Decision – making often involves consensus – building and may be slower as it requires buy – in from various levels of the hierarchy. Loyalty and long-term commitment are highly valued, encouraging stable workforces where employees develop deep connections and mutual trust over time.

Communication within Eastern teams tends to be more indirect, nurturing a non-confrontational

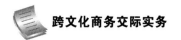

work environment that avoids conflicts and preserves "face". This subtlety in communication demands a high level of emotional intelligence and the ability to read between the lines, necessitating an implicit understanding of cultural norms and expectations.

On the other hand, team management in the West prioritizes individual accountability and direct communication. Performance is measured against clear, quantifiable metrics, and leaders are expected to provide explicit feedback that encourages continual self-improvement. Western teams typically have flatter structures, which can accelerate decision-making processes and foster a sense of ownership among team members. This structure also encourages innovation and independent thinking, as team members are empowered to contribute ideas and solutions without rigid hierarchical constraints.

Western culture also values transparency and open dialogue during team interactions. Issues are addressed openly, and conflicts are seen as opportunities for growth and improvement rather than impediments to harmony. Leaders in Western teams are often skilled in facilitating these discussions, ensuring everyone's voice is heard and considered.

In summary, team management styles in the East lean towards collective synergy, implicit communication, and hierarchical structures to maintain harmony, while their Western counterparts favor individual performance, direct communication, and flat structures to drive innovation and rapid decision-making. As the global business environment becomes increasingly interconnected, companies are starting to adopt hybrid management strategies that blend the strengths of both approaches. These mixed models attempt to balance the need for fast, results-driven decision-making with the benefits of a cohesive, harmonious team culture. Embracing diversity in team management not only enriches organizational practices but also enhances cross-cultural collaboration on a global scale.

Task 7: Furthering Your Understanding

Watch the video clip and talk about how to build a team.

---

3. The Stages of Team Development

The developmental stages of a team can vary significantly depending on the cultural context, reflecting disparate values, communication styles, and management philosophies. Understanding these differences can enrich cross-cultural collaboration and improve team dynamics in global environments.

In many Eastern cultures, influenced by Confucian principles, the formation and development of a team often prioritize group cohesion and hierarchical structure. During the forming stage, members may focus on establishing relationships and understanding their roles within the group rather than immediately diving into task assignments. The storming stage might be more subdued, with conflicts often addressed indirectly to avoid overt confrontation and preserve harmony. This approach can slow down conflict resolution but fosters a sense of belonging and loyalty over time.

The norming stage in Eastern teams is typically characterized by a strong sense of collective identity and shared responsibility. Decision-making may remain centralized, with leaders playing a crucial role in guiding the direction of the team. Performing stages in the East emphasize enduring stability and effective collaboration within established structures and processes.

Conversely, in the West, team development is often driven by individual contributions and direct communication. The forming stage may quickly transition to discussions about goals, responsibilities, and performance metrics. Storming stages in Western teams can involve robust debates and open expression of diverse opinions, viewed as integral to innovation and problem-solving. This openness may accelerate conflict resolution and enhance creative solutions but can also lead to shorter-term commitments as individuals defend their positions vigorously. During the norming stage, Western teams work on establishing agreed-upon rules and roles that streamline decision-making and enhance efficiency. Decentralized leadership and collective decision-making are encouraged, with an emphasis on empowering each team member. The performing stage in the West is marked by high autonomy and flexibility, where teams are results-oriented and rapidly adapt to change.

In conclusion, while Eastern team development tends to value harmony, hierarchy, and long-term relationships, Western approaches prioritize individualism, direct communication, and adaptability. Global teams, therefore, often require carefully balanced leadership that can synthesize these differing approaches. As companies embrace diversity and cultural intersections, they are increasingly likely to adopt hybrid models that combine the strengths of both Eastern and Western techniques to navigate the complexities of international teamwork effectively.

The Forming Stage

This is the initial phase where a team comes together. Members from diverse backgrounds tend to interact with a degree of formality, lacking personal familiarity. Without defined goals or clear expectations, the group has not yet become a functional team.

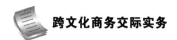
The Storming Stage

Unfamiliarity among members can lead to resistance and disagreements as they navigate different perspectives on goal achievement. These tensions may result in some members disengaging, either mentally or physically.

The Norming Stage

At this point, team members start to identify mutually accepted practices. They establish rules and principles that govern individual conduct and collective actions. A sense of unity begins to take precedence over individual agendas.

The Performing Stage

Following the challenges of storming and the consensus – building of norming, team members have each found their role in pursuing the shared objective. Recognizing the value of collaboration and support, the team operates efficiently and cohesively, reaching maturity in its functioning.

4. Effective Team Management

Effective team management is a critical component of organizational success in a globalized world. However, the approaches to achieve this effectiveness can differ significantly between Eastern and Western cultures due to divergent values, communication styles, and management philosophies.

Team management encompasses the spectrum of initiatives, strategies, and approaches that facilitate the synergy of individuals into an effective team, oriented toward the achievement of a mutual aim. As numerous undertakings necessitate collaborative efforts, teams become crucial for enhancing productivity. Enterprises depend on well – coordinated teams and adept management to ensure the continuity of their operations.

Obstacles such as inadequate communication or a lack of contribution from team members can impede a team's progress. Proficient team management serves to establish milestones that aid teams in commencing their endeavors successfully and sustaining constructive relationships and momentum from the project's inception through to the realization of the objective.

In many Eastern cultures, effective team management often revolves around ensuring group harmony and maintaining a hierarchical structure. Managers prioritize mutual respect and understanding among team members, which leads to an environment where individuals are less likely to openly disagree or voice contradictory opinions. This manages conflict by preventing it before it starts but might also mean that innovative ideas or dissenting views are not brought to the forefront. Decision-making tends to be top-down, with leaders making key decisions after considering input from various levels in the team, which can ensure everyone's needs are considered but may also slow down the decision process. Loyalty and long-term commitment are paramount, encouraging stable workforces where team members invest in long – term relationships and mutual growth.

Communication within effective Eastern teams is nuanced and indirect, requiring managers and team members to have a high level of emotional intelligence to interpret unspoken cues and maintain "face". Successful management, therefore, hinges on implicit understanding and the ability to navigate social complexities while upholding communal goals.

5. Why is Team Management Crucial?

Team management is an indispensable component of organizational success in the modern, interconnected world. It involves coordinating the efforts of individuals with diverse skills, experiences, and perspectives to achieve collective goals efficiently. The importance of team management cannot be understated, as it directly impacts productivity, innovation, employee satisfaction, and ultimately, the bottom line of any enterprise.

Effective team management starts with clear objectives that resonate with the overarching vision of the organization. When team members understand how their contributions align with broader goals, they are more motivated and likely to engage fully in their work. This clarity also helps minimize misunderstandings and ensures everyone pulls in the same direction.

A well-managed team fosters a sense of belonging and purpose among its members. As a result, employees are more committed and have higher job satisfaction, which reduces turnover rates and associated costs. Moreover, teams that operate with a shared purpose can adapt more readily to change and are better equipped to handle pressing challenges.

Communication is another key area where team management plays a pivotal role. Managers must ensure that information flows freely and that all team members are heard and understood. This open communication builds trust, encourages collaboration, and allows for the efficient resolution of issues that could otherwise impede progress.

Diversity within teams brings varied ideas and solutions but requires astute management to harness this potential. A skilled team manager recognizes the value of different perspectives and creates an environment where diversity is seen as a strength rather than a source of conflict. Such an inclusive approach enhances creativity and drives innovation, essential qualities for staying competitive in a rapidly evolving marketplace.

Finally, effective team management also encompasses recognizing and developing the talents within a team. By identifying individual strengths and providing opportunities for growth and advancement, managers can motivate team members and maximize their potential. This personal investment in employees' careers cultivates loyalty and long-term commitment to the team and the organization.

In conclusion, team management is crucial because it not only coordinates tasks but also molds a group of individuals into a cohesive, productive unit. It is through skilful management that teams can achieve superior results, thrive in dynamic environments, and push the boundaries of innovation. As Charles Noble once said, "The strength of the team is each individual member... The strength of each member is the team." This symbiotic relationship between the team and its members is what great management harnesses to drive organizations towards success.

Collaboration can present its challenges. Effective team management enhances the collaborative effort by establishing shared objectives, providing support, and devising strategies necessary to achieve these goals. Through task delegation, setting of incremental milestones, and additional measures, managers ensure that the team maintains focus and progresses coherently. Team management strategies also offer a mediation role in resolving conflicts among team members or when an external perspective is sought. Additional benefits of team management include:

- Cultivating a learning environment
- Elevating productivity levels
- Diminishing staff turnover rates
- Enhancing successful team dynamics
- Increasing employee contentment

6. What Defines a Team Leader?

A team leader is tasked with the responsibility of directing a group of individuals throughout a specific undertaking or towards the achievement of a well-defined objective. The role of a team leader does not necessarily equate to that of a team manager, as these functions typically diverge from personnel management duties. Specifically, a team leader is accountable for fostering a synergistic work atmosphere and charting the course for a particular venture or agenda.

Within their capacity, a team leader offers counsel and directions to the workforce regarding an initiative or a suite of related projects. They are entrusted with the allocation of tasks, monitoring the advancement toward set targets, and providing guidance to team members as circumstances require. Team leaders frequently assume the role of informal advisors for the team, irrespective of whether they hold a managerial position or not.

What defines a team leader can vary significantly depending on cultural context, reflecting distinct differences in values, management styles, and organizational philosophies between Eastern and Western approaches. These differences affect not only how leaders operate but also the expectations placed upon them by their teams and organizations.

In many Eastern cultures, a team leader is often defined by their role in maintaining harmony and upholding the collective good. Hierarchy and respect for authority are deeply ingrained, and leaders are expected to lead by example, making judicious decisions that consider the group's needs before individual desires. A strong emphasis on humility and servant leadership is prevalent, where the leader is seen as the facilitator of the team's success rather than the sole driver of it. The leader's effectiveness is measured by their ability to prioritize relationship-building, foster a loyal and cohesive team, and maintain stability and order within the group. Ambiguity in communication is also common, requiring leaders to have a high level of emotional intelligence to interpret unspoken cues and maintain "face" within the team.

On the other hand, in the Western context, a team leader is typically characterized by their ability to inspire and empower team members. Leaders are defined by their charisma, vision, and the capacity to encourage creativity and initiative among individuals. They are expected to be strategic thinkers who can foresee future opportunities and challenges, directly communicate goals, and motivate team members to achieve outstanding results. Leaders in the West are often evaluated based on their ability to drive innovation, handle change effectively, and secure tangible outcomes that contribute to the organization's success. Transparency and decisiveness are highly valued, as is the capacity to provide constructive feedback and promote continuous improvement.

While the East may emphasize communal achievements and indirect interactions, the West favors individual recognition and clear, direct communication. As globalization brings these diverse leadership styles into closer contact, there is an increasing recognition that effective leadership requires a nuanced blend of both approaches. Modern team leaders must balance the need for strong individual performance with the importance of collaborative effort, adapting their style to complement the diversity of their team and the demands of their environment. This amalgamation not only enriches leadership practices but also enhances the potential for building truly high-performing teams that excel in the complex, interconnected world of today's business.

To lead an effective team, the team leader must assume the role of a guide and mentor rather than simply a strict authority figure. Their responsibility extends beyond ensuring active participation from each team member; they should also facilitate the successful integration and performance of individuals from various cultural backgrounds within the team structure.

The team leader must embody fairness to ensure that all team members receive uniform information and have unimpeded access to higher-ups for any concerns or questions. Moreover, the leader should exhibit impartiality towards every member, regardless of their nationality or cultural heritage.

The team leader should possess the skill to regularly inspire and encourage team members, each with diverse cultural values and perspectives, thereby maintaining their morale and enthusiasm.

The team leader must unite the team members, fostering an environment where they can work harmoniously and experience contentment. It is crucial for the leader to nurture a spirit of collaboration that aligns with and honors the multicultural makeup of the team.

Task 8: Understanding the Concepts

Fill in the blanks with the serial numbers of the four keywords of a qualified team leader.

(1) fair   (2) motivate   (3) mentor   (4) satisfyingly

1. A team leader should be a _____ to his or her team members rather than just a strict boss.
2. A team leader should be _____ to every team member.
3. A team leader should _____ his or her team members to keep them in high spirits.
4. A team leader should bind the team members together and facilitate them to work _____ .

---

7. Effective Team Management Strategies

Effective team management often relies on timely and smart action. To enhance your team's dynamics, consider the following practical strategies that can be implemented immediately.

Challenges of Global Teams

<u>Create open channels of communication</u>: Cultivate a setting where all members feel at ease discussing their perspectives, innovative ideas, and concerns. This can be achieved by promoting transparency or utilizing platforms like Teamly for streamlined communication.

<u>Promote collaboration and engagement</u>: Create an environment that values everyone's input. This could involve actively soliciting contributions during meetings or employing shared project management tools.

<u>Conduct regular goal assessments</u>: Ensure that team goals are adaptable to reflect evolving

circumstances and capabilities. Consistent reviews allow for re – focusing efforts to maintain collective motivation.

Prioritize team wellness: A team that is overwhelmed or unhealthy will not perform optimally. Advocate for work – life balance, provide mental health resources, and ensure that team members take necessary time off. By embracing these clear strategies, you can step toward developing a more productive, involved, and cohesive team.

Task 9: Preparing for the Unit Project

1. Applying the Concepts

Rehearse developing a global team with your Chinese colleagues and the local employees in South America by following the four stages of forming, storming, norming and performing. Work in groups of four and have a discussion on the possible disputes and the rules that need to be formulated.

2. Applying Critical Thinking

Consider that team building and management are pivotal in multicultural business environments. To abbreviate the forming and storming phases within team development in South America, what targeted actions could be executed with the assistance of your team?

Part C   Business Ethics and Social Responsibilities

1. What Defines Business Ethics?

Business ethics represents the ethical standards, guidelines, and convictions that dictate how businesses and individuals behave within commercial interactions. It extends beyond mere legal obligations to create a framework of behavior that guides employees at every tier and fosters a trustful relationship between a company and its clients.

As a fundamental aspect of commerce, business ethics provides guidance for decision−making, behavior, and policies within companies. The definition and application of business ethics, however, can vary significantly between Eastern and Western cultures due to historical, philosophical, and cultural differences.

In the West, business ethics is often grounded in principles derived from philosophical traditions

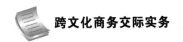
such as utilitarianism, deontology, and virtue ethics. These frameworks emphasize individualism, autonomy, and the importance of following universal moral rules or achieving the greatest happiness for the greatest number. Western corporations typically adopt codes of conduct that reflect these ethical principles, focusing on transparency, accountability, and respect for human rights. Issues such as environmental sustainability, consumer protection, and fair competition are paramount in Western business ethics.

Eastern conceptions of business ethics, particularly in Asia, are deeply influenced by Confucianism, Taoism, and Buddhism. These philosophies stress harmony, community welfare, and the importance of personal relationships. In Eastern cultures, the good of the collective often takes precedence over individual interests, and business practices are evaluated based on their contribution to societal and familial harmony. Loyalty to the company and long-term relationships with stakeholders are core values in Eastern business ethics, which also places significant emphasis on honor, face, and reciprocity.

One stark contrast between Eastern and Western business ethics lies in the treatment of corruption. In the West, corruption is viewed as a grave violation of ethical standards, often resulting in legal consequences and defamation. In some Eastern countries, however, building relationship, involves socially accepted beheaviors such as gift-giving and mutual favors. While these practices are seen as lubricants for business and social interactions, they can be perceived as forms of bribery in Western contexts.

Another difference is evident in leadership styles. Western corporate culture tends to advocate for transformational leadership, where ethical leaders inspire and motivate employees to achieve organizational goals. In contrast, Eastern cultures often prefer a more paternalistic approach, where leaders are seen as authority figures responsible for guiding and caring for their employees, similar to the head of a family.

Despite these differences, globalization has prompted a convergence of business ethics practices. Multinational corporations are increasingly adopting blended ethical standards that incorporate both Eastern and Western values to navigate diverse cultural landscapes effectively. Ethical issues such as labor rights, environmental stewardship, and anti-bribery initiatives have become universal concerns that transcend cultural boundaries.

In conclusion, while there are marked differences in how business ethics is defined and practiced in Eastern and Western contexts, there is also a growing recognition of the importance of integrating diverse ethical perspectives. As the global business environment continues to evolve, understanding and respecting these differences will be crucial for companies seeking to operate ethically and successfully across borders.

- Business ethics concerns the application of suitable policies and procedures to subjects that are often viewed as controversial.
- Common ethical issues include, but are not limited to, corporate governance, insider trading, bribery, discrimination, social responsibility, and fiduciary duties.
- Typically, it is the legal framework that sets the tone for business ethics, furnishing a foundational guideline businesses may elect to follow in order to earn public endorsement.

2. Why are Business Ethics Crucial?

Business ethics are critical for modern commercial success for numerous reasons. Primarily, a well-defined set of ethics creates a behavioral standard that influences employees at all levels, ranging from senior leaders to entry-level staff. As every team member commits to ethical decision-making, the firm solidifies its integrity, which enhances its standing in the industry. This growth in reputation brings about various advantages that an ethical organization can accrue:

- Enhanced brand recognition and expansion
- Improved negotiation capabilities
- Greater trust in offered products and services
- Customer loyalty and expansion
- Attraction of skilled personnel
- Appeal to potential investors

Why Study Ethics?

Task 10: Furthering Your Understanding

Watch a video clip and point out the importance of a Addis Ababa-Djibouti Railway.

---

3. Cross-cultural Ethical Standard

The United Nations has put forth a series of principles aimed at guiding the global business practices of multinational corporations. These guidelines encompass four key domains: human

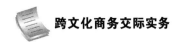
rights, labor standards, environmental protection, and anti-corruption.

Firstly, in terms of human rights, the United Nations emphasizes that businesses should respect and protect the basic rights of every individual, regardless of their location. This includes avoiding any form of discrimination, ensuring workplace safety and health, and respecting employees' freedom of association and collective bargaining rights. Secondly, in terms of labor standards, the United Nations advocates for businesses to comply with the core conventions of the International Labor Organization, ensure employees receive fair and reasonable wages, provide a safe working environment, and prohibit the use of child labor and forced labor. Thirdly, in terms of environmental protection, the United Nations encourages businesses to adopt sustainable business practices, reduce negative impacts on the environment, promote efficient resource utilization, and support ecosystem restoration and protection. Lastly, in the fight against corruption, the United Nations requires businesses to establish transparent governance structures, prevent bribery and corrupt practices, strengthen internal monitoring mechanisms, and cooperate with governments and other stakeholders to combat corruption.

These principles provide a moral and legal framework for global businesses to promote more just, sustainable, and responsible business practices.

4. Social Obligation and Social Responsibility

Social obligation is the basic principle that enterprises should follow when conducting business activities. This includes complying with laws and regulations, respecting human rights, protecting the environment, etc. Enterprises must ensure that their operations do not negatively impact employees, customers, or society, nor violate any moral and ethical standards. Social obligation is the fundamental responsibility of enterprises as members of society and the basis for their standing in society.

However, social responsibility is the further action taken by enterprises to make positive contributions to society on the basis of fulfilling their social obligations. These actions may include, but are not limited to: investing in community development projects, supporting education and training programs, promoting environmental protection initiatives, participating in charitable causes, etc. Social responsibility reflects the enterprise's concern and investment in social welfare and demonstrates the enterprise's values and sense of social responsibility.

In today's society, more and more enterprises are beginning to value social responsibility, considering it an important part of corporate strategy. By fulfilling social responsibilities, enterprises can not only enhance their brand image and reputation but also establish closer social connections and cooperative relationships. Additionally, social responsibility helps attract and retain excellent employees, improving employee satisfaction and loyalty.

In conclusion, social obligation and social responsibility are two important concepts that enterprises must confront in business operations. Social obligation is the basic norm for enterprises, while social responsibility is the proactive action taken by enterprises to promote social welfare. By fulfilling social responsibilities, enterprises can better give back to society, achieve sustainable development, and make positive contributions to building a more harmonious and prosperous society.

Task 11: Furthering Your Understanding

Watch the video clip and explain what CSR means.

Task 12: Preparing for the Unit Project

1. Applying the Concepts

What would you do when facing with a dilemma between making profits and the needs of the local society and customers? What can you learn from the traditional business values of China?

2. Critical Thinking

The couplet "善行孝义不欺天不欺人不欺自己，无忘仁慈须顾礼须顾信须顾先德" reflects the high ethical standards that ancient Chinese merchants were expected to follow. Comparing traditional Chinese wisdom with modern global ethics in a business context.

Assessment

1. *Decide whether the following statements are true (T) or false (F).*

_____ (1) The management of a multinational company should be based on understanding and interacting with people from different countries and cultures.

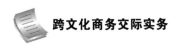

_____ (2) Different cultures have different perceptions of time due to their environment, history, traditions, and general practices.

_____ (3) In high-context corporate cultures, controlling tends to be task-driven in accordance with monitoring, with controlling procedures used to ensure the performance objectives.

_____ (4) A global team is a group of employees selected from two or more companies who work together to coordinate, develop, or manage certain aspects of the global operation of a project.

_____ (5) Social responsibility is the sorts of activities a business is willing to conduct in order to benefit society, which is beyond what is obligated by law.

_____ (6) In business contexts, standards of business ethics are the same around the world.

2. Read each of the following questions and choose the best answer.

(1) Which one is not a major function of management?

    A. Planning   B. Organizing   C. Motivating   D. Marketing

(2) Which cultural value is often associated with decentralized authority?

    A. The equality view   B. The monochronic view of time

    C. The hierarchy view   D. The polychronic view of time

(3) Which stage of team development may lead to some members' dropping out mentally or physically?

    A. The forming stage   B. The storming stage

    C. The norming stage   D. The performing stage

Unit Project

Re-examine the scenario of this unit and act as the secretary of the global team working in South America. Introduce the differences between Chinese culture and South America culture and tell your Chinese colleagues working there how to deal with the different ideas of the local employees. Record your introduction and present it in class. Your introduction may include the following points:

• Apply the theory of intercultural management on the basis of cultural values.

• Introduce the significance of common goals to all team members and present the ground rules for your team.

• Introduce traditional business ethics of China to the local employees and encourage your team to take social responsibility.

Case Analysis

Read the following case carefully and give your understanding of informality as well as the reasons why GE benefits from informality?

GE's Informality

At GE, informality is more than just an absence of managers parading around the factory floor in suits, or of reserved parking spaces and other trappings of rank and status. It's deeper than that. At GE, it's an atmosphere in which anyone can deliver a view, an idea, to anyone else, and it will be listened to and valued, regardless of the seniority of any party involved.

One of GE's management tenets has been the belief that businesses must be, or become, number one or number two in their marketplaces. But, this began to lead management teams to define their markets more and more narrowly. Then GE took a mid-level company management conference, in which some members point out, without shyness or sugar – coating, that cherished management idea had been taken to nonsensical levels. They told the high – level management that GE was missing opportunities, and limiting their growth horizons, by shrinking their definition of "the market" in order to satisfy the requirement to be number one or number two.

That fresh view shocked high-level management, and then shocked the system. Leaders began to redefine their markets. Rather than the increasingly limited market, they now had their eyes widened to the vast opportunity that lay ahead for their product and service offerings. This simple but very big change and their willingness to see it as "the better idea" was a major factor in their acceleration to double-digit revenue growth rates.

Further Reading

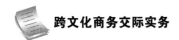

Five Intercultural Management Skills

As we have defined in our intercultural skills article, there are 5 management skills that can help along the cross-cultural management in an organization.

Learning about intercultural management skills is essential to develop a mindset that can work across international organizations with awareness and respect of the differences that exist.

That understanding and respect is what will help individuals to conduct in a manner that is able to resolve issues that might came across due to the different point of views in a multicultural group.

Therefore, working on the development of the followings skills is how intercultural management helps to know what to do in crucial moments within an international and culturally diverse environment.

Here we briefly mentioned intercultural management skills.

Speaking Several Languages

Senior level managers must know more than one language, especially if they are at an international business.

Yes, it is pretty common and comfortable to talk in the native language, but when the company already has a presence in multiple countries, then it is required for an effective intercultural communication to be able to have a good dialogue in a common language.

English can be considered a base language to do business world wide, but still businesses are located around the world, and so the language will be different.

A manager or business owner improves his intercultural competence by speaking different languages, especially when they deal with his or her customers native language.

Open Mindset

Intercultural business management requires an open mindset due to the differences that cultures will have.

Customs and behaviors vary from country to country, and businesses must understand that they can't fully impose their practices in other regions.

Having an open mindset of how to solve problems can help a business to find alternatives to improve their operations.

Empathy, Tolerance and Respect

Having the intercultural management skills of empathy, tolerance and respect will help managers to understand how to work with other cultures.

Of course business managers will prefer top performing employees, but acknowledging the differences and respecting them will create a better atmosphere for a proper intercultural communication.

Cultural Awareness

When a business unit decides to be set abroad from their headquarters, they must study the culture where they are going.

The day-to-day of normal life in a foreign country is where intercultural management skills are improved by getting to understand how the system and culture works.

As more time passes in another culture, especially if they don't speak your language, the intercultural communication skills are forced to be improved.

The language structure also described how the culture is created.

Critical Thinking

Among the intercultural management skills, critical thinking is required to be able to identify, evaluate, analyze and interpret the situations that happen around international business.

Critical thinking can support an intercultural competence that will help to take the proper decision in an international context for a better cross cultural management.

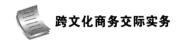

单元小结

1 学习目标

在学习本单元后，你将能够：
- 解释文化价值与跨文化管理之间的关系；
- 了解多元文化团队管理的特点；
- 阐明商业伦理和社会责任的概念；
- 将跨文化管理理论应用于特定的海外项目和影响跨文化谈判风格的文化因素。

2 情境假设

假设你在中国一家网络和电信跨国公司工作，该公司在国内外市场为客户提供专业设备和服务。你和几位同事被派往南美国家建立相关项目并探索与当地机构的合作。作为团队秘书，你需要帮助中国同事适应新文化环境，并与当地员工共同构建有效的多元文化团队。你和你的团队应确保可持续发展、满足当地需求，并与当地人保持长期合作关系。

3 什么是跨文化管理

管理是指涉及监督和协调个人或团队工作的过程和活动，其目标是有效且高效地实现组织目标。有效的管理对于任何企业或组织都至关重要，因为它直接影响到生产力、员工满意度和整体成功。

跨文化管理是全球商业运作的一个重要方面，特别在当今这个互联互通的世界中，企业往往拥有多元文化的劳动力，并在多个国家和区域开展业务。

4 如何与拥有不同文化背景的员工和客户合作

当你与拥有不同文化背景的人一起工作时，重要的是要保持开放的态度，准备好学习他们的思维和做事方式。不要猜测或批评他们与你不同的做事方式。在处理具有不同优先级和价值观的其他人时，过于执着于对自己信念的依赖可能会产生问题。

花时间了解你将要合作的人的习俗、信仰和生活方式。理解他们的过去、言语、庆祝活动和礼仪。了解这些有助于避免误解，并以他们的方式看待事物。始终考虑这三个问题：

宗教：我应该知道有关于饮食、休息、衣着或行为的规则，以免冒犯任何人。

性别：因为这一点，我应该改变行为或说话方式吗？

年龄和资历：这个人的文化是否特别重视年龄或资历？它们有多重要，我是否需要显得更加尊重？

5 化价值观对管理职能的影响

5.1 规划

在管理领域，设定目标的任务是管理者的首要功能。根据管理者的职责范围，目标可以为个人贡献者、部门或整个实体量身定制。除了设定目标之外，管理者还需要经常制定可执行的项目，进行策略和资源的分配，以促进组织任务的完成和目标的实现。

5.2 组织

组织包括制定组织架构以及工作角色和工作流程的层次结构。有时，管理者还必须提供针对性的培训，以使员工具备成功所需的知识和技能。

谈判可以说是一种对等对话，目的是在利益可能重叠或分歧的双方或多方之间达成共识。这是一个复杂而微妙的过程，涉及战略思维、情商和求同存异的意愿，以达成互惠互利的协议。

5.3 激励

管理者是员工激励的催化剂，确保他们的参与度和生产力。这包括分享共同愿景、鼓励力量发展以及激发持续的顶级表现。有效的沟通在此过程中不可或缺。

5.4 评估

管理者需要投入时间评估其团队的效能和目标实现情况。他们越能够分辨出成功与失败的因素，就越能为未来的决策做好准备。经理们必须吸收并重新调整策略，以符合公司的目标。

6 团队发展阶段

6.1 形成阶段

形成阶段是团队聚集在一起的初始阶段。拥有不同文化背景的成员会进行一定程度的正式性互动；由于缺乏个人熟悉度，也没有明确的目标或清晰的期望，这个群体还没有成为一个功能性的团队。

6.2 风暴阶段

在风暴阶段，成员之间的不熟悉可能会导致在目标实现的不同观点上产生抵抗和分歧。这些紧张关系可能导致一些成员在心理上或身体上产生疏离感。

6.3 规范化阶段

在规范化阶段，团队成员开始识别相互接受的实践。他们建立了指导个人行为和集体行动的规则和原则。团结感开始优先于个人议程。

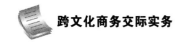

6.4 成熟阶段

在经历了风暴阶段的震荡和规范化阶段的共识之后，团队成员各自找到了在追求共同目标中的角色定位，认识到协作和支持的价值。团队高效而紧密地运作，其职能运作达到成熟。

7 什么是团队领导者

团队领导者负责在特定任务中指导团队实现一个明确的目标。团队领导者的角色并不一定等同于团队经理，因为这些职能通常与人事管理职责不同。具体来说，团队领导者负责营造协同工作的氛围，并为特定的项目或议程规划路线。

有效的团队管理往往依赖于及时和明智的行动。要提升团队的活力，可以考虑以下策略。

- 创建开放的沟通渠道；
- 促进合作和参与；
- 进行定期的目标评估；
- 优先考虑团队健康。

8 职业道德

职业道德代表了指导企业和个体在商业互动中行为的道德标准、准则和信念；它超越了单纯的法律义务，并创建了一个行为框架，指导每个层级的员工，致力于在公司与其客户之间培养信任关系。职业道德关注将适当的政策和程序应用于通常被视为有争议的主题。常见的问题包括但不限于公司治理、内幕交易、贿赂、歧视、社会责任和信托义务。通常，法律框架为职业道德设定了基调，提供了一个基础指南，企业可以选择遵循以获得公众认可。

职业道德对现代商业成功至关重要。首先，一套明确定义的伦理规范为所有级别的员工（从高级领导到初级员工）设定了行为标准。当每个团队成员都致力于做出符合伦理的决策时，公司就巩固了其诚信度，这增强了其在行业中的地位。这种声誉的增长带来了一个有道德的组织可以获得的各种优势：

- 增强品牌认知和扩张；
- 提高谈判能力；
- 对提供的产品和服务增加信任；
- 客户忠诚度和扩张；
- 吸引熟练人才；
- 吸引潜在投资者。

9 跨文化道德标准

联合国提出了一系列旨在指导跨国公司全球商业行为的原则，这些指导原则涉及四个关键领域：员工权利、劳工标准、环境保护和反腐败。

9.1 员工权利方面

联合国强调企业应尊重和保护每个人的基本权利，无论其身处何地。这包括避免任何形式的歧视，确保工作场所的安全和健康，以及尊重员工的自由结社和集体谈判的权利等。

9.2 劳工标准方面

联合国倡导企业遵守国际劳工组织的核心公约，确保员工获得公平合理的工资，提供安全的工作环境，并禁止使用童工和强迫劳动。

9.3 环境保护方面

联合国鼓励企业采取可持续的商业实践，以减少对环境的负面影响，促进资源的有效利用，并支持生态系统的恢复和保护。

9.4 反腐败方面

在反腐败斗争中，联合国要求企业建立透明的治理结构，防止贿赂和腐败行为，加强内部监督，并与政府和其他利益相关者合作打击腐败。

10 社会义务和社会责任

社会义务是企业在开展商业活动时应当遵循的基本原则。这包括遵守法律法规、尊重人权、保护环境等。企业必须确保其运营不会对员工、客户或社会产生负面影响，也不会违反任何道德和伦理标准。作为社会成员的企业，承担社会义务是其基本责任，也是其在社会中立足的基础。

社会义务和企业社会责任是企业在经营过程中必须面对的两个重要概念。社会义务是企业的基本规范，而企业社会责任则是企业为促进社会福利所采取的积极行动。通过履行社会责任，企业可以更好地回馈社会，实现可持续发展，并为建设更加和谐繁荣的社会做出积极贡献。

* 本单元智慧职教线上课程：https：//zyk. icve. com. cn/courseDetailed？ id = obbaaaqvo4doejfjffeicq&openCourse = obbaaaqvw79e5opp1bwbg.

Unit 7 习题参考答案

Unit 8   Intercultural Marketing

Ancient Chinese Wisdom

Xiao Gong, having employed Wei Yang, desired to implement reforms but feared the criticism from others. The decree was ready but not yet announced, as he worried about the people's disbelief. So, he placed a tall wooden pole at the southern gate of the capital city, offering a reward of ten gold pieces to anyone who could move it to the northern gate. The people were puzzled and no one dared to move it. He then announced, "Whoever can move it will receive fifty gold pieces". One person did so and was immediately rewarded with fifty gold pieces, proving that there was no deceit. Finally, the decree was issued.   （孝公既用卫鞅，鞅欲变法，恐天下议己。令既具，未布，恐民之不信，乃立三丈之木于国都市南门，募民有能徙置北门者予十金。民怪之，莫敢徙。复曰："能徙者予五十金。"有一人徙之，辄予五十金，以明不欺。卒下令。）

From *Shih Chi* （《史记》）

Learning Objectives

After learning this unit, you shall be able to：

- Know about the marketing styles of different cultures.
- Explain the strategies for solving intercultural marketing problems.
- Clarify the advantages and disadvantages of standardization and localization.
- Understand the concept of "thinking globally and acting locally".
- Apply intercultural marketing strategies and make marketing plans.

Project Scenario

After learning this unit, finish the unit project on the basis of the following scenario.

Suppose you are a director of sales department in a multinational corporation. Your company has designed a new electric car which will be launched onto the foreign market. You will make a business presentation on your new product to your international colleagues. You need to investigate the intercultural marketing situation and come up with specific marketing plans that can appeal to foreign consumers.

Lead-in

Watch the video clip about an advertisement of Chinese multinational company and answer the following question.

- What kind of corporate culture is this advertisement trying to convey?
- What marketing strategies do you adopt if you are responsible for the promotion?

Part A   Cross-Cultural Marketing

1. What is Marketing?

Marketing is the strategic set of actions a business implements to facilitate the exchange of its products or services. It involves initiatives such as advertising and aims to connect offerings with potential buyers, whether they are individual consumers, other companies, or various organizations.

The importance of marketing lies in its ability to create initial engagement with potential customers. Through marketing campaigns, a company can introduce its products to the market, providing opportunities to inform and persuade consumers about the value of their offerings. This introduction is often the first interaction a customer has with a product or service.

The 4 P's of Marketing

Furthermore, marketing is a pivotal tool for shaping the perception of a brand's identity. A business can strategically use marketing to convey specific qualities it wishes to be associated with. For example, if an outdoor camping gear company desires recognition for its durable and robust products, it can execute marketing strategies that reflect these qualities, ensuring that the brand's key messages resonate powerfully with the target audience.

2. Marketing Styles in Different Cultures

Marketing is the lifeline of business, and its effectiveness hinges on understanding the cultural nuances of target markets. Different cultures around the world have unique values, communication styles, and consumption habits, which necessitate tailored marketing approaches. This essay explores the divergence in marketing styles across cultures and underscores the importance of cultural sensitivity in global marketing strategies.

In individualistic societies, like those prevalent in the West, marketing messages often emphasize personal benefit, self-expression, and the realization of individual dreams. Advertisements in

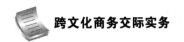

these cultures frequently portray independent characters achieving success through their efforts and the products they use. For instance, American advertising is known for its directness, clarity, and focus on the consumer's immediate gratification.

Conversely, in collectivist cultures found in many Asian countries, such as China and Japan, marketing communications tend to highlight family values, social harmony, and how products can contribute to group well-being. Ads may feature families or groups enjoying a product together, subtly suggesting how it enhances relationships and social status. For example, Japanese advertising typically employs indirect messaging and evokes emotion through storytelling and symbolism.

Furthermore, the level of context influences marketing styles significantly. High-context cultures, like those in the Middle East and Latin America, value implicit communication and nonverbal cues. Marketing messages in these regions might rely more on visuals, symbols, and indirect suggestions rather than explicit claims. In contrast, low-context cultures, such as Germany and the United States, prefer clear and direct verbal communication, making their advertising more explicit and straightforward.

Another crucial aspect is the attitude towards authority and hierarchy. In countries with a high power distance index, like India, advertisements may showcase respect for authority by featuring experts or celebrities endorsing products. In contrast, cultures with lower power distance, like Australia, might employ a more egalitarian approach, showing ordinary people using the products in everyday scenarios.

The role of gender varies widely across cultures, too. While Western marketing might emphasize gender equality and empowerment, other cultures may adhere to more traditional gender roles. For instance, Arabic advertising often depicts men in decision-making positions and women in caring roles, reflecting societal norms.

To sum up, the diversity in global cultures mandates that marketers adopt a culturally sensitive approach when crafting their campaigns. Understanding the values, communication styles, and social norms of different cultures is essential to create messages that resonate with specific audiences. As the marketplace continues to globalize, the capacity to adapt marketing strategies to local cultures will remain a critical skill for international businesses seeking to build connections and expand their reach across the world.

Chinese Style of Marketing

To ensure a retail venture's prosperity in China, it's important to understand the local culture and customs. This helps marketers cater to consumer preferences and avoid mistakes. In today's globalized world, consumers develop multicultural identities that impact their buying behavior. An excellent example of this is Starbucks' localization strategy in China. The company has introduced offerings like matcha latte and moon cakes during festive periods while creating a cozy environment inspired by traditional tea houses. Through such culturally sensitive strategies, Starbucks has emerged as one of the most successful foreign enterprises within China's coffee industry.

How does culture influence Chinese consumer buying habits?

Chinese consumer buying habits are deeply rooted in the country's rich cultural traditions, which have been evolving alongside rapid economic development and global influence. This essay will explore how culture shapes the purchasing behavior of Chinese consumers, emphasizing the importance of Confucian values, group orientation, and modernization.

Confucian philosophy plays a fundamental role in Chinese consumer behavior. One of the core principles is the concept of "li", which refers to proper conduct and rituals that maintain social harmony. This influences consumers to prefer brands that are respectful and contribute to social stability. Additionally, the emphasis on education and self-improvement encourages purchases related to personal development, such as educational products and services.

The group-oriented nature of Chinese society means that consumer choices often reflect communal preferences and expectations. Word-of-mouth recommendations and popularity within social networks significantly impact buying decisions. Brands that are perceived as widely accepted or endorsed by peers tend to be more trusted and preferred.

Furthermore, the rise of social media platforms has amplified the effects of electronic word-of-mouth (eWOM), where consumers share reviews and feedback instantaneously. In China, platforms like WeChat and Weibo are powerful tools for brands to engage with consumers and foster a sense of community around their products.

Another cultural factor is the balance between traditional values and modern lifestyles. As China has opened up to the world, Western influences have introduced new consumer trends. However, many consumers still hold traditional beliefs about health, family, and status. Health products that incorporate traditional Chinese medicine ingredients, for example, appeal to consumers seeking a blend of ancient wisdom and modern convenience.

Face, or "mian zi," which relates to dignity and social standing, also plays a crucial role in Chinese consumption patterns. Consumers may purchase luxury goods or high-status brands to enhance their social image and convey success. This trend has led to a thriving market for upscale products, from automobiles to cosmetics.

Finally, Chinese consumer buying habits are a complex interplay of cultural heritage and

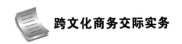

contemporary forces. Brands that understand and respect these cultural dynamics — be it the significance of harmonious interactions, group consciousness, or the balance between tradition and modernity — are better positioned to connect with Chinese consumers and thrive in this vast and vibrant market. As China continues to evolve, savvy marketers will adapt their strategies to align with the cultural pulse, leveraging both ancient wisdom and modern marketing techniques to capture the hearts and minds of Chinese consumers.

Guanxi, the essence of interpersonal relations: In China, "Guanxi" plays a pivotal role in achieving business success and fostering customer loyalty. It features personal trust and the strength of interpersonal bonds, significantly affecting how business transactions are conducted. For micro-entrepreneurial businesses to thrive in a competitive landscape, forging emotional ties with customers through close relationships becomes a strategic priority.

High-context communication: In China, consumer purchasing is often informed by implicit meanings and background information that hold significance. This communication style is characterized as high-context. Marketing messaging must be crafted with an understanding of this high-context communication style to resonate with potential customers effectively. The preference for indirect communication in China stems from its cultural values. Comprehending this helps establish an effective connection with the target customer.

The influence of "face" culture: The cultural notion of "face" exerts a significant influence on the behavior of Chinese consumers, shaping their purchasing decisions and brand preferences. Corporations must take this into account within their marketing strategies to prevent causing customers to lose face, which could negatively impact brand perception and loyalty.

Task 1: Furthering Your Understanding

Watch the video clip and learn about the Chinese culture.

American and European Style of Marketing

The United States' influence on the globe is overwhelming and its products are unavoidable. Whether it's through Hollywood films, music, or food, individuals from around the world tend to have a greater familiarity with American culture and its social landscape compared to Americans' knowledge of their respective cultures.

While countries like the UK and Ireland share a linguistic proximity with the US, each European country possesses its own unique business culture, which can differ considerably. By comprehending the differences between American and European business customs, one can prevent minor miscommunication that might hinder well-crafted strategies for business expansion.

The American business approach to collaboration exhibits both advantages and drawbacks. The ease of establishing new partnerships in the U. S. is favorable, yet these connections tend to be more fragile, ensuring that they do not hinder pragmatic decision-making. In Europe, the scenario differs considerably, with business relationships often spanning years or decades. Cultivating such bonds typically requires a heightened level of trust and, once formed, proves challenging to break.

American enterprises benefit from English being the common language of the business world, which facilitates their growth and expansion. Nevertheless, this does not absolve the need to tailor one's language according to the target market - or to learn the local language if venturing beyond initial introductions. The appropriate use of language is essential for creating a favorable first impression, a principle that holds true across the UK, Ireland, Spain, France, and beyond.

Although businesses may be cautious about forging new partnerships, customers are receptive to novel concepts. In comparison to their American counterparts, European consumers often demonstrate a more progressive perspective, which emboldens businesses to be more adventurous in their product offerings. Europeans have been quick to embrace e-commerce, click-and-collect services, mobile payment solutions, and internet banking. This trend is especially pronounced in the UK, where embracing innovation is prevalent.

Task 2: Furthering Your Understanding

Watch the video clip and try to figure out the office culture in the UK.

Task 3: Understanding the Concepts

According to the features of different marketing styles, fill in the two boxes with the serial numbers of the following words and phrases.

(1) relationship takes time (2) non-English environment (3) social harmony
(4) open to new things (5) "Face" culture (6) "guanxi"

European Style	Chinese Style

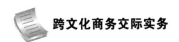

Part B   Intercultural Marketing Strategies

Intercultural marketing strategies bridge the gap between global brands and diverse cultural audiences. However, the approaches to intercultural marketing can significantly differ between Eastern and Western businesses due to disparate cultural values, communication styles, and consumer behaviors. This essay will delve into these differences, highlighting how each cultural block tailors its marketing efforts to resonate with its respective audiences.

One of the primary differences lies in the communication style. Western marketing often employs direct, clear, and explicit messages that quickly convey the product's benefits and USP (unique selling proposition). This approach aligns with Western values of individualism, practicality, and efficiency. In contrast, Eastern marketing strategies tend to be more indirect and subtle, utilizing symbolism, storytelling, and emotional connections to engage consumers. This method reflects the high‐context culture prevalent in many Eastern societies, where nuanced communication is valued.

Another significant area of difference is the role of collective identity. Eastern marketing frequently emphasizes family, community, and social harmony, reflecting the region's collectivist mindset. Ads may feature happy families or groups enjoying the product together, subtly suggesting how it enhances relationships. Meanwhile, Western advertising typically focuses on the individual, showcasing personal achievements and self‐expression enabled by the product.

The concept of "face" or reputation also influences intercultural marketing strategies. In

Eastern cultures, particularly in China, maintaining or enhancing one's social standing is crucial. As a result, marketing campaigns often position their products as status symbols, emphasizing luxury and prestige. Conversely, while Western cultures also value status, their ads may focus more on individual benefits, uniqueness, and innovation rather than solely on societal perception.

Furthermore, the interpretation of colors and symbols varies across cultures, impacting visual aspects of marketing materials. What signifies luck, wealth, or tranquility in one culture may have a different connotation in another. For instance, the color red is associated with good fortune in China but may signify danger or passion in Western contexts. Marketers must carefully select visual elements to avoid misinterpretations and negative associations.

Task 5: Telling China's Stories in English

What can you learn from the success of Haier's international marketing?

Corporation Profile of
HAIER INTRODUCTION

Haier's successful entry into the American market in 2000 was a significant milestone for the company, marking its expansion beyond Asia and onto the global stage. The factors that contributed to Haier's success in the U. S. market are multifaceted and provide valuable lessons for other companies looking to expand internationally. Here are some of the key elements that played a role in Haier's achievements:

Quality products: Haier's commitment to producing high-quality products was a fundamental aspect of its strategy. By ensuring that its products met stringent quality standards, Haier was able to gain the trust of American consumers who are known for their high expectations when it comes to product quality.

Individualistic design: In addition to quality, Haier also emphasized unique and individualistic design in its products. This approach allowed Haier to stand out in a crowded market and appeal to American consumers who value innovation and personalization.

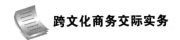

Consumer-centred approach: Haier demonstrated a deep understanding of American consumer wants and needs. By conducting thorough market research and actively listening to consumer feedback, Haier was able to tailor its products and services to meet the specific requirements of the American market.

Aggressive pursuit of quality assurance: Haier's relentless focus on quality assurance was another critical factor in its success. By consistently delivering products that exceeded quality expectations, Haier built a reputation for reliability and durability, which are highly valued attributes in the American market.

Adaptability: Haier showed a willingness to adapt its business practices and strategies to align with the cultural norms and market conditions of the United States. This flexibility allowed Haier to navigate the complexities of the American market effectively and maintain its competitive edge.

Strong branding: Haier invested in building a strong brand identity in the American market. Through effective marketing campaigns and advertising strategies, Haier established itself as a reputable and trustworthy brand among American consumers.

Global vision: Haier's success in the U. S. was part of a broader global strategy. By positioning itself as a global player, Haier was able to leverage its international experience and resources to compete effectively in the American market.

In today's globalized world, businesses face consumers from diverse cultural backgrounds. To succeed in this multicultural market, it is essential for companies to establish a concept of cross-cultural marketing. Cross-cultural marketing refers to the process where businesses take into account the needs, values, and behaviors of consumers from different cultural backgrounds when developing and implementing their marketing strategies, aiming to better satisfy their demands. Here are some recommendations to help businesses embrace the concept of cross-cultural marketing:

- Businesses need to deeply understand the values, beliefs, and consumption habits of consumers across various cultural backgrounds to better meet their needs. This can be achieved through market research, consumer interviews, social media analysis, etc. Understanding consumers' needs and expectations helps businesses develop more targeted marketing strategies.

- Respecting and understanding multiculturalism is crucial in cross-cultural marketing. Businesses should avoid stereotypes and prejudices towards specific cultures and instead adopt an open mindset to accept and understand different cultures. This facilitates building trust and positive relationships with consumers from diverse cultural backgrounds during interactions.

- Businesses should devise diversified marketing strategies based on the needs of consumers from various cultural backgrounds. This includes aspects such as product positioning, pricing strategies, promotional methods, and advertising creativity. For instance, businesses may launch products with regional characteristics or use advertising designs that align with local aesthetics for different cultural backgrounds.

- Employees of businesses need to possess cross-cultural communication skills to interact effectively with consumers from diverse cultural backgrounds. This involves developing language abilities, cultural sensitivity, and communication techniques. Businesses can enhance their employees' cross-cultural communication skills through training courses and exchange activities.

- Businesses should strive to establish a global brand image to build a positive reputation among consumers from different cultural backgrounds. This requires businesses to take into account the needs of consumers from diverse cultural backgrounds in product design, brand communication, customer service, etc., to achieve global development of the brand.

In summary, establishing a concept of cross-cultural marketing is vital for businesses to succeed in the globalized market. By understanding consumers from different cultural backgrounds, respecting and understanding multiculturalism, devising diversified marketing strategies, cultivating cross-cultural communication skills, and establishing a global brand image, businesses will be able to better meet consumers' needs and achieve sustainable development.

Task 6: Cross-cultural Comparison

Translate the following advertising slogans into Chinese, giving adequate consideration to the differences between customers' mindsets. Then work in groups of four and have a discussion with your group members.

- Nothing comes between me and my *Calvin's*. （CK 牛仔裤）
- Maybe she's born with it? Maybe it's *Maybelline*? （美宝莲化妆品）
- China Railways High-speed, a moving Great Wall in the world! （中国高铁）

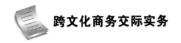

Task 7: Preparing for the Unit Project

1. Applying the Concepts

Find more information about existing cosmetic advertisements of different cultures, and then examine the aspects of languages, gestures, colors, appearances, rituals and religions. Design an advertising slogan for the product l in the scenario. Share your idea with your partner.

2. Critical Thinking

Suppose you are an employee of Huawei overseas marketing department and the company asks you to design a sports watch advertisement for the Indian market. What intercultural marketing strategies will you use?

Part C Standardization and Localization

Global standardization and global localization are two distinct strategies that companies employ when expanding their operations into international markets. Each approach has its advantages and disadvantages, and the choice between them often depends on the nature of the product or service, the company's resources, and the characteristics of the target markets. Here's a detailed comparison.

Standardization and Localization

1. Global Standardization

Global marketing standardization is an approach that involves the use of uniform marketing strategies, messages, and campaigns across different countries and regions. This method aims to create a consistent global brand image and reduce costs associated with customized marketing for each individual market.

The primary impetus for global standardization is the increasing homogenization of consumer needs and wants worldwide. As technology, travel, and media democratize access to information and culture, consumers in different countries exhibit similar behaviors and preferences. This phenomenon allows companies to deploy uniform marketing strategies globally, thereby realizing economies of scale and reducing complexity.

One notable advantage of global standardization is cost efficiency. By adopting a standardized approach, businesses can reduce production and marketing costs associated with customized products or campaigns for each region. For instance, a multinational corporation like Coca-Cola can use the same advertising campaign in multiple countries, saving on creative and distribution expenses.

Another benefit is the strengthening of brand identity. Consistent branding fosters global recognition and loyalty. For example, Apple's sleek and minimalistic design language is uniform across its products, creating an instantly recognizable brand image worldwide.

However, global standardization also presents challenges. Cultural differences can significantly impact product acceptance and consumer engagement. A product that thrives in one market may fail in another due to local tastes, traditions, or laws. Thus, thorough market research is essential before rolling out standardized campaigns.

Furthermore, language and translation issues can create communication barriers. A message that resonates in one language might not translate effectively into another, potentially altering the intended meaning or emotion.

While global standardization offers numerous benefits, including cost efficiency and unified branding, it requires careful consideration of cultural nuances and local preferences. Successful standardization strategies often result from a blend of centralized principles and local adaptations, balancing the consistency of the brand's core values with the diversity of global markets. As the business landscape continues to evolve towards globalization, the ability to standardize while remaining sensitive to cultural differences will be paramount for international marketing success.

Advantages

Cost savings: By using the same products, packaging, and marketing campaigns globally, companies can achieve economies of scale in production and advertising.

Brand consistency: A standardized approach ensures that the brand message remains consistent across all markets, which can help strengthen brand recognition worldwide.

Simplicity: This strategy is easier to manage as it involves fewer variations to keep track of.

Speed to market: With less need for local adaptation, products can be launched more quickly in new markets.

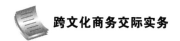

Disadvantages

Cultural insensitivity: One size may not fit all, and what works in one country may not work in another due to cultural differences.

Limited customization: Standardized products may not meet the specific needs or preferences of local consumers.

Competitive disadvantage: Local competitors who offer products tailored to local tastes may have an advantage.

> **Examples**
> • Apple maintains a consistent design and user interface across all its products, with only minor adjustments for power sources and language.
> • Coca-Cola has a universally recognizable brand image and product formulation, though it does offer some local flavors.

2. Global Localization

Localization in global marketing refers to the strategy of adapting products, services, and marketing messages to suit the language, culture, and preferences of specific local markets. This approach recognizes the diversity among global consumers and seeks to engage with them on a more personal and relevant level.

Localization in global marketing is a crucial strategy for companies looking to expand their reach and appeal to customers across different regions. It involves adapting products, services, marketing materials, and even the overall brand image to meet the unique needs, preferences, and cultural contexts of each target market.

The impetus for localization arises from the fact that despite trends towards globalization, individual markets retain unique characteristics. Consumer behavior, language, cultural norms, and legal requirements can vary widely, necessitating a tailored approach to market effectively.

One significant advantage of localization is enhanced customer engagement. By understanding and respecting local customs, companies can create stronger emotional connections with their consumers. For example, McDonald's adapts its menu in different countries to include items that cater to local tastes, such as the McSpaghetti in Switzerland or the Samurai Pork Burger in Japan.

Another benefit is the avoidance of cultural insensitivities that can damage a brand's reputation. A marketing campaign that is well-received in one country could be offensive or ineffective in another. Localization allows for the contextualization of messages to prevent such faux pas.

However, localization also presents challenges. It requires substantial research and insight into each local market, resulting in increased costs and complexity. Additionally, maintaining consistency across multiple localized campaigns can be difficult, potentially diluting the brand's global identity.

Furthermore, localization demands linguistic expertise to ensure accurate translation and adaptation of marketing materials. Poor translations can lead to embarrassing errors that undermine the brand's credibility.

As a result, localization is a crucial aspect of global marketing, enabling companies to connect with consumers on a deeper level by acknowledging and respecting their cultural identities. While it entails additional costs and complexities, the payoff comes in the form of stronger market presence and customer loyalty. As the marketplace continues to fragment into niche segments, the capacity to localize effectively will remain a critical skill for international marketing success.

Advantages

Cultural relevance: Products and marketing messages are tailored to resonate with local cultures, increasing appeal and acceptance.

Greater flexibility: The ability to adapt to local market conditions allows for greater responsiveness to changes and opportunities.

Stronger competitive position: By addressing local preferences directly, companies can compete more effectively against local brands.

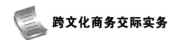

Enhanced customer loyalty: Customers are more likely to engage with a brand that understands and respects their cultural nuances.

Disadvantages

Higher costs: Localization can be expensive, requiring additional research, development, and marketing efforts for each market.

Complexity: Managing multiple variations of products and campaigns can be logistically challenging.

Consistency issues: Maintaining a unified global brand image while adapting to local markets can be difficult.

Examples

- Spotify adjusts its playlists and recommendations based on regional music preferences.
- McDonald's offers localized menu items in many countries, such as the "Teriyaki Burger" in Japan or the "Maharaja Mac" in India.

Both global standardization and global localization strategies have their places in international marketing. The choice between them should be informed by a thorough understanding of the product, the target markets, and the overall goals of the company. Often, a blend of both strategies — known as "glocalization" — can provide the best of both worlds, allowing for global efficiency while still catering to local tastes and preferences.

Task 8: Understanding the Concepts

Judge which of the following marketing principles or strategies are related to standardization and which are related to localization.

- The more national, the more international.

- The name of a multinational food company is transliterated into the local language.
- One advertisement could be used for all markets and all cultures.
- A Western shoe company uses the Temple of Heaven as the background of its advertisement for Chinese consumers.

Task 9: Preparing for the Unit Project

1. Applying the Concepts

According to Part C, standardization and localization are two important views of intercultural marketing. How are you going to use appropriate strategies to promote the newly designed mobile phone? Explore the cultural elements that can support the standardization or localization of products in the specific culture you have chosen.

2. Critical Thinking

After learning this part, which view do you think is better for intercultural marketing in general—standardization or localization? Give your reasons.

Part D　Strategies for International Marketers

Entering new markets overseas offers both substantial opportunities and significant challenges for international marketers. To succeed, they must employ a suite of strategies that balance global uniformity with local adaptation, cultural sensitivity with brand consistency, and efficiency with customization.

Challenges in International Marketing

Thorough market research is the cornerstone of successful international marketing. Understanding the socioeconomic conditions, consumer behavior, competition, and legal environment of target markets is essential. This knowledge enables companies to identify potential opportunities and threats, tailor their offerings, and devise effective promotional strategies.

Product adaptation is another critical strategy. What works in one country may not translate well to another due to differing cultural norms and needs. Therefore, making appropriate adjustments to products or services to better suit the tastes and preferences of the local population is vital. This could involve changes to the product itself, its packaging, or even the way it is used.

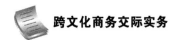
Communication strategy also requires careful consideration. Language differences and cultural nuances necessitate adapting advertising copy, slogans, and visual elements to resonate with the local audience. Moreover, selecting the right channels to reach the target demographic — be it print, television, digital, or social media — is crucial for maximizing impact.

Pricing strategy involves more than simply converting currency. It demands an understanding of the local economy, price sensitivity of consumers, and the positioning of competing products. In some cases, this might mean adopting a penetration pricing strategy to gain market share initially at a lower cost or adjusting prices to align with local purchasing power.

1. Adapting Marketing Strategy to Culture

Adapting marketing strategy to culture is a vital process that ensures the effectiveness and relevance of campaigns in diverse cultural landscapes. This essay will explore why cultural adaptation is necessary, how it can be achieved, and the benefits and challenges that come with this approach.

The necessity for cultural adaptation arises from the core truth that consumers' beliefs, values, and behaviors are shaped by their cultural backgrounds. Ignoring these factors in marketing can lead to messages that are misunderstood, offensive, or simply ignored by the target audience. By adapting to local cultures, marketers can craft more impactful and respectful campaigns that resonate deeply with consumers.

To achieve cultural adaptation, marketers must first engage in extensive research to understand the nuances of the target demographic. This includes aspects such as language, traditions, social norms, and consumer habits. For instance, understanding the high value placed on family in many Latin American cultures could influence the portrayal of families in advertising, making them more relatable to the audience.

Another key aspect is language adaptation. This goes beyond simple translation to ensure that the tone, humor, and connotations of the message align with local sensibilities. For example, what might be considered humorous sarcasm in one culture could be seen as rudeness in another.

Benefits of cultural adaptation include increased brand relevance, enhanced customer engagement, and stronger market positioning. A campaign that respects and reflects the local culture can foster trust and loyalty among consumers, leading to better acceptance of products and services.

However, challenges also exist. Cultural adaptation can be time – consuming and costly, requiring significant resources to get it right. Additionally, there is always a risk of oversimplifying or stereotyping a culture, which can backfire and harm the brand's image.

The approach of adapting marketing strategies to fit the specific values and behaviors of different cultures is known as localization. This method contrasts with a more standardized approach that emphasizes a common message across all markets. Localization recognizes that consumers in different countries have unique needs, wants, preferences, attitudes, and values, which can significantly influence their shopping, purchasing, and consumption behaviors. By tailoring their products, promotions, and overall marketing strategies to align with these local cultural nuances, companies can increase their appeal and success in international markets.

Key Aspects of Localization in International Marketing

Research: Extensive research into each local market's cultural characteristics is essential for effective localization. This includes understanding language nuances, social norms, consumer behaviors, and regulatory environments.

Product adaptation: Products may need to be modified to suit local tastes and preferences. For example, food products often require flavor adjustments to match local palates.

Promotional tailoring: Marketing messages and advertising campaigns should be tailored to resonate with local audiences. This might involve using local celebrities, symbols, or cultural references that are meaningful to the target market.

Branding flexibility: Brand image and positioning may need to be adjusted to better connect with local consumers. This could mean emphasizing different brand attributes that are more valued in the local culture.

Channel strategy: The distribution channels used in different countries can vary greatly. Companies must identify and utilize local channels that are most effective and efficient for reaching their target customers.

Pricing considerations: Pricing strategies may need to be adapted to reflect local economic conditions, purchasing power, and competition.

Legal compliance: Adherence to local laws and regulations is crucial, especially regarding labeling, packaging, and advertising practices.

<u>Continuous assessment</u>: Markets are dynamic, and ongoing monitoring and evaluation are necessary to ensure that localization efforts remain effective over time.

Examples of Successful Localization in Global Marketing

<u>McDonald's</u>: As mentioned, McDonald's has successfully localized its menu in many countries, offering items like the "Teriyaki Burger" in Japan or the "Maharaja Mac" in India. These adaptations not only respect local culinary traditions but also make the brand more appealing to local customers.

<u>Levi's</u>: Levi's adjusts its brand messaging based on cultural differences. In the U. S. , it might focus on a social-group image, while in Europe, it might highlight individuality and sexuality, reflecting differing cultural values and consumer preferences.

<u>Nestlé</u>: Nestlé modifies the taste of its Nescafé coffee and promotions between France and Switzerland to accommodate varying preferences in each country, demonstrating sensitivity to subtle yet important differences in consumer tastes.

Localization in international marketing requires a deep understanding of local cultures, preferences, and market dynamics. By adapting their marketing strategies to meet these local needs, companies can enhance their global presence and competitiveness, building stronger connections with consumers around the world. This approach ensures that marketing efforts are not only effective but also respectful of the diverse cultures they aim to serve.

Task 10: Furthering Your Understanding

Watch the video clip about advertisements of MacDonald's in different countries and find about marketing strategies used in the video clip.

---

2. Standardizing Global Strategy Across Cultures

The approach described here is global marketing, which contrasts with localization. Global marketing involves standardizing products and marketing strategies across different countries, assuming that consumer needs and preferences are converging globally due to increased world travel and telecommunications capabilities. Here's a detailed breakdown of the key aspects and considerations of global marketing.

Advantages

Cost efficiencies: Standardized products and marketing campaigns can lead to economies of scale, reducing production and marketing costs.

Brand consistency: A unified brand image and message can help strengthen brand recognition and loyalty worldwide.

Simplicity in management: Managing one global strategy is often simpler than tailoring multiple local strategies.

Speed to market: Global strategies can facilitate faster product launches in new markets without the need for extensive localization.

Capitalize on global trends: By adopting a global approach, companies can quickly capitalize on emerging global trends and consumer behaviors.

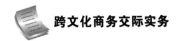

Disadvantages

Cultural insensitivity: A "one – size – fits – all" approach may overlook critical cultural differences, leading to misunderstandings or offense.

Reduced relevance: Standardized products and messages may not resonate as strongly with local consumers compared to locally tailored strategies.

Limited flexibility: Fixed global strategies may struggle to adapt quickly to changing local market conditions or competition.

Regulatory risks: Not all countries have the same regulations, and a global approach may face legal challenges in certain markets.

Key Considerations

Consumer convergence: Assess the extent to which consumer needs and preferences are becoming more homogeneous across different cultures.

Brand positioning: Determine if a consistent global brand positioning will be effective across diverse markets.

Product standardization: Evaluate the feasibility and desirability of offering the same product worldwide without significant adaptation.

Communication strategies: Decide on the appropriate balance between global consistency and local customization in advertising and promotions.

Distribution channels: Consider whether global distribution channels are suitable for reaching target consumers in various countries.

Pricing strategy: Develop a pricing strategy that considers global competitiveness while being sensitive to local purchasing power and market conditions.

Legal compliance: Ensure that global products and marketing strategies comply with local laws and regulations across all target markets.

Monitoring and adaptation: Continuously monitor global markets and be prepared to adapt the global strategy when necessary to respond to local market changes.

Examples of Global Marketing

Coca-Cola: With its "one sight, one sound, one sell" approach, Coca-Cola has long been a proponent of global marketing, offering essentially the same product and messaging worldwide.

General Motors (GM): GM uses global advertising for various products and services, demonstrating a commitment to a unified global brand message.

Global marketing strategies aim to leverage the increasing homogenization of consumer tastes and preferences across different cultures. By adopting a standardized approach, companies can achieve cost efficiencies and maintain a consistent brand image worldwide. However, this approach requires careful consideration of potential cultural insensitivities and the flexibility to adapt when necessary to address local market nuances.

3. Mixed Strategy

The "mixed" strategy that some firms have adopted is often referred to as glocalization. This approach combines the efficiency and consistency of global marketing with the sensitivity and relevance of localization. Glocalization recognizes that while certain aspects of a product or brand can be standardized globally, other elements must be adapted to reflect local culture, tastes, and preferences effectively. Here's a breakdown of the key considerations and strategies involved in glocalization.

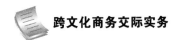

Key Considerations

Cultural sensitivity: Understanding and respecting local cultural norms and values is essential for effective glocalization. This includes adapting products, packaging, messaging, and advertising to align with local customs and expectations.

Consumer behavior: Researching and analyzing local consumer behavior can provide insights into how products should be positioned and marketed to maximize appeal.

Linguistic differences: Language adaptation is crucial, as direct translations may not convey the intended message. Ads and marketing materials should be created by native speakers or professionals familiar with the local dialects and idiomatic expressions.

Aesthetic preferences: Visual elements such as colors, symbols, and images may need to be adjusted to resonate with local aesthetic preferences.

Regulatory requirements: Compliance with local laws and regulations is necessary, especially regarding product safety, labeling, and advertising practices.

Market access: Identifying and utilizing local distribution channels that are most effective for reaching target consumers in each market.

Pricing strategies: Pricing must be adapted to reflect local economic conditions, purchasing power, and competition.

Technology and media: Leveraging local technology platforms and media outlets to reach consumers where they are most active and receptive.

Continuous learning: Staying attuned to shifting local trends and consumer needs through ongoing market research and feedback mechanisms.

Strategies for Glocalization

Product adaptation: Modify products to suit local tastes, sizes, and specifications, ensuring they meet local regulatory requirements.

Communication tailoring: Craft messages that speak to local values and aspirations, using local languages and cultural references.

Brand customization: Adjust branding elements like logos, slogans, and brand stories to connect more deeply with local audiences.

Promotional activities: Design promotions and advertising campaigns that resonate with local consumers, potentially featuring local celebrities or influencers.

Partnerships and alliances: Build relationships with local businesses and organizations to enhance market access and credibility.

Customer service: Provide customer service in local languages and according to local service standards.

Supply chain optimization: Ensure supply chain efficiency by localizing production or warehousing, reducing transportation costs and times.

Monitoring and evaluation: Continuously monitor the effectiveness of globalized strategies and make data-driven adjustments as needed.

Examples of Globalization

Coca-Cola: While maintaining a unified global brand image, Coca-Cola offers localized flavors like "Green Tea" in Japan or "Bitter Lemon" in Australia, tailoring its advertising to reflect local cultural nuances.

Unilever: Unilever adapts its products to suit local tastes and needs, such as offering maggi seasonings tailored to Indian cuisine or creating detergents suitable for various water hardness levels around the world.

Black & Decker: This company modifies its power tool designs to meet local electrical standards and user preferences, such as providing different voltage options for different markets.

Glocalization allows companies to balance the benefits of global standardization with the need for local customization. By adopting this strategy, firms can achieve global efficiency while also catering to the unique needs and preferences of local markets, thus enhancing their competitiveness on a global scale.

Task 11: Understanding the Concepts

According to your understanding of standardization and localization, find more examples of "thinking globally and acting locally" in intercultural marketing.

Assessment

1. Decide whether the following statements are true (T) or false (F).

_____ (1) The marketing interaction is not only between people, but also between people and messages, between people and products.

_____ (2) The Italian style of marketing can be depicted as being fundamentally based on emotion and sensitivity.

_____ (3) The similarities of human beings are the base for advertisements to succeed internationally. Standardization is based on cultural universals.

_____ (4) Global marketing may combine standardized and localized approaches.

_____ (5) Intercultural marketing may be the greatest challenge facing international businesses, and errors can be very costly.

2. Read each of the following questions and choose the best answer.

(1) The government of Thailand protested against Sony and forced Sony to stop the advertisement of the recorder and make public apologies because _____.

A. Sony's advertisement did not respect the religious belief in Thailand

B. The Sony recorder had a quality problem

C. Sony's advertisement did not respect the prime minister of Thailand

D. Sony's advertisement used inappropriate vocabulary

(2) Coca-Cola's "Diet Coke" was renamed as "Coca-Cola Light" in _____ because the word diet has negative associations there when used to describe soft drinks.

A. China

B. Australia

C. Canada

D. many European countries

(3) _____ is not an advantage of standardization in marketing and advertising.

A. Significant reduction in cost

B. Dissemination of national cultures

C. Ensuring consistency

D. Diversification of intercultural advertising styles

Unit Project

Re-examine the scenario of this unit and act as the director of sales department of the multinational company. Develop the advertising campaign for the newly designed electric car for a specific culture. Prepare a poster and introduce the marketing strategies used in your advertisement design. Your introduction may include the following points:

- Choose one specific culture and analyze the customer needs.
- Analyze the verbal and nonverbal elements involved in existing advertisements, and then design an advertising slogan for your new product.
- Apply the marketing concepts and strategies introduced in this unit and propose a marketing plan.

Case Analysis

Analyze the following case with the intercultural marketing theories learned in this unit.

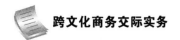

Then answer the questions.

Cross-Cultural Marketing Examples — McDonald's

McDonald's could make up a textbook full of cross-cultural marketing examples. Let's study the differences between Facebook advertisements from McDonald's USA and McDonald's Guatemala.

McDonald's Guatemala is currently promoting meal plans for 4 people or more and their Happy Meal, or Cajita Feliz.

This is a young child's product yet the minimum age to create a Facebook account is 13 years old which tells me that this advertisement is probably targeted to parents.

McDonald's understands that adults in Guatemala, a collectivist society, are more likely to treat the children in their family to a fast food meal than themselves.

In the USA, on the other hand, McDonald's is promoting a Buy One Get One meal and rewards for downloading their app.

As an individualist society, this promotion plays into their need for individual benefits and rewards.

Questions
• What are the differences between Facebook advertisements from McDonald's USA and McDonald's Guatemala?
• Why do McDonald's choose different advertisement on Facebook in Guatemala?
• What do you know about individualism and collectivism? Is it individualistic or collectivist in your country?

Further Reading

Benefits of Improved Intercultural Communication

In an increasingly globalized world, intercultural communication has become an indispensable aspect of both business operations and social interactions. The ability to effectively communicate across cultural divides not only fosters understanding but also opens doors to numerous benefits that extend from individual relationships to organizational success and beyond. This essay will explore the multifaceted advantages of improved intercultural communication, focusing on business productivity, societal cohesion, innovation, and global diplomacy.

Firstly, improved intercultural communication significantly enhances business productivity. In today's global marketplace, companies often have teams that span different countries and cultures. When team members understand each other's communication styles and cultural contexts, they can collaborate more efficiently. Misunderstandings are reduced, and conflicts are resolved quicker. This mutual understanding also helps in tailoring products and services to fit the diverse needs and preferences of international markets, leading to increased sales and market share.

Secondly, within the society at large, improved intercultural communication promotes cohesion and harmony. It helps dispel stereotypes and prejudices that often arise from ignorance or misinformation about other cultures. Greater understanding leads to more inclusive communities where individuals from various backgrounds can coexist peacefully and contribute to the society's development. This is particularly important in multicultural societies where diversity is a norm rather than an exception.

Thirdly, intercultural communication drives innovation. Exposure to different cultures and ideas can spark creative thinking and problem−solving approaches that might not have been considered in a monocultural setting. Cross − cultural teams bring together a wealth of knowledge and experiences, which can lead to innovative solutions and products that resonate with a broader range of consumers. Companies that embrace cultural diversity are often better positioned to navigate the complexities of globalization and stay ahead in the competitive market.

Fourthly, improved intercultural communication is vital for effective global diplomacy. In international relations, the ability to understand and respect different cultural perspectives is crucial for negotiating treaties, resolving conflicts, and fostering cooperation. Diplomats who are skilled in intercultural communication can build trust and find common ground amidst divergent interests, thereby promoting peace and stability worldwide.

Fifthly, intercultural communication supports the personal growth of individuals. Engaging with different cultures enriches one's perspective, challenging preconceived notions and encouraging open‐mindedness. This personal development can lead to more satisfying professional and social relationships, as individuals become more adaptable and empathetic towards others.

However, achieving improved intercultural communication comes with its challenges. Language barriers, non‐verbal misinterpretations, and cultural assumptions can all pose significant obstacles. Moreover, it requires ongoing effort and education to keep up with the fluid nature of cultures.

In conclusion, the benefits of improved intercultural communication are vast and varied, encompassing business, society, innovation, global relations, and personal growth. While it demands a commitment to learning and adaptation, the rewards of enhanced cross‐cultural dialogue are well worth the investment. As the world becomes more interconnected, the ability to communicate effectively across cultures will remain a valuable asset for individuals and organizations alike.

单元小结

1　学习目标

在学习本单元后，你将能够：
- 了解不同文化的市场营销风格；
- 解释解决跨文化营销问题的策略；
- 阐明标准化和本土化的优缺点；
- 理解"全球化思维，本土化行动"的概念；
- 应用跨文化营销策略并制订营销计划。

2　情境假设

假设你是跨国公司销售部门的主管。你的公司设计了一款新型电动汽车，即将推向国外市场。你需要向你的国际同事介绍这款新产品。你需要调查跨文化市场营销情况，并提出能够吸引外国消费者的特定营销计划。

3　什么是市场营销

市场营销是企业实施的一系列战略性行动，其目的在于促进其产品或服务的交换。它涉及诸如广告等举措，并旨在将产品与潜在买家（无论是个人消费者、其他公司还是各种组织）联系起来。

市场营销的重要性在于其能够创造与潜在客户的初次接触。通过营销活动，公司可以将产品引入市场，提供机会向消费者介绍关于其产品的价值。这种介绍通常是客户与产品或服务的首次互动。

此外，营销是塑造品牌认知的关键工具。企业可以策略性地使用营销来传达其希望被关联的特定品质。例如，如果一家户外露营装备公司希望其耐用且坚固的产品得到认可，它可以执行反映这些品质的营销策略，确保品牌的核心信息与目标受众产生强烈的共鸣。

4　不同文化中的营销风格

4.1　中式营销风格

文化如何影响中国消费者的购买习惯？中国消费者的行为深深植根于中国文化，如关系、间接沟通的艺术以及"面子"文化等概念及因素。

关系：在中国，关系在实现商业成功和培养客户忠诚度方面发挥着关键作用。它以个人信任和人际关系亲疏为特征，并显著影响着商业交易的进行方式。对于微型创业企业来说，为了在竞争激烈的环境中蓬勃发展，与顾客建立情感联系成为战略优先事项。

高语境沟通：在中国，消费者购买往往受到隐含意义和背景信息的影响，这些信息具有重要性。这种沟通风格被描述为高语境。营销信息必须理解这种高语境沟通风格，以便有效地与潜在客户产生共鸣。中国偏好间接沟通的特征源于其文化价值观。理解这一点有助于与目标客户建立有效的联系。

"面子"文化的影响："面子"这一文化观念对中国消费者的行为产生重大影响，也在一定程度上塑造了他们的购买决策和品牌偏好；企业在制定营销策略时必须考虑这一点，要防止使顾客失去"面子"，否则可能会对品牌感知和忠诚度产生负面影响。

4.2 美国和欧洲的市场营销风格

美国对全球的影响是全面性的，其产品无处不在。无论通过好莱坞电影、音乐还是食物，世界各地的人们往往对美国文化及其社会有较深的了解，相比之下，美国人对其他文化的了解却较少。

虽然像英国和爱尔兰这样的国家与美国在语言上有接近性，但每个欧洲国家都有其独特的商业文化（这些文化可能会有很大的不同）。通过理解美国和欧洲商业习俗之间的差异，可以防止误解，而这些误解可能会阻碍相应的商业扩张策略。

美国的商务合作方式既有优点也有缺点。在美国，建立新的合作伙伴关系很容易，但这些联系往往更加脆弱，通常不会妨碍务实的决策。在欧洲，情况大相径庭，商业关系通常跨越数年甚至数十年。培养这样的关系通常需要更高程度的信任，一旦形成，就很难打破。

美国企业受益于英语是商务世界的通用语言，这有助于它们的增长和扩张。然而，这并不意味着它们不需要根据目标市场调整其语言或者在初次介绍之外使用当地语言。恰当使用语言对于创造良好的第一印象至关重要，这一原则在英国、爱尔兰、西班牙、法国等地都适用。

尽管企业在建立新的合作伙伴关系时可能会谨慎行事，但消费者往往对新概念持开放态度。与美国消费者相比，欧洲消费者通常表现出更开放的态度，这鼓励企业在产品提供上做法更加大胆。欧洲人迅速接受了电子商务、信息收集服务、移动支付解决方案和互联网银行。这一趋势在英国尤为明显，那里接受创新的情况很普遍。

5 全球营销

在当今全球化的世界里，企业面临着拥有多元文化背景的消费者。为了在这个多文化的市场中取得成功，公司必须建立跨文化营销的概念。跨文化营销是指企业在制定和实施市场营销策略时，考虑到不同文化背景的消费者的需求、价值观和行为，以更好地满足他们的需求的过程。以下是一些建议，帮助企业接受跨文化营销的理念：

● 企业需要深入了解不同文化背景下消费者的价值观、信仰和消费习惯，以更好地满足他们的需求。这可以通过市场调研、消费者访谈、社交媒体分析等方式实现。了解消费者的需求和期望有助于企业制定更具针对性的营销策略。

- 尊重和理解多元文化在跨文化营销中至关重要。企业应避免对特定文化的刻板印象和偏见，采取开放的心态接受和理解不同的文化。这有助于在与不同文化背景的消费者互动过程中建立信任和积极的关系。

- 企业应根据不同文化背景下消费者的需求制定多样化的营销策略。这包括产品定位、定价策略、促销方式和广告创意等方面。例如，企业可以针对不同的文化背景推出具有地域特色或符合当地审美的广告设计的产品。

- 企业员工需要具备跨文化沟通能力，以便有效地与拥有多元文化背景的消费者进行互动。这涉及发展语言能力、文化敏感性和沟通技巧。企业可以通过培训课程和交流活动来提高员工的跨文化沟通能力。

- 企业应努力建立全球品牌形象，以在拥有不同文化背景的消费者中建立积极的声誉。这要求企业在产品设计、品牌传播、客户服务等方面考虑拥有多元文化背景的消费者的需求，以实现品牌的全球发展。

6 标准化与本土化

全球标准化和全球本土化是企业在将业务扩展到国际市场时采用的两种不同策略。每种方法都有其优点和缺点，选择何种方法通常取决于产品或服务的性质、公司的资源以及目标市场的特点。

6.1 全球标准化

全球营销标准化是一种在不同国家和地区使用统一营销策略、信息和活动的方法。这种方法旨在创造一致的全球品牌形象，并减少为每个单独市场定制营销相关的成本。

优势：

- 成本节约：通过全球使用相同的产品、包装和营销活动，公司可以在生产和广告上实现规模经济。

- 品牌一致性：标准化的方法确保品牌信息在所有市场保持一致，这有助于加强全球品牌识别度。

- 简单性：这种策略更容易管理，因为它涉及的变种较少，易于跟踪。

- 上市速度：由于对本地适应的需求减少，产品可以更快地在新市场推出。

劣势：

- 文化不敏感：一种尺寸可能不适合所有人，在一个国家有效的方法在另一个国家可能因文化差异而无效。

- 定制有限：标准化产品可能无法满足当地消费者的具体需求或偏好。

- 竞争劣势：提供符合当地口味产品的本地竞争对手可能具有优势。

6.2 全球化与本土化

在全球营销中，本土化是企业扩大影响力并吸引不同地区客户的重要策略。它涉及调整产品、服务、营销材料甚至整体品牌形象，以满足每个目标市场的独特需求、偏好

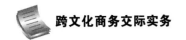

和文化背景。

优势：

- 文化相关性：产品和服务以及营销信息经过定制，以与当地文化产生共鸣，增加了吸引力和接受度。
- 更大的灵活性：能够适应当地市场条件的能力，使得企业对变化和机会的反应更加迅速。
- 更高的竞争地位：通过直接满足地方偏好，公司可以更有效地与当地品牌竞争。
- 更强的客户忠诚度：客户更有可能与一个理解并尊重他们文化的品牌互动。

劣势：

- 成本更高：本土化可能成本很高，因为需要为每个市场进行额外的研究、开发和营销努力。
- 复杂性：管理多个产品和营销活动在物流上和管理上极具挑战性。
- 难以保持一致性：在适应本地市场的同时保持统一的全球品牌形象可能很难。

7 国际市场经营者的策略

7.1 适应市场策略以适应文化

将市场策略调整以适应不同文化的具体价值观和行为的方法被称为本地化。这种方法与强调在所有市场中传递共同信息的标准方法形成对比。不同国家的消费者具有独特的需求、欲望、偏好、态度和价值观，这些因素可以显著影响他们的购物、购买和消费行为。通过根据这些当地文化特点定制其产品、促销和整体市场策略，公司可以增加其在国际市场上的吸引力和成功的可能性。

7.2 跨文化统一全球战略

全球营销涉及在不同国家都采用标准化产品和营销策略；同时，由于世界旅行和通信的日益普及，消费者的需求和偏好正在全球范围内趋同。

全球营销策略旨在利用不同文化中消费者品位和偏好日益同质化的趋势。通过采用标准化的方法，公司可以实现成本效益并在全球范围内保持统一的品牌形象。然而，这种方法需要仔细考虑潜在的文化不敏感问题，并在必要时灵活调整以应对本地市场的特点。

7.3 混合策略

一些公司采用的混合策略通常被称为全球本土化。这种方法结合了全球营销的效率和一致性以及本土化的敏感性和相关性。虽然产品或品牌的某些方面可以在全球范围内标准化，但其他元素必须进行调整，以有效地反映当地文化、口味和偏好。

全球化策略让企业能够在享受全球标准化带来的利益的同时满足地方定制化的需求。通过采用这一策略，公司可以提升全球营销的效率，同时也能迎合本地市场的独特需求和偏好，从而在全球范围内提升他们的竞争力。

　　* 本单元智慧职教线上课程：https：//zyk. icve. com. cn/courseDetailed？ id = obbaaaqvo4doejfjffeicq&openCourse = obbaaaqvw79e5opp1bwbg.

Unit 8　习题参考答案

Unit 9　Intercultural Business Negotiation

Ancient Chinese Wisdom

Industry is skilled in diligence, wasted in play; action is accomplished by thinking, and destroyed by following. (业精于勤，荒于嬉；行成于思，毁于随。)

From *Jin Xue Jie* (《进学解》)

Learning Objectives

After learning this unit, you shall be able to:

- To understand the importance of intercultural communication in global business negotiations.
- To identify and compare cultural dimensions that influence negotiation styles across cultures.
- To develop strategies for effective cross-cultural negotiation.
- To enhance awareness of one's own cultural biases in a negotiation context.

Project Scenario

After learning this unit, finish the unit project on the basis of the following scenario.

Suppose you are the project manager of ABC company in China. A multinational corporation based in the United States is interested in expanding its operations into the Chinese market. The company has identified ABC company as a potential partner, a Chinese firm with a strong presence in the local market. Both parties need to initiate discussions to explore the possibility of a joint venture, so as to establish a successful business relationship through effective cross-cultural communication and negotiation.

Lead-in

Watch the video clip from Wall Street: Money Never Sleeps and answer the following questions.

- What aspects did the negotiation between the salesperson and the Chinese client cover?
- How does the salesperson (Jake Moore) get the Chinese client's interest and willingness to cooperate in the negotiation?

Video Capture of Wall Street

246

Part A   What is Negotiation?

Negotiation is a process by which two or more parties communicate in an attempt to reach an agreement that is mutually beneficial. It involves discussing the terms of a transaction, resolving disputes, and finding compromises between differing viewpoints.

In the context of business, negotiation typically centers on issues such as price, delivery dates, quality, contract terms, and other conditions of a sale, purchase, partnership, or joint venture. Successful negotiation requires effective communication skills, the ability to understand and empathize with different cultural perspectives, and strategic planning to achieve one's goals while maintaining good relationships with the other party or parties involved.

1. Nature of Negotiation

Negotiation is a fundamental aspect of human interaction, permeating every facet of our lives. Whether we are haggling over the price of a second-hand car, discussing terms of employment, or engaging in international diplomacy, negotiation serves as the bridge between divergent interests and goals. At its core, negotiation is a process by which two or more parties attempt to reach a mutually acceptable agreement. This process is characterized by elements such as communication, bargaining, persuasion, and sometimes, concession.

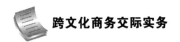

Negotiation is not only a part of people's professional lives but also an integral aspect of their personal interactions. It encompasses scenarios ranging from simple one-on-one discussions to intricate engagements involving multiple parties and crossing national boundaries.

The nature of negotiation can be multifaceted, encompassing both cooperative and competitive dynamics. On one hand, parties may approach negotiations with a win-win attitude, seeking outcomes that satisfy everyone involved. Such an approach often emphasizes understanding and addressing each party's underlying needs and priorities, fostering trust and long-term relationships. On the other hand, negotiations can also adopt a zero-sum or win-lose mentality, where gains for one side are perceived as losses for the other. In these cases, tactics such as strategic ambiguity, psychological leverage, and brinkmanship may come into play.

Effective negotiation requires a deep understanding of both the substance of the issue at hand and the psychology of the individuals involved. It demands strong communication skills — the ability to listen actively, articulate clearly, and empathize genuinely. Furthermore, it hinges on the capacity to identify and capitalize on areas of agreement while minimizing points of contention. Successful negotiators are often those who can navigate complex emotions and power dynamics, maintaining composure and creativity even in the face of resistance or impasse.

Negotiation constitutes a form of interaction wherein individuals engage in dialogue.

Negotiation involves the exchange of ideas between individuals aimed at reaching a mutual agreement. It can occur in personal contexts, such as with family members or neighbors, as well as in professional settings like negotiations with colleagues, supervisors, or business associates.

Negotiation serves to fulfill the interests of all involved parties.

A party's fundamental requirements, desires, and impulses are typically defined as their interests, which are the primary catalyst for negotiation.

The concept of interests encompasses a broad spectrum, including tangible objectives like monetary gain, timelines, or assurances, as well as emotional needs such as the desire for respect, acknowledgment, or the sense of being equitably treated.

Task 1: Understanding the Concepts

According to the features of substantive interests and emotional interests that could be met during negotiations, fill in the two boxes with the serial numbers of the following words.

---

(1) profit	(2) recognition	(3) delivery	(4) respect
(5) maintenance	(6) fairness	(7) packages	(8) warranties

Substantive interests	Emotional interests

In the course of negotiations, it is inevitable that the interests of both sides will collide, including conflicting interests and shared interests. Both parties should be firm about their primary interests but flexible about how to meet these interests.

Negotiation works out when both parties perceive that they have been treated justly.

Fairness is one of the strongest human motivators. At times, negotiations collapse not due to an unacceptable proposal on the table but because it seems unjust to one or both parties involved.

Often, the pursuit of legitimacy or fairness stands as the primary catalyst in a dispute. For instance, aircraft company should outsource as much work as possible while the suppliers reduce the price.

Task 2: Understanding the Concepts

Decide whether the following statements are true (T) or false (F).

_____1. Negotiators should look out for verbal and nonverbal clues because nonverbal communication also reveals the negotiator's intended meaning.

_____2. The negotiating parties sit down to settle differences in interests; thus both parties only have conflicting interests.

_____3. Sometimes negotiation fails not because the option on the table is unacceptable, but because it does not sound fair to one or both parties.

---

2. Definition of Negotiation

Negotiation can be characterized as a reciprocal dialogue aimed at achieving consensus among two or more parties, each with interests that may overlap or diverge. It is a complex and nuanced process that involves strategic thinking, emotional intelligence, and a willingness to find common ground in order to reach a mutually beneficial agreement.

3. Intercultural Business Negotiation

Business negotiation involves a series of interactions where participants in business activities engage in dialogue, debate, and modify their perspectives to resolve disparities, ultimately

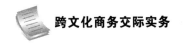

arriving at a consensus that is agreeable to all parties, with the objective of finalizing a transaction or attaining a predetermined financial objective.

<u>Intercultural business negotiation</u> involves discussions between parties with vested interests from diverse nations or areas.

Therefore, in the process of intercultural business negotiation, there must be some problems caused by cultural differences between different countries and regions. In view of our study of the definition of culture and cultural differences in the first unit, one can not only better understand and master the styles and skills of negotiation, but can also avoid possible misunderstandings in negotiation in advance by clarifying the cultural differences between the two sides of negotiation.

The style of negotiation differs among individuals, influenced by their personal beliefs and abilities, as well as the broader context in which they take place. Negotiation styles can also be significantly impacted by cultural variances, such as differences in communication methods and decision-making processes. In fact, every negotiator possesses a distinct negotiation style. These range from competitive and avoidant to compromising, accommodating, and ultimately collaborative; individuals tend to gravitate towards one of these inherent styles.

In this book, generally speaking, intercultural business negotiation requires a deep cultural competency, effective cross-cultural communication skills, patience, and a willingness to bridge differences to achieve successful outcomes.

Task 3: Preparing for the Unit Project

1. Applying the Concepts
According to Part A, there could be shared, differing, and conflicting interests in business negotiation. Work in groups of four and draw a mind map on the basis of what you have learned in this part to predict in detail what could be the possible interests for both parties in the scenario.

2. Critical Thinking
Negotiation typically entails a reciprocal dialogue between two entities aiming to forge an accord. Numerous subjects can be explored to draw the parties closer and foster a harmonious relationship. Undertake online research and engage in discussions with your team members to identify potential topics that could be effective.

Part B   Preparing for Negotiation

Many negotiators may err by concentrating solely on a singular issue during negotiations. Often, this issue revolves around monetary matters (such as the sales price, salary, etc.). However, it is a critical oversight to concentrate on just one issue during negotiations because, in reality, multiple issues are typically at play in most negotiation scenarios. By recognizing additional issues, negotiators can enhance the value of negotiations.

Negotiation, a universal business practice, is influenced significantly by cultural factors. The way Eastern and Western cultures approach negotiation preparation can differ substantially, reflecting their respective values and business philosophies. Here are some of the key differences.

Preparing for Negotiation

1. Different Communication Styles

Western negotiators often value directness and clarity in communication, preparing to state their intentions and goals explicitly right from the start. In contrast, Eastern negotiators, particularly those from Asia, may take a more indirect approach, focusing on building relationships first and gradually revealing details through the process.

Decision-Making Hierarchy

In the West, negotiators are often empowered to make decisions autonomously or with minimal consultation. Preparation involves having all necessary data at hand to facilitate quick decisions. In Eastern cultures, decision-making tends to be more collective, requiring consensus-building. Negotiators may spend more time preparing for group discussions and aligning internal stakeholders.

Time Orientation

Time is considered a valuable commodity in the West, and preparation often emphasizes efficiency and deadlines. This can lead to a preference for shorter negotiations with clear timelines. In Eastern traditions, especially in countries like China, time is viewed more flexibly. Preparation may involve creating a schedule that allows for prolonged engagement to build trust.

Relationship Building

While relationship-building is important globally, it takes center stage in Eastern negotiation preparation. There's an emphasis on personal connections and social etiquette which can greatly influence the negotiation outcome. Preparation includes learning about the counterpart's

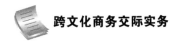

background and finding common ground for rapport.

Risk Assessment

Western negotiators tend to rely heavily on data and risk assessment during preparation, using historical examples and market analysis to predict outcomes. Conversely, Eastern negotiators might place more emphasis on intuition and face-saving elements, preparing strategies that ensure dignity for all parties.

Information Access

Western negotiators prepare by ensuring access to information, striving for transparency, and assuming that both parties have equal knowledge. In Eastern cultures, information may be more guarded, and preparation involves being prepared to uncover information gradually while maintaining a cautious approach.

Understanding these differences is crucial for cross-cultural negotiation success. It allows parties to adapt their preparation accordingly, creating a more respectful and effective negotiation environment that acknowledges diverse cultural norms and practices.

2. Preparation Work

We are aware that various cultural groups exhibit diverse negotiating objectives, attitudes, personal attributes, and communication styles. Consequently, we can devise specific negotiation strategies tailored to a country with a particular culture. International business negotiations encompass multiple facets, making the content intricately complex. Before the negotiation, proper preparation work should be done.

Organizing a Negotiation Team

In general, a negotiation team may be composed of the lead negotiator, technical experts, business professionals, legal advisors, and individuals responsible for documenting the proceedings, among others.

- The technical staff, such as technicians or engineers, is responsible for negotiating technical details.
- The business professionals, including factory directors or managers, handle negotiations regarding price, quantity, delivery, payment terms, warranties, and similar matters.
- Legal advisors are responsible for overseeing the contractual terms and conditions.

Organizing a negotiation team is a critical step in preparing for and executing a successful negotiation. It requires careful consideration of individual strengths, strategic alignment, and effective communication both within the team and with the other negotiating party.

Setting a Negotiation Space

Setting a negotiation site or space involves creating a physical or virtual environment that is conducive to effective communication and decision – making between parties. Generally, one party's own place, the other party's place and the third party's place are three common selections for negotiation places. Each of them has its own advantages.

- If the negotiation is set at one party's own place, support can be obtained easily and there are more chances of using aggressive tactics. The issue on Hong Kong's Sovereignty perfectly explains the statement.
- If the negotiation is set at the other party's place, it is a good opportunity to know more about the counterpart and use tactics for postponing the talk.
- If the negotiation is set at the third party's place, it is fair to both parties.

Regardless of the nature of the space — whether it's an open office, a compact area, or a meeting room with chairs arranged against the walls — it will be familiar to the hosts. The visitors will have to acclimate to a new environment. This unfamiliar setting could potentially distract them from focusing on their work and adjusting to new food, which might lead to indigestion and sleeping difficulties due to unfamiliar beds. Additionally, jet lag may further exacerbate these issues for the visiting party.

Task 4: Furthering Your Understanding

Translate the following sentences regarding a negotiation agenda into Chinese.

(1) Here is the itinerary we have worked out for you during your stay here. And I'd like to have your comments on it.

(2) I can see that you have put a lot of time and energy into the plan. But there are a few details I would like to mention.

(3) I don't think it is fair to us to start the negotiation tomorrow morning. We have not yet overcome the jet lag.

(4) If you don't mind, we'd rather have the talks held in the hotel instead of in your company. Never mind the necessary expenses. We shall cover them.

(5) Last but not least, you don't need to arrange the sightseeing on the last day. We might need the time to attend to some of the questions we might overlook in the talks.

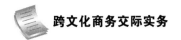
Making Logistic Arrangement

Organizing and coordinating the practical details and requirements are necessary for a successful negotiation process. Making logistic arrangements in advance helps to ensure that the negotiation can proceed smoothly and efficiently, allowing all parties to focus on the discussion and agreement-building process without being hindered by avoidable disruptions or discomforts.

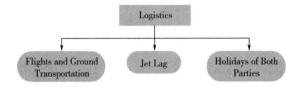

Comfortable flight refers to being smart at the negotiation table, while ground transportation reflects a company's image and standing. An international journey exceeding ten hours in duration can significantly impair cognitive processes and may even adversely affect physical well-being. Therefore, scheduling meetings immediately upon arrival or early the next day is not advisable.

Careful consideration to traditional holidays of both parties should also be taken for a successful negotiation. For instance, discussions held in London during the Christmas period or in Rio de Janeiro during Carnival are unlikely to be productive.

Task 5: Furthering Your Understanding

Suppose you are heading a team to negotiate with your counterpart. You need to start the negotiation, covering the following information including the objective the main issues, the schedule, and the roles of your team members.

Your presentation should be clear, concise, and professional, establishing an atmosphere of transparency and collaboration that will facilitate effective communication and help steer the negotiation towards a successful conclusion.

Objective

To reach an agreement about the terms and conditions for a revised annual printing contract.

Main Issues

(1) The existing contract: advantages and disadvantages;

(2) The problems: payment and delivery;

(3) The revised contract: main elements.

Schedule

10: 00-11: 30 Issue (1) & Issue (2);

11: 30-13: 30 Lunchtime;

13: 30-16: 00 Issue (3).

Roles

Peter: take the minutes;

Margarita: present the revised contract.

Task 6: Furthering Your Understanding

Decide whether the following statements are true (T) or false (F).

_____1. Agendas don't need to be set beforehand; they could be worked out during the negotiations.

_____2. Sometimes the host party may use the tactic of deliberately diverging from the schedule to leave less time for the most important issue.

Task 7: Preparing for the Unit Project

1. Applying the Concepts

The negotiation team sent to Los Angeles in the scenario will be composed off our members. As the chief negotiator for this equipment negotiation, how will you organize your team? How will you arrange the agenda for the negotiation?

2. Critical Thinking

Which kind of negotiation team may work better for intercultural business negotiation, a big one or a small one? Give your reasons.

Part C Strategies for Making Concessions

1. Negotiation is a Matter of Give-and-take

Negotiation is a process of mutual exchange, where both parties involved make compromises and concessions to reach a common agreement. It involves a balance of offering and receiving, where

A Matter of Give-and-take

each side strives to meet their needs while also considering the needs and interests of the other party. Successful negotiation requires flexibility, open communication, and a willingness to find solutions that are beneficial to all involved. Therefore, in the process of negotiation, certain concessions are necessary.

Labeling Concessions

The first strategy involves explicitly identifying our concessions. During negotiations, we cannot simply expect that our actions will be self-evident. To prevent the possibility of the other party feeling obligated to reciprocate, they might choose to ignore or diminish the significance of our concessions. Consequently, it becomes our duty to ensure that our concessions are unmistakably clear to the opposing side. We must expressly inform our negotiating partner about the sacrifices we have made and emphasize their cost to us.

Task 8: Furthering Your Understanding

Company A is negotiating a contract with Company B for the supply of electronic components. Company A wants to secure a lower price per component, while Company B is insisting on maintaining their current pricing structure. Company A has identified that meeting delivery deadlines is a significant concern for Company B.

Find out the expressions used to label out concessions in their talk.

Company A: We've reviewed your pricing proposal, and while we appreciate the value you provide, we were hoping to achieve a more competitive cost per component.

Company B: I understand your position, but our costs have gone up significantly due to raw material prices. We simply can't afford to lower our prices any further.

Company A: We understand your constraints regarding costs, and we're willing to be flexible. How about we meet halfway on the price? In exchange, we could agree to a more frequent delivery schedule, which would help us maintain a steadier stock and reduce the risk of stockouts on our end.

Company B: That's certainly a creative solution. Can you give me an idea of what you had in mind for the delivery schedule?

Company A: We were thinking of shifting from monthly deliveries to bi-weekly. This would give us more time to adjust our inventory based on sales fluctuations and ensure that we never miss a production window due to lack of components.

Company B: Bi-weekly deliveries would indeed help us ensure timelier shipments. Let me run some numbers, and I think we can make that work on our end.

Company A: Great, I'm glad we could find a solution that works for both of us. We value our partnership with Company B, and we believe this adjustment will strengthen our collaboration in the long run.

Demanding and Defining Reciprocity

During negotiations, after making a concession, a party may explicitly state what they expect in return for their compromise. This can be done diplomatically to avoid creating a confrontational or adversarial atmosphere. The goal is to ensure that both parties feel the negotiation is balanced and that each concession made leads to some form of compensation or benefit.

For instance, if Company A gives in on price, reducing their initial asking figure, they might "demand and define reciprocity" by stating something like, "If we agree to this price point, we would appreciate it if you could offer us expedited delivery times to help us better manage our inventory".

In essence, "demanding and defining reciprocity" involves clearly articulating the desired outcome or action you expect from the other party in exchange for the concession you have made. It's a way to ensure that both sides benefit from the negotiation and that the process remains fair and balanced.

2. Making Conditional Concessions

Making conditional concessions refers to the practice of offering a compromise or giving in on a particular issue during negotiations, but only if certain conditions are met by the other party. This strategy allows a negotiator to maintain control over the give-and-take process and ensures that their concessions lead to specific, desired outcomes.

Conditional concessions can help both parties feel like they are achieving their goals while also maintaining a balance of power in the negotiation. It's a way to ensure that any compromise made is <u>mutually beneficial</u> and moves both parties closer to a final agreement.

Many experienced negotiators caution that once a concession has been accepted and the conversation has shifted to a different topic, it is inappropriate to revisit the previous issue to ask for a counter-concession. Occasionally, negotiations culminate in a final agreement sooner than anticipated. There are cultural differences whereby some prefer not to conclude negotiations definitively.

In contrast, negotiators from Western backgrounds often show a desire to expedite the signing of agreements.

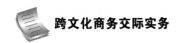

Task 9: Understanding the Concepts

Make conditional concessions for the situations below to demand some benefits in return.

Situation	Concession	Condition
a company to a supplier	placing a large order	offering a favorable price
a company to IT providers	signing a contract for three consecutive years	offering a round-the-clock service
a company to a retailer	offering a discount	increasing the order quantity substantially
a company to a retailer	bringing down the price	making the payment within 30 days
an agent to a principal	increasing the annual sales volume in the contract	improving the craftsmanship

---

Breaking Down Concessions

Breaking down concessions refers to the process of dividing larger concessions into smaller, more manageable parts during negotiations. This strategy can be beneficial for several reasons as follows.

Maintaining leverage: By parceling out concessions gradually, negotiators can retain leverage throughout the negotiation process. This prevents them from giving away too much at once, which might reduce their bargaining power later on.

Building trust: Smaller concessions can help build trust between negotiating parties. As each small concession is granted and reciprocated, both sides may become more comfortable with the negotiation process and more willing to make further concessions.

Enhancing flexibility: Breaking down concessions allows for more flexibility in adjusting to new information or changed circumstances during negotiations. It provides opportunities to reassess the situation and make necessary adjustments without feeling like a significant commitment has been made that cannot be altered.

Improving clarity: Dividing concessions into clear, distinct parts can help both parties understand exactly what is being offered and what is expected in return. This can lead to more precise and satisfying agreements.

Managing risk: Smaller concessions allow negotiators to test the waters and gauge the other party's response before committing to larger compromises. This can help mitigate risks associated with making assumptions about the other side's intentions or reactions.

Overall, breaking down concessions is a way to approach negotiations strategically, ensuring that both parties feel like they are making progress and maintaining a balanced give-and-take dynamic throughout the negotiation process.

Task 10: Preparing for the Unit Project

1. Applying the Concepts

Observe the concessions made in the following dialog, where representatives from Company A and Company B are talking about the sale of software. On the basis of your observation and the strategies introduced in Part C, rehearse the negotiation in the scenario, in which concessions should also be properly made.

Company A: Thank you for considering our software solution. We believe it will significantly improve your operations. Our standard fee is $10,000 per year for a license.

Company B: That's quite a bit higher than we were expecting. We have a limited budget this fiscal year.

Company A: I understand your concern. How about we break it down? We can offer the license for $8,000 this year, and you can decide whether to renew next year based on its performance.

Company B: That sounds more reasonable. What kind of support can we expect for that price?

Company A: For 8,000, we include basic support during business hours. For 24/7 support, we usually charge an additional 8,000, we include basic support during business hours. For 24/7 support, we usually charge an additional 2, 000 per year.

Company B: 24/7 support is essential for us. However, we're already stretching our budget with the license fee.

Company A: Given your needs, let's make a concession on the support. We can offer 24/7 support for an additional $1, 500 this year, and we'll review the fee next year based on the level of support required.

Company B: That's a fair compromise. Now, regarding customization...

Company A: We include minor customization in the license fee. For extensive customization, there's an additional charge.

Company B: We'll need some extensive customization to fit our workflows.

Company A: Considering our commitment to your satisfaction, we can include the extensive customization you need within the current license fee structure. This is a one-time exception based on the good faith of our negotiations.

Company B: That's very accommodating. I think we have a deal then.

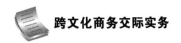

2. Critical Thinking

If the counterpart looks aggressive and insists on the original requirements even if you have already shown the willingness to take a step back, what will you do to bring the negotiation out of the deadlock?

Part D   Different Negotiation Styles

Different negotiation styles refer to the various approaches and tactics that individuals or teams use when engaging in negotiations. The approach individuals take to negotiation can differ significantly based on their personal beliefs, skills, and the specific context in which the negotiation takes place. These styles can also be strongly influenced by cultural factors, such as variations in communication norms and decision-making processes. It is important to recognize that each negotiator brings their unique style to the table. This can range from being highly competitive, to avoiding conflict altogether, to easily complying with demands, to being overly accommodating, and

Negotiation Styles

ultimately, to seeking a collaborative solution where both parties' needs are met.

Each style has its strengths and weaknesses, and understanding these can help in navigating negotiations more effectively.

1. Negotiation Styles

Negotiation styles differ significantly between the East and West, reflecting deeper cultural variations in communication, values, and business practices. Understanding these disparities can enhance cross-cultural interactions and help forge more effective negotiation outcomes. Here are some of the key differences:

Communication Directness

Western negotiators typically value direct, explicit communication. They often come straight to the point and express their interests and objectives openly. Conversely, Eastern negotiators, particularly those from Asia, may employ a more indirect or circular communication style, focusing on cues and context to convey messages.

Relationship vs. Task Orientation

In the East, particularly in countries like China, building a relationship is a crucial step before diving into the task at hand. This relationship-first approach is less common in the West, where negotiations tend to be more task-oriented, getting down to business quickly after initial niceties.

Decision-Making Structure

Western negotiations often involve individuals or smaller teams with clear decision-making authority. In contrast, decisions in Eastern negotiations may require consensus from larger groups or upper management, which can lengthen the process and necessitate more consultation during talks.

Confrontation and Conflict

Western negotiators are generally more comfortable with direct confrontation and addressing conflicts head-on during negotiations. Eastern cultures, influenced by Confucian philosophy, emphasize harmony and avoidance of overt conflict, which can lead to a more indirect handling of disagreements.

Time Sensitivity

Time is often viewed as a commodity in the West, with negotiations planned rigorously to fit into tight schedules. In the East, time may be seen as more fluid, allowing negotiations to unfold at a pace that accommodates relationship building and thorough discussion.

Bargaining and Toughness

While bargaining is not exclusive to any culture, Western negotiators might engage in hard bargaining and exhibit a take-no-prisoners attitude at the negotiation table. In Eastern cultures, there's often a preference for a gentler approach that maintains respect and harmony, even during tough discussions.

Agreement Formality

Western cultures often favor formal, legally binding contracts with detailed terms. Eastern negotiations may place more emphasis on the relationship and trust built during the process, sometimes resulting in more flexible or less specific agreements initially, with details to be worked out later.

Recognizing and adapting to these stylistic differences can create a more understanding and respectful negotiation environment. By bridging cultural gaps, negotiators can improve communication, build stronger relationships, and increase the likelihood of successful outcomes in international dealings.

2. Cultural Variations of Negotiation Styles

Certainly, negotiation styles can differ significantly across countries due to cultural variations. Here are some examples of how negotiation styles can vary among different countries:

Negotiators in the U. S. often favor a direct, explicit, and efficient style. They tend to focus on the task at hand, aim for quick decisions, and value clarity and transparency.

In Japan, negotiations are typically more indirect and formal. Relationship-building is crucial, and decisions are often made through consensus. Patience and respectfulness are highly valued.

Chinese negotiations also emphasize relationship-building and trust. The process can be slow and involve multiple meetings and social gatherings. Face-saving and group harmony are important considerations.

German negotiators are known for their directness, precision, and punctuality. They often focus on facts, details, and logical arguments, with less emphasis on emotional aspects.

Negotiators from Nordic countries (e. g. , Sweden, Norway) often prefer a collaborative, consensual style. They value equality, honesty, and transparency in negotiations.

Russian negotiators can be perceived as pragmatic and may prioritize strategic interests over personal relationships. Negotiations can sometimes involve opaque communication and a focus on gaining leverage.

These are generalizations, and individual negotiators may not strictly follow the cultural norms of their country. It's essential to recognize that people are diverse within cultures and that negotiation styles can vary greatly even within a single country. Understanding these cultural tendencies, however, can help negotiators prepare for interactions with individuals from different cultural backgrounds.

Task 11: Furthering Your Understanding

Please match the exact country's names in the left column with the proper negotiation styles in the right column.

Countries	Negotiation styles/characteristics
China	relationship-focused
America	detail-oriented
Japan	direct
South Korea	indirect
Germany	emotional
India	factual
France	time-sensitive

Task 12: Furthering Your Understanding

Work in groups of four. Study the following case and have a discussion with your group members: What do you think leads to the American's loss in the negotiation?

A multinational company based in the United States is looking to expand its operations in India. They send a team to negotiate a joint venture with a local firm. The American team is led by John, who has had great success negotiating deals in the U. S. but has limited experience with Indian business culture.

John arrives in India with a detailed, time-bound agenda. He expects a quick, efficient negotiation process focused on the facts and figures. During the first meeting, he presents his proposal directly, highlighting the financial benefits and potential profits for both parties.

In the course of the negotiations, the attitude of the Indian side was not clear, and it was somewhat incompatible with the directness of the US side. John didn't notice this and kept pushing to end the collaboration as soon as possible.

Task 13: Preparing for the Unit Project

1. Applying the Concepts

According to Part D, each culture has its unique negotiation style. Form groups of four and discuss the specifics of the American negotiation approach. Afterward, plan how your team can handle potential scenarios in the negotiation ahead.

2. Critical Thinking

Cultures vary in the importance they place on protocol during negotiations. Research online and find examples that illustrate these differences in negotiation protocols across cultures.

Assessment

1. *Read each of the following questions and choose the best answer.*

(1) What is typically considered a critical first step in intercultural negotiation?

    A. Directly discussing the financial terms.

    B. Building a relationship and establishing rapport.

    C. Presenting your strongest argument upfront.

    D. Focusing on non-verbal communication cues.

(2) Which of the following countries is known for a more indirect communication style during

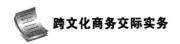
negotiations?

    A. United States   B. Germany   C. Japan   D. Netherlands

（3）In which country would you expect negotiations to proceed at a slower pace, with less emphasis on time-bound agendas?

    A. Switzerland   B. Brazil   C. China   D. New Zealand

（4）During negotiations, what is an important factor to consider when dealing with teams from Arab countries?

    A. The importance of physical gestures.

    B. The directness of communication.

    C. The role of seniority and hierarchy.

    D. The avoidance of personal relationships.

（5）When negotiating with teams from France, what should you be prepared for?

    A. A focus on consensus and group harmony.

    B. A direct, confrontational discussion style.

    C. An emphasis on individualism and self-expression.

    D. A preference for avoiding conflict and saving face.

（6）Which kind (s) of interests could different parties of business negotiations have?

    A. Shared interests.

    B. Different interests.

    C. Conflicting interests.

    D. All of the above.

（7）Which of the following statements about making concessions is NOT true?

    A. Negotiators should reserve concessions until they are needed.

    B. It's better for the pace of concessions to be as little as possible and the frequency of concessions to be as low as possible.

    C. In general, a concession made by one party should be matched by a concession made by the other party.

    D. A one-time concession might show our sincerity to make the deal, but sometimes the other party may not believe that is all we could do.

（8）In general, which kind (s) of personnel should be included in a negotiation team?

    A. Technical personnel.

    B. Business personnel.

    C. Legal personnel.

    D. All of the above.

（9）In intercultural business negotiations, which cultural characteristic leads negotiators to tend to avoid expressing their needs and intentions directly?

    A. High-context culture.

    B. Low-context culture.

C. Direct communication culture.

D. Indirect communication culture.

（10） When negotiating with counterparts from a collectivist culture, which approach is beneficial?

A. Focusing on individual achievements and rewards.

B. Involving key members of their team in discussions.

C. Highlighting the needs of your own company exclusively.

D. Imposing strict deadlines for agreement.

2. Decide whether the following statements are true（T）or false（F）.

_____ （1） In Japan, it is common to engage in direct confrontation during negotiations.

_____ （2） In the United States, negotiations typically move at a slower pace compared to many other countries.

_____ （3） During negotiations with teams from Saudi Arabian cultures, it is important to avoid physical contact, especially between genders.

_____ （4） In China, relationships and personal connections（known as "guanxi"）play a minor role in business negotiations.

_____ （5） Negotiators from Brazil generally prefer a detailed, contract-focused approach with little room for flexibility.

_____ （6） French negotiators tend to prioritize group harmony and consensus over individual achievement.

Unit Project

Re-examine the scenario of this unit and play the role of he project manager of ABC Company. Re-examine the scenario of this unit. Work in groups and start the simulated negotiation with your group members in class. Your simulated negotiation should include the following points：

- Introduce the members of your negotiation team.
- Introduce the agenda for the negotiation.
- Apply your analysis of the possible interests for both parties to the negotiation.
- Use the strategies for making concessions.
- Take the American negotiation style into consideration and take effective countermeasures.

Case Analysis

Analyze the following case with the intercultural business negotiation theories learned in this unit.

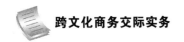
Walmart, the world's largest retailer, initially entered Germany through acquisitions, buying up existing retail chains such as Wertkauf and Interspar, and later opened its first Walmart store in 1997.

- Walmart faced significant cultural challenges in adapting to the German market, which differed greatly from the U. S. market in terms of consumer preferences, shopping habits, and labor laws.
- German consumers prioritize quality and service over low prices, which was contrary to Walmart's discount focus.
- Walmart also struggled with local regulations, including strict opening hour laws and labor union influences, which made it difficult to implement its efficient, cost-cutting operations model.
- There were issues related to the brand name as well. The company initially used the name "Wal-Mart", which sounded too American, potentially alienating local customers. It later changed the name to "Wallmart" to sound more localized.

Walmart's attempt to expand into the German market failed due to significant cultural and regulatory challenges. The company struggled to adapt its cost-cutting operating model to local consumer preferences, labor laws, and regulatory frameworks, which prioritized quality, service, and employee rights over low prices. Walmart also faced branding issues, competition from local retailers, and criticism over its labor practices, leading to its withdrawal from the market in 2006.

Further Reading

Navigating Intercultural Business Negotiations

A Comprehensive Guide

In the intricate tapestry of global commerce, intercultural business negotiations stand as a critical thread, weaving together disparate threads of economic opportunity and cultural diversity. As businesses reach across borders in pursuit of partnerships and agreements, a deep understanding of intercultural negotiation strategies becomes indispensable. This passage serves as a foundational overview, aiming to enrich your knowledge and equip you with insights for successful intercultural business negotiations.

Cultural Intelligence: The Compass of Negotiation

At the heart of intercultural negotiation lies cultural intelligence (CQ) — the capability to understand, respect, and effectively interact with individuals from diverse cultural backgrounds. High CQ enables negotiators to anticipate and adapt to cultural differences, thereby fostering harmonious negotiations. It encompasses strategic thinking, behavioral adaptability, emotional regulation, and an open, inquisitive mindset toward cultural norms and practices.

The Pivotal Role of Communication

Communication is the lifeblood of negotiation, transcending mere verbal exchange to encompass nonverbal cues, silences, and contextual nuances. Intercultural business negotiations demand a keen awareness of communication styles, including direct versus indirect communication, contextual meaning, and the use of silence. For instance, while explicit, direct communication may be valued in Western cultures, indirect communication that relies on subtlety and contextual understanding is often favored in Eastern cultures.

Building Trust: The Cornerstone of Successful Negotiations

Trust acts as the bedrock of effective negotiations, especially in cultures that place a high value on relationship-building. Techniques to establish trust include demonstrating credibility through consistent behavior, showing respect for cultural values and norms, and engaging in open, transparent communication. Moreover, displaying empathy and understanding, particularly by acknowledging and respecting cultural holidays and practices, can significantly enhance trust and rapport.

The Art of Concession and Consensus

Concession-making is an integral part of negotiations, yet its approach varies culturally. In some cultures, a direct, upfront style of concession is appreciated, signaling clarity and transparency. However, other cultures may view this as confrontational, favoring a gradual, indirect approach that allows both parties to save face and maintain harmony. Recognizing these differences enables negotiators to craft strategies that align with cultural expectations, facilitating consensus and agreement.

The Power of Patience: A Strategic Asset

Patience emerges as a crucial virtue in intercultural negotiations, often determining the

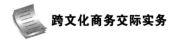

outcome. In many cultures, the negotiation process is viewed as a means to build relationships and understand each other's needs fully, which may extend discussions. Western cultures, prioritizing efficiency, may advocate for swift conclusions. However, embracing patience can demonstrate respect for the negotiation process, fostering trust and potentially leading to more favorable outcomes.

Leveraging Technology: A Double-Edged Sword

Technology has revolutionized negotiations, enabling remote communication and streamlining processes. However, technological advancements also introduce challenges, such as misinterpreting nonverbal cues via video conferencing or misunderstandings due to language nuances in written communications. Technological proficiency must therefore be balanced with cultural sensitivity to harness its benefits without compromising the human element of negotiations.

Further Your Journey

To delve deeper into the realm of intercultural business negotiations, consider exploring resources like *The Culture Map* by Erin Meyer, offering insights into managing cross-cultural teams and negotiations, or *Kiss, Bow, or Shake Hands* by Terri Morrison and Wayne Conway, providing practical strategies for navigating international business interactions. Additionally, participating in negotiation workshops and simulations can offer practical experience and enhance your intercultural negotiation skills.

In conclusion, intercultural business negotiations require a delicate balance of strategic insight, cultural sensitivity, and communicative finesse. As you embark on cross-cultural negotiations, let cultural intelligence be your guide, trust your anchor, and patience your ally. With preparation and an open mind, you can navigate the complexities of intercultural negotiations, fostering lucrative partnerships and collaborations that transcend cultural boundaries.

单元小结

1　什么是谈判

谈判是有关各方为了各自的目的、利益和需要，在一项涉及各方的事务中进行磋商，并通过调整各自的条件以达成一定共识的过程。

1.1　学习目标

在学习本单元后，你将能够：
- 了解跨文化交流在全球商务谈判中的重要性；
- 识别和比较影响跨文化谈判风格的文化因素；
- 制定有效的跨文化谈判策略；
- 提高在谈判中对自身文化偏见的认识。

1.2　情境假设

假设你是 ABC 公司在中国的项目经理。一家总部设在美国的跨国公司有意将业务拓展到中国市场，该公司已确定 ABC 公司为潜在合作伙伴，这是一家在当地市场拥有强大影响力的中国公司。双方需要展开讨论，探讨建立合资企业的可能性，以便通过有效的跨文化沟通和谈判建立成功的业务关系。

2　谈判是什么

谈判是双方或多方进行沟通，试图达成互利协议的过程。它包括讨论交易条款、解决争议以及在不同观点之间寻求妥协。在商业领域，谈判通常围绕价格、交货日期、质量、合同条款以及销售、购买、合作或合资企业的其他条件等问题展开。成功的谈判需要有效的沟通技巧、理解和同情不同文化观点的能力，以及在与对方保持良好关系的同时实现自身目标的战略规划。

2.1　谈判的本质

谈判不仅是人们职业生活的一部分，也是个人交往中不可或缺的一个方面。它包含的场景从简单的一对一讨论到涉及多方、跨越国界的复杂约定。
- 谈判是个人进行对话的一种互动形式。
- 谈判的目的是实现所有相关方的利益。
- 如果双方都认为自己受到了公正的对待，谈判就会成功。

2.2　谈判的定义

谈判可以说是一种对等对话，目的是在利益可能重叠或分歧的双方或多方之间达成共识。这是一个复杂而微妙的过程，涉及战略思维、情商和求同存异的意愿，以达成互

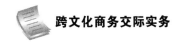

惠互利的协议。

2.3 跨文化商务谈判

商务谈判涉及一系列互动，商务活动的参与者通过对话、辩论和修改观点来解决分歧，最终达成各方都同意的共识，目的是最终完成交易或实现预定的财务目标。

3 谈判的准备

许多谈判者在谈判过程中可能会犯一个错误，那就是只关注一个问题。通常情况下，这个问题围绕着金钱问题（如销售价格、工资等）。然而，在谈判过程中只专注于一个问题可能是一种严重的疏忽，因为实际上，在大多数谈判场景中，通常有多个问题在起作用。通过认识并关注更多的问题，谈判者可以提高谈判的价值。

3.1 组织谈判小组

谈判小组可由首席谈判代表、技术专家、商业专业人士、法律顾问和负责记录谈判过程的成员等组成。

3.2 谈判场所的选择

设置谈判地点或空间涉及创造一个有利于各方有效沟通和决策的物理或虚拟环境。一般来说，己方场所、另一方场所和第三方场所是谈判场所的三种常见选择。它们各有各的优势。

- 谈判地点设在己方场所：容易获得支持，也更有可能使用激进策略。
- 谈判地点设在另一方场所：是了解对方的好机会，也是使用拖延战术的好机会。
- 谈判地点设在第三方场所：对双方都公平。

3.3 后勤安排

组织和协调实际细节和要求是谈判进程取得成功的必要条件。提前做好后勤安排有助于确保谈判顺利、高效地进行，使各方都能专注于讨论和达成协议的过程，而不会受到本可避免的干扰或不适的阻碍。

4 让步策略

谈判往往是一个有得有失的过程。

谈判是一个相互交流的过程，参与谈判的双方都要做出妥协和让步，以达成共同协议。它涉及提供和接受的相互平衡，即每一方都努力满足自己的需求，同时也考虑到另一方的需求和利益。成功的谈判需要灵活、坦诚的沟通，以及找到对各方都有利的解决方案的意愿。

4.1 给让步"贴标签"

首要的策略是明确指出我们的让步。在谈判过程中，我们不能简单地期望我们的行动是不言自明的。为了防止对方忽视我们的让步，我们有责任确保将我们的让步明确无误地传达给对方。我们必须明确告知谈判对手我们所做出的牺牲，并强调我们为此付出的代价。

4.2　要求和确定互惠

在谈判过程中，一方做出让步后，可以明确说明他们期望得到什么作为其妥协的回报。这可以通过外交途径进行，以避免造成对抗或敌对气氛。这样做的目的是确保双方都能感受到谈判是平衡的，每一次让步都会带来某种形式的补偿或利益。

4.3　有条件的让步

有条件的让步是指在谈判过程中，只有在对方满足某些条件的情况下，才会在特定问题上做出妥协或让步。这种策略可以让谈判者保持对取舍过程的控制，并确保他们的让步能带来具体、理想的结果。

有条件的让步可以让双方都感觉自己实现了目标，同时也保持了谈判中的权力平衡。这能确保任何妥协都是互惠互利的，使双方更接近达成最终协议。

4.4　分解让步

分解让步是指在谈判过程中将较大的让步分割成较小的、更易于管理的部分。

● 保持影响力：通过逐步分解让步，谈判者可以在整个谈判过程中保持影响力。这可以防止他们一次让步过多，从而削弱他们日后的讨价还价能力。

● 建立信任：较小的让步有助于在谈判双方之间建立信任。随着每一个小让步的达成和回报，双方可能会对谈判过程更加适应，也更愿意做出进一步的让步。

● 增强灵活性：在谈判过程中，将让步细分可以使我们更灵活地根据新信息或变化的情况对其进行调整。它提供了重新评估形势并做出必要调整的机会，而不会让人觉得已经做出了无法改变的重大承诺。

● 提高清晰度：将让步划分为清晰明确的部分，可以帮助双方准确了解所提出的条件和期望得到的回报。这样可以达成更精确、更令人满意的协议。

● 管理风险：较小的让步可以让谈判者在做出较大的妥协之前先试探一下，观察一下对方的反应。这有助于降低假设对方意图或反应而带来的风险。

5　不同的谈判风格

不同的谈判风格是指个人或团队在参与谈判时使用的各种方法和策略。不同个人所采取的谈判方式可能因其个人信仰、技能和谈判的具体环境而大相径庭。这些风格也会受到文化因素的强烈影响（如沟通规范和决策过程的差异）。重要的是要认识到，每个谈判者都有自己独特的风格。这种风格可以是高度竞争的，可以是避免冲突的，可以是轻易满足要求的，可以是明显迁就的，还可以是寻求双方需求都能得到满足的合作式的。

每种风格都有其长处和短处，了解这些长处和短处有助于更有效地驾驭谈判。

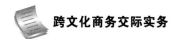

● 美国：美国的谈判者通常喜欢直接、明确、高效的风格。他们往往专注于手头的工作，力求快速决策，重视清晰度和透明度。

● 日本：在日本，谈判通常更加间接和正式。建立关系至关重要，通常通过协商一致做出决定。耐心和尊重受到高度重视。

● 中国：中国的谈判也强调建立关系和信任。谈判过程可能比较缓慢，涉及多次会议和社交聚会。面子和团体和谐是重要的考虑因素。

● 德国：德国谈判者以直接、精确和守时著称。他们通常注重事实、细节和逻辑论证，较少强调情感因素。

● 北欧国家（如瑞典、挪威）：北欧国家的谈判者通常喜欢合作、协商一致的风格。他们重视谈判中的平等、诚实和透明度。

● 俄罗斯：俄罗斯的谈判者可能被认为是务实的，可能会将战略利益置于个人关系之上。谈判有时会涉及不透明的沟通，并注重获取筹码。

＊本单元智慧职教线上课程：https：//zyk. icve. com. cn/courseDetailed？ id＝obbaaaqvo4doejfjffeicq&openCourse＝obbaaaqvw79e5opp1bwbg.

Unit 9 习题参考答案

Unit 10　Intercultural Business Etiquette

Ancient Chinese Wisdom

Explain the following quote and reflect on its contemporary relevance.

Give a man a fish and you feed him for a day. Teach a man to fish and you feed him for a lifetime. （授人以鱼，不如授人以渔。）

From *Huai Nanzi* （《淮南子》）

Learning Objectives

After learning this unit, you shall be able to:

- Explain the importance of etiquette in international business settings.
- Discuss the process of establishing initial connections in multicultural business environments.
- Outline the steps for organizing social events in a intercultural business context.
- Describe the appropriate methods for presenting gifts in different cultural business scenarios.
- Evaluate the role of humor in fostering relationships within diverse cultural business interactions.

Project Scenario

After learning this unit, finish the unit project on the basis of the following scenario.

Suppose You are the CEO of a medium-sized Chinese technology company that has recently expanded its operations to include offices in America, Japan and India. With this expansion, you are planning invite potential clients to a business dinner before intercultural business negotiation, where you have encountered several challenges related to cultural differences in business etiquette. To address these challenges, you need to prepare a detailed plan on appropriate business etiquette to help enhance the image of your company.

Lead-in

Watch the video clip about cross-culture dining etiquette and answer the following questions.

- How do you interpret the man's reaction to the Japanese family's behavior?
- If you at the the scene, how will you introduce the dining etiquette to the others?

Cross-culture Etiquette
(video capture)

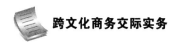

Part A   The Significance of Etiquette

Etiquette encompasses the norms of conduct and comportment that are deemed appropriate in social and professional contexts. Mastering appropriate social conduct entails an understanding of cultural nuances in introductions, the exchange of business cards, the acknowledgment of rank and stature, dining customs, gift – giving, and more. Therefore, understanding and practicing proper etiquette can have several positive impacts on both personal and professional levels.

1. Case about Etiquette

A British delegation led by Lord George Macartney was sent by King George III to establish diplomatic and trade relations with the Qing Dynasty in China.

The embassy arrived in China with gifts for the Qianlong Emperor, including clocks, telescopes, and other Western inventions. However, the British delegation encountered difficulties due to cultural differences in business etiquette. For example, the Chinese expected the British to perform the kowtowing ceremony, which involved kneeling and touching one's forehead to the ground as a sign of respect. The British, however, considered this practice degrading and refused to perform it.

This refusal caused offense to the Chinese officials and led to tensions between the two sides. Despite these challenges, the embassy eventually met with the Qianlong Emperor and presented their gifts. However, they were unable to secure a trade agreement or establish lasting diplomatic relations with China.

This event highlights the importance of understanding and respecting cultural differences in business etiquette when engaging in international negotiations and relationships. It also serves as a reminder that failure to do so can lead to misunderstandings, conflicts, and missed opportunities for cooperation and growth.

Background Information
of the case

The differences in etiquette between China and the West reflect deeper cultural values and social customs. Chinese communication tends to be more indirect and subtle, with a strong emphasis on the concept of "face", favoring non – verbal cues to convey intentions, while western communication is typically more direct and explicit, where clarity and candor are highly valued.

Task 1: Telling China's Story in English

China has always been a land of ceremony and propriety, which can be seen from the following story. Translate it into English and reflect on what you can learn from it.

三顾茅庐

臣本布衣，躬耕于南阳，苟全性命于乱世，不求闻达于诸侯。先帝不以臣卑鄙，猥自枉屈，三顾臣于草庐之中，咨臣以当世之事，由是感激，遂许先帝以驱驰。后值倾覆，受任于败军之际，奉命于危难之间，尔来二十有一年矣。

诸葛亮《出师表》

The story of "Repeated a Whole-hearted Invitation" is not merely a historical anecdote but a rich tapestry of traditional Chinese etiquette woven with threads of respect, humility, patience, propriety, and sincerity. It serves as a powerful lesson on how these virtues, when practiced by leaders and individuals alike, can foster mutual respect, build strong partnerships, and contribute to achieving broader goals with wisdom and integrity. These teachings from ancient China continue to resonate in modern times, providing guidance on leadership, interpersonal relationships, and the pursuit of collaborative excellence.

When engaging in business activities overseas or within a different cultural context, an understanding of specific social and business etiquette rules becomes extremely important. Understanding and applying intercultural etiquette is crucial for building trust, respect, and successful business relationships globally.

Case Study

IBM's "Laptop Gift" Fiasco

In 2004, IBM faced criticism when it launched a campaign offering free laptops to teachers in Turkey. The promotion included the Turkish flag modified with IBM's logo. While the intent was to show appreciation for the host country, the altered flag was seen as disrespectful, leading to public outrage and an eventual apology from IBM.

This incident highlights the importance of understanding and respecting national symbols in intercultural contexts.

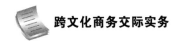

Task 2: Preparing for the Unit Project

1. Applying the Concepts

Analyze the cases in Part A with your partner. Then discuss what you should pay special attention to when attending the business dinner in the scenario.

2. Critical Thinking

Give some examples of business etiquette in China. Then discuss the significance of etiquette in intercultural business context.

---

2. A Comparative Analysis of Eastern and Western Politeness Norms

Etiquette serves as a cultural compass, guiding individuals through the intricate landscape of social interactions. The divergent etiquette practices between the East and West reflect deeper cultural values and social norms. Here are some salient differences.

Greetings

In the West, a firm handshake is a common greeting, symbolizing confidence and equality. It's usually accompanied by direct eye contact and a smile. In Eastern cultures, such as in Japan, a lighter, briefer handshake or a bow may be used. The depth of the bow can indicate respect, with a lower angle signifying higher respect.

Western etiquette encourages the use of first names quite early in professional relationships, promoting a friendly, informal atmosphere. In Eastern traditions, particularly in Asia, people often address each other by their titles and surnames until a significant level of familiarity is established.

Hierarchy and Respect

Social hierarchy plays a critical role in Eastern etiquette. This manifests in the way conversations are initiated and how respect is shown to elders or those in positions of authority. In the West, there's generally a more egalitarian approach, with less emphasis on formalities dictated by hierarchy.

Table Manners

Western dining etiquette emphasizes the use of specific cutlery for different courses and keeping them organized in a certain way. In Eastern etiquette, the rules can differ; for example, in China, it's customary to have all the dishes placed at the center of the table for sharing, and it's polite to offer food to others before serving oneself.

Gift Giving

Gift giving is an essential aspect of Eastern etiquette, imbued with symbolism and understated respect. Gifts are often modest and carefully chosen to reflect the giver's consideration. In Western cultures, while gifts are also significant, they tend to be more straightforward and the gesture is appreciated rather than the item itself.

Personal Space

Western cultures value personal space and privacy. In contrast, Eastern cultures, especially in places like Middle Eastern countries, have a broader definition of personal space, and physical contact during conversation is not uncommon.

Communication Style

Directness is a key component of Western communication, where clear and explicit expression is valued. In the East, maintaining harmony often leads to a more indirect style of communication, where nuances and non-verbal cues carry significant weight.

Dealing with Disagreement

In the West, disagreements are often addressed openly and resolved through discussion. In Eastern cultures, conflicts might be handled more subtly to avoid causing someone to "lose face", which can harm the relationship.

Understanding these etiquette differences is crucial in today's globalized world, where cross-cultural interactions are increasingly common. Being aware of these nuances can help individuals adapt, showing respect and fostering effective communication across cultural boundaries.

Part B   Initial Business Relationships

Establishing initial business relationships is a multifaceted process that involves understanding, respect, and communication across potential cultural divides. It's the beginning phase of forming professional connections and can set the tone for future interactions and collaborations. Here are some key elements to keep in mind.

Etiquette on Business Relationship

1. Addressing People

Names distinguish individuals from each other. It's both vital and hard to remember and use these names properly when talking to others as part of good manners. Figuring out when and how to use someone's name can be especially difficult.

When it comes to addressing people in initial business encounters, adhering to proper etiquette can make a significant difference in how your relationship begins and evolves. Here are some key points to keep in mind.

- Use appropriate titles:

Professional titles: if you're addressing someone with a professional title (e. g. , Dr. , Prof. , Mr. , Ms. , or specific job titles like Director or Manager), be sure to use it. This shows respect for their professional status.

Academic titles: in academic or research settings, using titles like "Dr. " for individuals who have doctoral degrees is expected.

Cultural titles: in some cultures, specific titles reflect familial status or respect (e. g. , "elder" or "auntie/uncle" in Asian communities). Understanding and using these correctly can demonstrate cultural sensitivity.

- Get names right:

First name vs. last name: different cultures have different customs regarding the use of first and last names. in many Western cultures, it's common to use the first name once a certain level of familiarity is established, while in other cultures (like Japan and Korea), people may consistently use last names with appropriate honorifics.

Pronunciation: take care to learn the correct pronunciation of names. If not sure, don't hesitate to ask the person how to pronounce their name correctly.

- Be aware of cultural differences:

Forms of address: in some cultures, it might be appropriate to use more formal language and address people by their title and surname until invited to do otherwise. in other cultures, moving to a first-name basis quickly is a sign of friendliness and openness.

Avoid assumptions: never assume that someone prefers a nickname or diminutive of their name unless they offer that information themselves or it is clearly indicated by their company or context.

- Listen for cues:

Often, how you should address someone will be modeled by others around them or by hints they drop during conversation. Pay attention to these cues and adapt your address accordingly.

- Ask if unsure:

If you're unsure about how to address someone, it's usually best to ask. you might say something like, "Please forgive me, but I'm not certain how I should address you. would you prefer. . . ?" This shows respect for the individual and their preferences.

In conclusion, when addressing people in initial business situations, always aim for respect, accuracy, and cultural sensitivity. Building these elements into your etiquette can help establish positive and professional relationships from the outset.

2. Making Appointments

Scheduling appointments is a crucial aspect of establishing business relationships for the first time, and it's also very common in most business interactions. There are several ways to make business appointments, and the appropriate method may depend on the context, the relationship with the other party, and cultural norms.

Here are some common methods.

- A brief phone call:

A brief phone call is direct and personal. It's best used when you have an established relationship with the other person or if timeliness is crucial.

- A formal letter:

A formal letter (sent through email or traditional mail) is appropriate for scheduling initial meetings or for particularly formal contexts. This method is more time-consuming but can leave a lasting professional impression.

- A "go-between":

A "go-between" is someone who acts as an intermediary between you and the person with whom you want to meet. This could be a mutual contact, a colleague, or a business associate familiar with both parties.

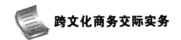
- An emissary:

An emissary is similar to a go-between but typically refers to someone officially delegated to represent your interests. This could be a company representative, a diplomat, or even a professional service that specializes in making business connections.

Making appointments is a common practice in many countries, but the way it is done can vary significantly from one culture to another.

In Mexico, it is often beneficial to try to make appointments with the highest-ranking official you can access. This approach is taken because decisions are typically made by higher-level managers or executives in Mexican organizations. By going directly to the top, you can expedite the decision-making process and demonstrate the importance you place on the meeting.

In Egypt, business relationships are built on personal connections and trust. Therefore, before scheduling a meeting or an appointment, it is customary to send a formal letter of introduction. This letter should outline your intentions for wanting to meet and provide some background on yourself or your company. It helps establish a preliminary connection and can pave the way for a successful meeting.

In many African countries, using an intermediary or local agent to set up business appointments can be very effective. This person can help navigate the social and business networks, understand local customs, and facilitate communication. They can also vouch for you and your credibility, which is important in building trust among business associates.

When in China, establishing contacts before physically visiting is essential. Business is conducted based on personal relationships and trust, known as "guanxi". Before planning a business trip to China, it's crucial to spend time building these relationships through various communications like emails, video calls, or WeChat. Doing so ensures that your visit will be productive and that you have a clear agenda once you arrive.

3. Using Business Cards

Business cards are used for convenience at the beginning of a business interaction, helping people you meet for the first time learn more about you in written form rather than orally. Knowing how to exchange business cards properly can leave a positive and lasting impression on the business people you meet.

Presenting a business card with both hands shows respect and acknowledges the significance of the ritual in Asian cultures. It's best to hold the card by its upper corners when presenting it.

Similarly, you should receive a business card with both hands. Once you have it, take some time to read it thoroughly, not just glance at it. This is an excellent opportunity to repeat the person's name, which will help you remember their face and name.

Handle the card with care. Ideally, carry a small pocket cardholder or case.

While you may write on your own card, writing on someone else's card is considered rude and disrespectful. In Islamic countries, the left hand is considered unclean.
Even in many non-Islamic areas of Africa and Asia, the right hand is preferred over the left. So, use the right hand when presenting or receiving a business card.

In Europe and North America, business cards are less formalized and are used primarily to keep track of who's who during busy meetings. If you're selling in these societies, your hosts will focus on your product, not your business card.

Business cards are used for convenience at the beginning of a business interaction, helping people you meet for the first time learn more about you in written form rather than orally. Knowing how to exchange business cards properly can leave a positive and lasting impression on the business people you meet.

Task 3: Understanding the Concepts

Read each of the following questions and choose the best answer.

1. When meeting someone for the first time in a business setting, what is the appropriate way to greet them?

    A. "Hey there!"

    B. "Nice to meet you!"

    C. "Good morning/afternoon/evening, my name is Li Hua. "

    D. "What's up?"

2. How should you address a person in a business setting if you are unsure of their title or position?

    A. Use their first name.

    B. Use their last name with Mr. /Ms. /Mrs.

    C. Ask them how they prefer to be addressed.

    D. Assume they hold a higher position and use a formal title.

3. When making an appointment with a potential client or partner, what is the best way to do so?

    A. Call them at any time, even if it's outside of business hours.

    B. Send them an email without checking their availability first.

    C. Schedule a meeting through their assistant or secretary.

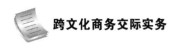

D. Text them to set up a meeting.

4. What is the proper way to exchange business cards in a business setting?

    A. Hold the card with one hand and quickly give it to the other person.

    B. Hold the card with both hands and present it to the other person with a smile.

    C. Put the card in your pocket or purse before the other person has a chance to look at it.

    D. Hand the card to the other person without saying anything.

5. When receiving a business card from someone, what should you do after looking at it?

    A. Put it away immediately without saying anything.

    B. Make a comment about the design or information on the card.

    C. Ask the person to repeat their name and job title.

    D. Write notes on the back of the card.

Task 4: Preparing for the Unit Project

1. Applying the Concepts

Choose a specific cultural background for the other attendees in the scenario. Then consider how to address them appropriately, and rehearse presenting your business cards to them.

2. Critical Thinking

Discuss with your partner on the examples of how Chinese people build initial business relationships and strategies for building initial business relationships with Americans.

Part C   Social Entertainment

Social entertainment in intercultural business etiquette often involves a wide range of activities, from formal business dinners and corporate events to more informal gatherings like networking receptions or team-building exercises. Understanding and respecting the diverse cultural norms and expectations is crucial when engaging in social entertainment in a global business context.

Etiquette of Social
Entertainment

1. Dining Practices

Dining practices in intercultural business etiquette are a critical aspect of building and maintaining professional relationships across different cultures. Meal times offer a unique opportunity for individuals to interact in a more relaxed setting, which can facilitate the development of trust and understanding.

While each culture possesses its unique dining customs, there are foundational dining etiquette guidelines that are widely applicable across nations. By adhering to these standards, business professionals can swiftly become better acquainted, facilitating the continuation of their business endeavors in the days ahead. The subsequent list of essential dining etiquette suggestions combines well-recognized global norms with basic wisdom. Your conduct during a meal will undoubtedly leave an imprint on your associates.

Dining practices encompass the timing and location of meals, the methods of eating, and the selection of food. Broadly, these practices can illuminate numerous collective traits of a specific culture.

Selection of Time and Places

The selection of time and place for a business meal should take into account cultural norms, religious practices, personal preferences, and the nature of the business interaction. Proper planning can help ensure a successful and enjoyable dining experience that facilitates positive business relationships.

- Selection of time:

Respect for meal times: In many cultures, there are specific times when meals are traditionally eaten. For example, in Spain, lunch is typically between 2:00 PM and meals at non-traditional times may be seen as disrespectful.

Work hours vs. meal breaks: In many countries, there's a clear distinction between work hours and meal breaks. Lunch, in particular, is often a significant break during the day. In some Latin American countries, for instance, it's common to take a two-hour lunch break, which is a cherished part of the daily routine.

Religious observances: Some religions have specific fasting periods or require meals to be consumed within certain time frames. For example, during Ramadan, Muslims fast from dawn until sunset. Scheduling a business meal during this period would need to accommodate these religious requirements.

Weekends and holidays: In some cultures, weekends and public holidays are reserved for family meals and not for business entertaining. It's important to be aware of these days when planning a business meal.

- Selection of places:

Formal vs. informal: The choice of restaurant can convey the level of formality intended for the meal. A high-end restaurant signals a desire to impress or celebrate, whereas a more casual

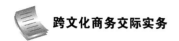

venue suggests a relaxed atmosphere for conversation.

Cultural significance: Selecting a restaurant that serves local cuisine can show respect for the local culture and provide an opportunity to experience authentic dishes.

Location: The location of the restaurant can also be significant. Being centrally located or easily accessible by public transport shows consideration for your guests' convenience.

Noise level: The noise level at the chosen restaurant can impact the ability to converse. A quieter setting is usually preferred for business meals, as it allows for better communication.

Private rooms: For important business discussions or when privacy is needed, selecting a restaurant with private rooms can be beneficial.

Dietary restrictions: Consideration should be given to any dietary restrictions or preferences of the attendees. Choosing a restaurant that can accommodate these needs shows thoughtfulness and respect.

Atmosphere: The overall atmosphere of the restaurant — including its decor, music, and service style — should align with the purpose of the meal and the cultural expectations of the guests.

Visibility and exposure: Depending on the nature of the business discussion, you might choose a more discreet location to ensure privacy, especially if sensitive business matters will be discussed.

Dining Rules

Dining in intercultural business etiquette involves a set of rules and customs that vary significantly across different cultures. Here are some general guidelines.

• Arrival and seating:

Arrive on time: Punctuality is appreciated in most business settings, though in some cultures like Mexico or Italy, arriving slightly later than the specified time is acceptable.

Seating arrangements: Pay attention to where you are directed to sit, as seating arrangements can be hierarchical in many cultures, especially in Asia.

• Dining customs:

Utensil use: In Western cultures, knife and fork are typically used, but in Asian cultures, it may be chopsticks, and in Ethiopian culture, it's customary to eat with your hands.

Meal structure: The order and structure of courses can vary. For example, in France, cheese is served after the main course before dessert, while in the US, it's uncommon to have cheese as a course in a formal dinner.

• Table manners:

Wait to be served: In many cultures, it's polite to wait for the host or the most senior person to start eating before you begin.

Observe and follow: If unsure about how to eat a particular dish or use a certain utensil, observe and follow the lead of your host or fellow diners.

- Conversation:

Appropriate topics: Avoid controversial or personal topics. Stick to business-related discussions or neutral topics unless your host introduces other subjects.

Compliments: Complimenting the food or the hosting can be a nice gesture in most cultures, showing appreciation for the effort made.

- Drinking:

Beverages: Know when and how to drink alcohol if it is offered. In some cultures, toasts are common, and refusing a drink can be seen as impolite.

Toasts: If toasts are made, know the proper way to participate. For instance, making eye contact during a toast is important in many Western cultures.

- Bill and payment:

Who pays: In many cultures, especially Asian cultures, the person who issues the invitation pays the bill. However, in the US, it's common to split the bill evenly among colleagues.

Gratuity: Tipping practices vary widely. In Japan, it's considered rude, whereas in the US, it's expected.

- Post-meal etiquette:

Thank your host: Always thank your host at the end of the meal. This can be done verbally or through a thank-you note sent afterwards.

Follow up: A follow-up note or call after the meal is a good way to continue building the relationship.

In a word, the key is to be respectful, observant, and adaptable. When in doubt, mimic the behavior of your host or the most senior member of your group.

Selections of Food and Drinks

Dining etiquette involves an understanding of not only the correct utensils to use and appropriate behavior, but also awareness of dietary restrictions and taboos that vary across cultures. Here are some examples of food and drink-related prohibitions in different countries.

Many Indians do not eat beef, especially those who are Hindu, as cows are sacred.

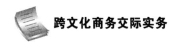

In many Middle Eastern countries, particularly those that are predominantly Muslim, alcohol is prohibited.

It's considered an insult to the chef to ask for Parmesan cheese to be added to seafood dishes in Italy. Cappuccino and milky coffees are typically only consumed before 11 a. m. Do not cut your bread; it should be torn by hand and used to mop up sauces.

Unlike in Italy, it is common to cut the bread rather than tearing it in France.

Leeks, called "spring onions" in S. Korea, they are often used as a garnish and should not be removed from the dish and placed on the side of your plate.

In all cases, it's essential to observe the cues of your host and fellow diners, follow their lead, and show respect for the cultural norms and dietary restrictions.

Task 5: Understanding the Concepts

1. *Mark the following statements about dining etiquette as True (T) or False (F).*

_____ (1) In China, it is considered rude to make noise while eating noodles.

_____ (2) In France, it is customary to cut your bread instead of tearing it.

_____ (3) In the Middle East, it is acceptable to consume alcohol during a meal.

_____ (4) In the United States, it is common to split the bill evenly among restaurant diners.

_____ (5) In a formal dinner setting, it is appropriate to start eating before everyone has been served.

2. *Fill in the blanks with the appropriate word or phrase.*

(1) In Mexico, refusing food when offered can be seen as _____.

(2) In Korea, laying your chopsticks across your plate is similar to the gesture used for _____.

(3) In India, using the _____ hand to eat is considered unclean.

(4) In Italy, adding _____ to seafood dishes is generally frowned upon.

---

2. After-hours Gathering

After-hours gatherings in a business context often serve as an opportunity for professionals to network, build rapport, and strengthen working relationships outside of the formal office environment. These events can include a wide range of social activities, such as attending cocktail parties, restaurants, or other recreational venues. Here are some specific considerations and examples.

Cocktail Parties

Activity: A cocktail parties in the context of intercultural business etiquette are social events typically held before or after work hours, often in a relaxed environment that allows for networking and socializing. They can range from small gatherings to larger receptions and are common in international business settings.

Intercultural considerations: Pay attention to the dress code (business attire, cocktail attire, etc.), be mindful of your alcohol consumption, and understand that the purpose is often to facilitate introductions and casual conversations rather than to close business deals.

Industry Nights

Activity: Special events where professionals from a certain industry gather at a designated club or bar.

Intercultural considerations: Be aware of the music and noise levels which can affect communication, and be respectful of the fact that not everyone might enjoy loud environments or certain types of music.

Sporting Events

Activity: Attending a baseball game, soccer match, or other sports event with colleagues.

Intercultural considerations: Remember that not everyone might be interested in the same sports, so choose events that are likely to be enjoyable for the entire group. Additionally, be prepared for the outdoor environment and provide information on what to expect (e. g. , weather, duration of the game).

3. Tipping

In some countries, it is customary or anticipated to leave a tip, but elsewhere, this practice is neither obligatory nor permitted. These disparities emphasize the need to recognize and honor diverse cultural norms in international business interactions.

In cultures where it is customary to leave gratuities, such practices function as a form of non-verbal communication and are frequently viewed as gestures of goodwill. Nonetheless, the custom of tipping differs across nations. In societies where tipping is infrequent, offering a tip

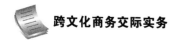

might even be taken as a insult.

The U. S. and Canada: Tipping is expected in the U. S. and Canada for services such as dining, hotel staff, taxi drivers, and hair salons. The standard tip is around 15%~20% of the total cost for restaurant meals and hotel housekeeping.

Europe: In Northern European countries like Sweden, Denmark, and Norway, a service charge is often included in the bill, so additional tipping is not necessary. However, in Southern and Eastern European countries like Italy, Greece, and Russia, tipping is more common and appreciated.

Asia: Tipping culture varies widely across Asia. In Japan and South Korea, tipping is not customary or even considered rude in some cases. In China and Vietnam, tipping is not expected but can be appreciated if offered discreetly.

Middle East: In countries like the UAE and Qatar, a 10%~15% service charge is usually added to the bill, making additional tipping unnecessary. However, it is common to give small tips to hotel staff, taxi drivers, and porters.

Australia and New Zealand: Tipping is not customary in Australia and New Zealand, as service charges are often included in the bill. However, leaving a small tip for exceptional service is appreciated.

Africa: Tipping culture varies across Africa, with some countries like Egypt and Morocco expecting tips for services rendered, while others do not have a strong tipping culture.

Latin America: Tipping is common in most Latin American countries, with a standard tip of 10%~15% for restaurant bills and other services.

When doing business in an intercultural setting, it's important to research the local tipping customs and follow them accordingly. This shows respect for the local culture and can help build positive relationships with business partners and clients.

Task 6: Furthering Your Understanding

Tipping culture can vary significantly across different countries and regions. Please conduct an online research in groups on how much tip is suitable for in different situations in English-speaking countries today?

Task 7: Preparing for the Unit Project

1. Applying the Concepts

Suppose your colleague from the Chinese technology company is attending another company's reception, as described in the scenario, it's crucial to discuss with them beforehand the etiquette for dining, behavior during the reception, and the customary way to handle tipping. This preparation will help ensure they conduct themselves appropriately at the event.

2. Critical Thinking

Compare and contrast the dining etiquette and tipping customs in Chinese and American cultures, providing pertinent examples to illustrate the differences.

Part D   Gift Giving and Receiving

Gift giving etiquette refers to the unwritten rules or social norms that govern the act of presenting gifts to others, playing an significant role in international business. It includes guidelines on what to give, how to give, when to give, and even how to receive gifts appropriately. This etiquette helps to ensure that the gesture is well-received and does not inadvertently offend the recipient.

For instance, gift giving etiquette might dictate that one should give a gift that is appropriate to the occasion, matching the level of formality or intimacy of the relationship with the recipient. It also often involves considering cultural customs, as different cultures have varying traditions and expectations surrounding gift exchanges. Additionally, this etiquette can include aspects like wrapping the gift in an appropriate manner, delivering it at a suitable time, and expressing gratitude upon receiving a gift in return.

Gift giving and receiving etiquette in international business can vary significantly across cultures and regions. Understanding these differences is crucial to avoid misunderstandings and to build strong relationships. Here are some general guidelines.

1. Gift Giving

In many companies, there are established guidelines for gift-giving within a business context. These guidelines often include a selection of items that managers can choose from for gifts; common choices include calendars, pans, clocks, and golf balls, as these are well-received in a business setting. Business professionals in the United States must be mindful of legal restrictions imposed by the *Foreign Corrupt Practices Act*. This act prohibits bribery and places

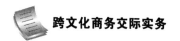

strict limits on the value of gifts that can be given and accepted. However, these laws and company policies may not provide clear guidance on how to handle situations where an employee is invited to attend a social event, such as a dinner party.

Appropriateness: Choose a gift that is appropriate for the recipient and the context. Avoid overly personal or extravagant gifts that could be misconstrued as bribery or inappropriate attention.

Cultural sensitivity: Be aware of cultural norms and sensitivities. What is considered a polite gift in one culture might be inappropriate or even offensive in another.

Timing: Gifts are typically given during specific times, such as holidays, after signing a significant deal, or upon meeting a new business contact. Be mindful not to give gifts at times when they might be seen as an attempt to influence a business decision.

Transparency: In some industries or regions, giving gifts might be subject to legal or corporate guidelines. Ensure that your gift-giving is transparent and compliant with any such regulations.

Card included: Always include a card with the gift to provide a personal touch and to avoid any misunderstandings about the intention behind the gift.

Quality: Aim for high-quality gifts that reflect well on you and your company, without being too lavish.

Paperwork: Depending on the value of the gift, there may be tax implications or requirements to declare the gift. Ensure you understand and comply with these requirements.

Reciprocity: While it's polite to appreciate a gift with gratitude, don't feel obliged to reciprocate with a gift of equal value. The focus should be on building a relationship, not on one-upmanship.

Personal touch: If possible, add a personal touch to the gift to show that you've put thought into it and are not just going through the motions.

Delivery: Consider how and when the gift will be delivered. Hand delivering a gift can show sincerity, but for long-distance relationships, mailing a gift is also acceptable.

Remember, the goal of gift giving in a business setting is to build goodwill, strengthen relationships, and show appreciation — not to create obligations or suggest ulterior motives.

2. Gift Receiving

When receiving a gift, always express gratitude regardless of the gift's nature or value. If you are not supposed to accept gifts per your company policy or personal principles, tactfully decline without causing embarrassment to the giver. Be mindful of the timing and setting in which you open a gift, as some cultures prefer it to be done in private.

Gift Receving

Japan: Express gratitude but do not open the gift immediately in the presence of the giver.

China: Receive gifts with both hands and appreciate the thought behind it, even if you do not open it immediately.

Saudi Arabia: Accept gifts graciously, but remember that some may not be appropriate to open immediately.

Germany: Open gifts immediately upon receipt to show appreciation.

United States: It is appropriate to open a gift when received, expressing thanks for the gesture.

Brazil: Receive gifts with enthusiasm and open them immediately.

India: Receive with gratitude, potentially declining once as a sign of respect before accepting.

Task 8: Understanding the Concepts

Read each of the following questions and choose the best answer.

1. In which country is it considered impolite to open a gift immediately in the presence of the giver?

    A. United States   B. Japan   C. Germany   D. Brazil

2. What should you do if you are a man wanting to give a gift to a businesswoman in Saudi Arabia?

    A. Give it to her directly at the meeting.

    B. Send it to her office later.

    C. Have it delivered to her home.

    D. Avoid giving gifts to prevent misunderstandings.

3. Why might a gift be declined initially in China?

    A. Because it is too expensive.

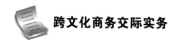
B. As a sign of modesty and humility.

C. Because the recipient does not accept gifts.

D. Due to dissatisfaction with the gift choice.

4. Which of the following is an appropriate gift in German business culture?

   A. An extravagant luxury item.

   B. A personalized, practical gift.

   C. An item related to your company's products.

   D. A gift voucher for a very high amount.

5. In India, which of the following should be avoided when giving a gift?

   A. Spicy food items.   B. Leather goods.

   C. Handicrafts from your region. D. Chocolates.

Task 9: Furthering Your Understanding

Work in groups. Study the following case and have a discussion with your group members: Why did the executives refuse the New Year gift? What different views on gift-giving etiquette does the case show?

Elaine, an international business development manager for a medium-sized enterprise in China, embarked on a week-long business trip that includes stops in Dubai, Beijing, and Berlin. The trip involved meetings with top-level executives from important partner companies. She chose *Moutai*（茅台）as a New Year gift for Dubai's executives. The top-level executives from Dubai partner company were grateful for that but firmly refuse to accept it.

Task 10: Preparing for the Unit Project

1. Applying the Concepts

The following is a list of gifts for your business partners in the scenario. Cross out the ones that are definitely unacceptable. Then choose proper gifts from the list or think of other suitable gifts. Work in groups of four and share the reasons for your choices with your group members.

A. A high-quality leather briefcase

B. A set of luxury wine glasses

C. A box of assorted gourmet chocolates

D. A smartwatch

E. A bottle of single malt scotch whiskey

F. A book on Canadian wildlife

G. A silk scarf featuring traditional Chinese motifs

H. A New Year calendar

I. A coffee machine

J. A personalized journal

2. Critical Thinking

Provide specific instances to demonstrate the contemporary practices of presenting gifts within Chinese business and social contexts. Following this, engage in a group discussion to explore the deep-rooted customs and values associated with gift-giving in Chinese culture.

Part E Humor and Taboos in Business

The use of humor in intercultural business etiquette is a complex and nuanced aspect that requires careful consideration. Humor, when used appropriately, can help to build rapport, diffuse tension, and create a friendly atmosphere. However, what is considered funny can vary widely across cultures, and humor that is well-received in one culture may be perceived as offensive or inappropriate in another.

Superstitions represent beliefs that contradict the established principles of science or the truths and rationality recognized by a society.

Taboos, on the other hand, are actions or verbal expressions deemed inappropriate or unacceptable by a particular society or culture. These taboos usually stem from the deeply-held convictions of the people within a specific region or cultural group and are transmitted across generations.

1. Humor

If humor is incorporated effectively in commercial endeavors, entrepreneurs may accomplish their objectives more efficiently. Each culture possesses distinct elements that stimulate amusement in individuals.

In the U.S., humor is often used to break the ice and establish a more casual, friendly atmosphere during business meetings. Jokes and light-hearted banter are common, but it's important to avoid controversial topics like politics or religion.

Japanese culture values humility and respect, so humor is used more subtly and indirectly. It's common to use self-deprecating humor to show modesty and build rapport with colleagues.

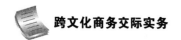

However, making jokes at someone else's expense is generally considered rude.

<u>Germans</u> tend to be more direct and straightforward in their communication, so humor is often used in a more matter-of-fact way. Jokes that play on words or involve puns are popular, but it's important to avoid humor that could be seen as insulting or disrespectful.

<u>Indian culture</u> places a high value on hospitality and warmth, so humor is often used to create a welcoming atmosphere during business interactions. Jokes and anecdotes are common, but it's important to avoid humor that could be seen as critical of other cultures or religions.

<u>Brazilians</u> are known for their lively and expressive communication style, which includes a love of humor. Jokes, puns, and wordplay are all common ways to add humor to business interactions, but it's important to avoid humor that could be seen as offensive or disrespectful.

Humor can be universally appealing, but it often takes on unique forms in different cultures. For instance, slapstick, jokes about restaurants, and humorous anecdotes about golfers can evoke laughter across borders. Yet, even with globally recognized jokes, individuals often add cultural nuances to make the humor resonate with their compatriots. In America, for example, humor frequently incorporates sarcasm（讽刺）and playful teasing. Meanwhile, Australian humor tends to be more barbed and provocative（挑衅性的）.

While humor is often used to help ease tension and create a more comfortable atmosphere with international colleagues, there is a significant risk of inadvertently offending someone from another culture or telling a joke that simply doesn't translate. Simply put, what amuses one culture may not resonate with another. It's important to be aware of cultural sensitivities and adapt your humor accordingly to ensure it is well-received by all.

2. Taboos

In intercultural business etiquette, it's important to be aware of potential taboos or cultural sensitivities that could inadvertently offend your international counterparts. Taboos represent actions or statements deemed inappropriate or unacceptable by a particular society or cultural group. These prohibitions are frequently grounded in the belief systems of specific regions or cultures and are transmitted from one generation to the next.

Intercultural Taboos

In order to avoid such taboos, two basic rules of humor etiquette are shown as follows.

- Properly research and preparation before engaging in business interactions are recommended. It helps to ensure if you understand the cultural norms, expectations, and sensitivities of your international colleagues.

● Never do or say anything that will bring unfavorable attention or embarrassment to another person. Always strive to maintain respectful and considerate behavior in all your interactions, avoiding actions or words that could cause offense, shame, or discomfort to others, particularly in cross-cultural settings where different standards and sensitivities may apply.

Specifically, for more information on humor-related taboos in cross-cultural business etiquette, please refer to the following guidelines.

● Avoid ethnic jokes: Refrain from making jokes that target or stereotype specific ethnic or cultural groups, as they can be highly offensive and damage business relationships.

● Carefully choose subjects or incidents: Be cautious and selective in the topics you discuss or the events you reference, ensuring they are appropriate and will not unintentionally offend your international colleagues.

● No interpretation, or don't tell jokes: Avoid making assumptions about what others mean or intend, and refrain from telling jokes that may not translate well cross-culturally or could be taken out of context.

● Avoid the spur-of-the-moment decision: Do not make important decisions impulsively, especially in a cross-cultural business setting, where hasty choices can overlooked critical cultural considerations and lead to misunderstandings or conflicts.

By understanding these cultural nuances, you can avoid unintentionally offending your international colleagues and build stronger, more respectful relationships.

Task 11: Preparing for the Unit Project

Applying the Concepts

In Part E, you have learned about the importance and rules of using humor. Work in groups of four. Discuss with your group members how you are going apply humor in the business dinner in the scenario and what cultural taboos you need to avoid when using humor.

Task 12: Telling China's Stories in English

Translate the following paragraph related to Chinese traditional etiquette into English. And share with your classmates what you have learned from it.

在中国传统文化中，尊敬长者是礼节的基石。在不同的情境下，这种尊敬表现在多种形式上。例如，当进入一个房间时，年轻人习惯让年长的人先走。在用餐时间，

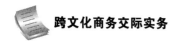

邀请年长的人先开始吃是一种尊重的表现，年轻人在长辈未动筷子之前先吃会被认为是不礼貌的。此外，在递接物品时，应该用双手作为礼貌和敬重的姿态。这些行为不仅反映了个人品格，也体现了儒家思想中关于社会层级和秩序的理念。

Assessment

1. *Read each of the following statements and choose the best answer.*

（1）Which of the following is considered rude in a Japanese business setting?

　　A. Direct eye contact.

　　B. Turning down a small gift.

　　C. Keeping your business card in your pocket.

　　D. Using both hands when giving or receiving a gift.

（2）In which country is it customary to remove shoes before entering a business meeting?

　　A. United States

　　B. Japan

　　C. United Kingdom

　　D. Australia

（3）What is the appropriate title to use when addressing a German businesswoman with a PhD?

　　A. Ms. Schmidt

　　B. Dr. Schmidt

　　C. Frau Schmidt

　　D. Professor Schmidt

（4）In which culture is it common to eat with your hands?

　　A. France

　　B. Japan

　　C. India

　　D. United States

（5）Which gesture is considered offensive in many Western cultures?

　　A. Thumbs-up

　　B. OK sign

　　C. Bowing slightly

　　D. Waving hello

2. *Decide whether the following statements are true（T）or false（F）.*

_____（1）In Japan, it is considered rude to refuse a gift immediately in front of the giver.

_____（2）In China, the color red is associated with death and mourning.

_____（3）In the Middle East, it is appropriate to use the index finger to point at people or objects.

_____ (4) In India, the "namaste" gesture, which involves pressing palms together and nodding, is a common way to greet someone.

_____ (5) In Brazil, punctuality is strictly enforced in business meetings.

_____ (6) In Germany, it is customary to use first names immediately upon meeting someone in a business setting.

_____ (7) In the United States, it is appropriate to discuss religion and politics openly in business conversations.

_____ (8) In Arab countries, it is acceptable to consume alcohol during business meals.

Unit Project

Re-examine the scenario of this unit and play the role of the CEO at the business dinner. You should pay attention to the following points:

- Be careful about the business etiquette as to what to do, what to say, and how to best present yourself.
- Study the identity of the other attendees and find appropriate ways to address them and exchange business cards.
- Show appropriate table manners and give tips properly.
- Choose suitable business gifts and present them decently.
- Use humor during the business dinner and avoid possible cultural taboos.

Case Analysis

Analyze the following case with the cultural models and theories learned in this unit.

Miscommunication in a Multinational Team

A multinational corporation with headquarters in the United States launched a new project that required collaboration between teams from the U. S. , Mexico, and India. The goal was to develop a new software application within a tight deadline. During the cooperation period, misunderstandings arising from differences in etiquette were brought out.

The American team was direct and used phrases like "this needs to be done yesterday", which was perceived as aggressive by the Mexican and Indian teams.

The Indian team worked during their daytime hours, which overlapped with the last few working hours of the American team but was outside the Mexican team's work hours. This led to delays in communication.

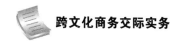

The American team provided direct feedback on performance, which the Mexican and Indian teams found overly harsh and disrespectful according to their cultural norms.

By addressing these issues, the multinational team can foster a more inclusive and understanding work environment, leading to improved morale and productivity on the project.

Further Reading

Intercultural Business Etiquette

Global Greetings and First Impressions

In the dynamic world of international business, first impressions are critical, and they often begin with the simple act of greeting. However, what is considered polite and appropriate in one culture could be perceived as cold or even rude in another. Understanding the nuances of greetings across different cultures can significantly impact how you are perceived by international clients and business associates. This passage explores various greeting customs, aiming to equip business professionals with the knowledge to make a positive and respectful first impression.

- Greeting in Japan:

In Japan, bowing is a central element of greetings and shows respect. The depth of the bow and the length of time it is held can indicate the level of respect being shown. A lighter bow, around a 15-degree angle, might be used for casual meetings, while a deeper bow, up to a 45-degree angle, is reserved for more formal occasions or to show significant respect. Handshakes are also common but are usually lighter and accompanied by a bow.

- Greeting in Middle Eastern countries:

In many Middle Eastern countries, the handshake is the customary greeting but comes with its own set of cultural protocols. For instance, it is common for men to shake hands using only their right hands, as the left hand is considered unclean. Additionally, the handshake might be longer than what Westerners are accustomed to, sometimes lasting several seconds, and it may be accompanied by a light grasp or pat on the shoulder or back. In some contexts, especially when dealing with older or highly respected individuals, it is not uncommon to use both hands to shake, demonstrating additional respect.

● Greeting in France:

In France, the norm is a gentle, brief cheek-to-cheek kiss upon meeting, known as "la bise" (the kiss). The number of kisses varies by region, from one to four. In a professional setting, it is always acceptable to offer a handshake instead, especially if uncertain about the other person's preference. French greetings also involve a substantial amount of verbal pleasantries, inquiring about one's health and well-being before diving into business topics.

● Greeting in India:

India offers a diverse range of greetings depending on the region and the relationship between the individuals. A namaste, performed by placing your hands together in front of your chest and nodding, is a common and respectful way to greet, particularly in Hindu-majority regions. Among Muslims, a salaam or slight bow with a hand over the heart is customary. In more westernized areas or business settings, a simple handshake will suffice, but it should be initiated by the senior or higher-ranking individual.

The Art of International Business Greetings

Mastering the art of greeting in international business requires research, cultural sensitivity, and often, a willingness to adapt. It involves understanding the subtle cues and customs that can vary significantly from what you might be accustomed to in your home country. By taking the time to learn and adopt the proper greeting etiquette, you demonstrate respect and build a foundation of goodwill that can pave the way for successful international business interactions.

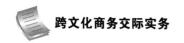

单元小结

1. 学习目标

学习了这个单元之后，你将能够：

- 解释国际商务环境中礼仪的重要性；
- 讨论在多元文化商务环境中建立初步联系的过程；
- 概述在跨文化商务环境中组织社交活动的步骤；
- 描述在不同文化商务环境中赠送礼品的适当方法；
- 评估幽默在不同文化商务互动中促进关系的作用。

2 学习情境

在完成这个单元后，根据以下情景完成该单元项目：

假设你是中国的一家中型科技公司的首席执行官，该公司最近将业务扩展到美国、日本和印度。随着业务的扩展，你计划在跨文化商务谈判前邀请潜在客户参加商务晚宴，但在商务礼仪方面遇到了一些与文化差异有关的挑战。为了应对这些挑战，你需要准备一份有关适当商务礼仪的详细计划，以帮助提升公司的形象。

3 礼仪的意义

礼仪包括在社交和职业环境中被认为适当的行为和举止规范。掌握适当的社交礼仪需要了解介绍、交换名片、承认等级和地位、用餐习俗、赠送礼品等方面的文化差异。因此，了解和实践正确的礼仪可以在个人和职业层面产生若干积极影响。

中西方礼仪的差异反映了更深层次的文化价值观和社会习俗。中国人的交流往往更加间接和含蓄，非常强调"面子"概念，更倾向于通过非语言线索来传达意图；而西方人的交流通常更加直接和明确，非常重视清晰和坦率。在现代世界中，数字沟通变得越来越普遍，包括社交媒体、即时消息、视频会议以及其他形式的电子沟通。

4 初步业务关系

建立初步业务关系是一个多方面的过程，涉及理解、尊重和跨越潜在文化鸿沟的沟通。这是建立专业联系的起始阶段，可以为未来的互动与合作奠定基调。

4.1 称呼语

姓名是人与人之间的区别。在与他人交谈时，作为良好礼仪的一部分，记住并正确使用这些名字既重要又困难。弄清何时以及如何使用他人的姓名尤其困难。在初次商务接触中称呼他人时，遵守正确的礼仪会对你们关系的开始和发展产生重大影响。以下是一些需要牢记的要素：

4.1.1　使用适当的称谓

专业头衔：如果某人有专业头衔（如教授或总监或经理等具体职称），请务必使用。这表示对其专业地位的尊重。

学术头衔：在学术或研究环境中，对拥有博士学位的人应使用 Dr. 等头衔。

文化称谓：在某些文化中，特定的称谓反映了家庭地位或尊重（例如，亚洲社区中的"长辈"或"阿姨/叔叔"）。正确理解和使用这些称谓可以体现文化敏感性。

4.1.2　正确使用姓名

名与姓：不同的文化对使用名和姓有不同的习俗。在许多西方文化中，人们一旦建立了一定程度的熟悉关系，通常就会使用名，而在其他文化中（如日本和韩国），人们可能会一直使用带有适当敬语的姓。

读音：注意学习姓名的正确读音。如果不确定，不要犹豫，询问对方如何正确发音。

4.1.3　注意文化差异

称呼形式：在某些文化中，使用较为正式的语言和称呼别人的头衔和姓氏可能是合适的。在某些文化中，迅速转为直呼其名是友好和开放的表现。

避免假设：永远不要假设某人喜欢自己名字的昵称或缩写，除非他们自己提供了这一信息，或者他们的公司或上下文清楚地表明了这一点。

● 倾听暗示：通常情况下，周围的人或他们在谈话中的暗示会给你示范如何称呼某人。注意这些暗示，并相应地调整你的称呼。

● 不确定时询问：如果你不确定如何称呼某人，通常最好先问一下。可以这样说："请原谅，我不确定应该如何称呼您，您更喜欢……吗?"这表示对个人及其喜好的尊重。

4.2　预约

预约是首次建立商务关系的一个重要方面，在大多数商务交往中也很常见。商务预约有几种方法，合适的方法可能取决于具体情况、与对方的关系以及文化规范。

简短电话：简短的电话既直接又私人。当你与对方已经建立了良好的关系或者需要及时联系时，最好使用这种方式。

正式信函：正式信函（通过电子邮件或传统邮件发送）适用于安排初次见面或特别正式的场合。这种方法比较耗时，但可以留下持久且专业的良好印象。

中间人：中间人是指在你和你想见面的人之间充当中间人的人。中间人可以是双方的联系人、同事或熟悉双方的商业伙伴。

使者：使者类似于中间人，但通常是指正式授权代表你利益的人。使者可以是公司代表、外交官甚至专门负责建立商业联系的专业服务机构。

4.3　使用商务名片

名片是在商务交往开始时为方便起见而使用的，它可以帮助初次见面的人通过书面形式而不是口头形式更多地了解你。掌握正确交换名片的方法，可以给你遇到的商务人

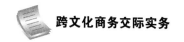

士留下积极而持久的印象。

用双手递交名片表示尊重，也是对亚洲文化中这一仪式的认可。递交名片时，最好握住名片的上角。同样，你也应该双手接过名片。拿到名片后，请花一些时间仔细阅读，不要只看一眼。这是重复对方姓名的绝佳机会，可以帮助你记住对方的长相和姓名。

最好随身携带一个小巧的卡片夹或卡片盒。尽管你可以在自己的卡片上写字，但在别人的卡片上写字被认为是不礼貌和不尊重的行为。在伊斯兰国家，左手被视为不洁之物；在非洲和亚洲的许多非伊斯兰地区，右手也比左手更受欢迎。因此，在递交或接收名片时要用右手。在欧洲和北美，名片没有那么正式，主要在繁忙的会议中用来记录谁是谁。如果你在这些地方推销产品，主人会把注意力放在产品上，而不是名片上。

5 社交娱乐

跨文化商务礼仪中的社交娱乐往往涉及范围广泛的活动，从正式的商务晚宴和企业活动到更非正式的聚会，如交流招待会或团队建设活动。在全球商务背景下参与社交娱乐活动时，了解和尊重不同的文化规范和期望至关重要。

5.1 用餐礼仪

跨文化商务礼仪中的用餐惯例是在不同文化间建立和维持专业关系的一个重要方面。用餐时间为个人在更轻松的环境中互动提供了一个独特的机会，可以促进双方的互信任和理解。

虽然每种文化都有其独特的用餐习俗，但有一些基本的用餐礼仪准则在各国广泛适用。通过遵守这些标准，商务人士可以迅速熟悉起来，从而促进他们在未来的日子里继续开展业务。下面列出的基本用餐礼仪建议结合了公认的全球规范和基本智慧。毫无疑问，用餐时的举止会给他人留下深刻印象。用餐礼仪包括用餐的时间和地点、用餐的方法和食物的选择。从广义上讲，这些做法可以揭示特定文化的许多集体特征。

5.2 下班后聚会

商务环境中的下班后聚会通常是专业人士在正式办公环境之外建立联系、建立融洽关系和加强工作关系的机会。这些活动可以包括各种社交活动，如参加鸡尾酒会、餐馆聚餐或其他休闲场所活动。

• 鸡尾酒会：跨文化商务礼仪中的鸡尾酒会通常是指在上班前或下班后举行的社交活动，通常在轻松的环境中进行。鸡尾酒会可以是小型聚会，也可以是大型招待会，在国际商务环境中比较常见。

注意事项：注意着装要求（商务装、鸡尾酒装等），注意饮酒量，并了解其目的通常是促进介绍和闲聊，而不是达成业务交易。

• 行业之夜：某个行业的专业人士聚集在指定俱乐部或酒吧的特别活动。

注意事项：注意音乐和噪声水平可能会影响交流，要尊重并非每个人都喜欢喧闹环境或某些类型音乐的事实。

• 体育赛事：与同事一起参加棒球赛、足球赛或其他体育赛事。

考虑因素：并非每个人都对相同的体育运动感兴趣，因此要选择可能会让整个团队都感到愉快的活动。此外，要为户外环境做好准备，并提供预期信息（如天气、比赛时间）。

5.3　小费

在一些国家，习惯上或预期中会给小费，但在其他地方，这种做法既不是强制性的，也不被允许。这些差异凸显了在国际商务交往中承认和尊重不同文化规范的必要性。

在有给小费习俗的文化中，这种做法是一种非语言交流形式，通常被视为善意的表示。尽管如此，各国给小费的习惯却不尽相同。例如，在不习惯给小费的社会，贸然给小费甚至可能被视为一种侮辱。

6　礼物的赠送与接受

送礼礼仪是指向他人赠送礼品行为的不成文规定或社会规范，在国际商务中发挥着重要作用。它包括赠送什么礼物、如何赠送、何时赠送，以及如何恰当地接受礼物等方面的准则。这种礼仪有助于确保礼物受到欢迎，并且不会无意中冒犯收礼人。

6.1　赠送礼品

许多公司有既定的商务送礼准则，这些准则通常包括经理们可以选择的礼品。常见的礼品包括日历、平底锅、钟表和高尔夫球，因为这些礼品在商务活动中很受欢迎。

6.2　接受礼物

收到礼物时，无论礼物价值如何，都要表示感谢。如果根据公司政策或个人原则，你不应该接受礼物，则应委婉地拒绝，但要注意避免让送礼者感到尴尬。注意打开礼物的时机和环境，因为在有些文化下人们喜欢在私下打开礼物。

7　商务中的幽默与禁忌

在跨文化商务礼仪中使用幽默是复杂而微妙的，需要仔细斟酌。如果使用得当，幽默有助于建立融洽关系、缓解紧张气氛和营造友好氛围。然而，在不同的文化背景下，人们对幽默的理解可能大相径庭，在一种文化背景下广为接受的幽默，在另一种文化背景下可能会被视为冒犯或不恰当。迷信代表着与既定的科学原则或社会公认的真理和理性相矛盾的信仰。另一方面，禁忌是特定社会或文化认为不恰当或不可接受的行为或语言表达。这些禁忌通常源于特定地区或文化群体中人们根深蒂固的信念并世代相传。

* 本单元智慧职教线上课程：https：//zyk. icve. com. cn/courseDetailed？id = obbaaaqvo4doejfjffeicq&openCourse = obbaaaqvw79e5opp1bwbg.

Unit 10　习题参考答案

Unit 11   Intercultural Business Workshop

Ancient Chinese Wisdom

The world endures for eons, but this life won't come again; a human life spans just a century, and today passes most swiftly. （天地有万古，此身不再得；人生只百年，此日最易过。）

From *Cai Gen Tan* （《菜根谭》）

Learning Objectives

After learning this unit, you shall be able to:

- Create an employee requisition form.
- Create an employment requisition form.
- Draft a job advertisement.
- Apply for a job and go for an interview.
- Apply cross-cultural awareness for a job interview.

Project Scenario

After learning this unit, finish the unit project on the basis of the following scenario.

Suppose you are a job candidate named Alex, who has applied for a position in an international company based in a different country than your own. The company is known for its diverse workforce and global business operations. You have been invited to a job interview, which will be conducted via video conference by a panel consisting of representatives from different cultural backgrounds. You need to get well prepared for the up-coming interview.

Lead-in

Introductory background: P&T, a high-tech company, is going to start a new employee recruitment program for the next financial year. The following file is an employee requisition form from R&D Department.

Response Email Sample

Department: Research and Development (R&D)

Date: 1st June 2024

Requisition for new employee

Job Title: Software engineer

Number of Positions: 2

Job Description: The Software engineer will be responsible for designing, developing, and maintaining software applications that align with the company's products and services.

Responsibilities

- Collaborate with cross-functional teams to define, design, and develop software solutions.
- Conduct thorough testing and debugging to ensure quality and performance.
- Maintain and update existing software systems to improve functionality and performance.
- Stay up-to-date with emerging technologies and industry trends.
- Provide technical support and training to colleagues and clients as needed.

Required Skills and Qualifications

- Bachelor's in computer science or related field.
- Proficiency in programming languages such as Java, C++, or Python.
- Strong problem-solving and critical thinking skills.
- Experience with software development methodologies and tools.
- Excellent communication and interpersonal skills.

Budget Details

Annual Salary Range: 70,000-90,000.

Bonus/Incentives: Performance-based bonus of up to 10% of the annual salary.

Other Benefits: Comprehensive health insurance, retirement plan, paid time off, and professional development opportunities.

Part A   Recruitment and Selection

1. Employee Requisition Form

Language Points

An employee requisition form is used whenever a specific department needs to fill a staff position. It contains a description of job opening and qualifications required for the position. It is prepared by the department that has the vacancy and mainly presented to the human resources

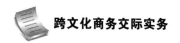

department which advertises the opening. The following are the detailed information which should be contained in an employee requisition form:

Questions for discussion:

What are the key elements of an employee requisition form?

What might be the essential qualification requirements according to the information in the form?

If you are the recruitment manager, what else would you like to know from an employee requisition form apart from the information given in the form?

- Job description:

Department, job title, location (or multiple locations), title of the supervisor, date the position was documented; Position summary (one or two sentences summarizing the primary function and general purpose of this job); Essential duties and responsibilities; Position type (new requirement or replacement, if it is the latter, the person being replaced and the reason for the replacement should be in the form); Position category (full-time, part-time or temporary); Number of applicants to be interviewed and hired; Working hours, pay rate and compensation.

- Job qualifications and special considerations:

Education requirement (e. g. a bachelor's degree, a college degree or equivalent education in a related field); Special skills (e. g. advanced IT degrees, communication skills, etc.) Licenses or certifications; Experience required (e. g. 2-3 years of working experience directly related to position responsibilities); Physical requirements (e. g. an ability to lift a certain amount of weight, or to sit or stand for long periods of time).

Business Know-how

How to complete an employee requisition form for Approval when a supervisor finds there is a need to hire new employees? The first step will be to complete an employee requisition form and forward it to the administrative manager for approval. The purpose of an employee requisition form is to establish a valid need for a new position, indicate that funding and space are available, and provide a source document for posting the position. Bear this purpose in mind and pay attention to the following points when completing the form:

List all the prerequisites of the job. For example, if you need applicants who have the ability to lift a certain amount of weight, drive certain vehicles or use special tools or machinery, you should contain the physical duties in the form, in order to hire the candidates whom you believe can hit the ground running in your company.

Be sure to write the qualifications for the position you need, not the person who may currently be in the position. If a job requirement is listed, then those applicants not meeting the minimum standards are not viable for the position.

Make sure that all your job requirements meet those rules which are set by the state and local laws to prohibit job discrimination based on race, color, religion, sex, national origin, sexual orientation, and age. It is important not to violate these rules.

Tips:
Avoid inflating position descriptions and titles. Doing so could result in confusion regarding the nature and level of work being performed as well as performance expectations.

One of the useful tricks when writing a job description is to find free examples of job descriptions on any popular job boards. Just cut and paste pieces and parts of similar jobs you see on job boards, and then modify the specific information to fit your needs.

Avoid arbitrary education and experience requirements. If one of the minimum qualifications for a job is a bachelor's degree, you need to be able to show the relationship between that requirement and the job.

Task 1: Understanding the Concepts

The personnel manager of P&T, Mrs. Becker, is interviewing Sam. Read the following conversation between Mrs. Becker and Sam and role-play the interview with a partner. After that, discuss the questions below in pairs.

(*Now Sam is sitting across the desk from Mrs. Becker, the personnel manager.*)

Mrs. Becker:	So your resume says you've worked at a number of companies.
Sam:	Yes. And in my last job, I worked for Digit sky. So I have a little experience working in the high-tech industry.
Mrs. Becker:	That's good. How are your computer skills?
Sam:	Excellent. I won the gamers' award and nobody can beat me at kungfu Battle.
Mrs. Becker:	I mean for the office.
Sam:	Oh, pretty good. I am proficient in word processing, creating spreadsheet and setting up data basis. And I have experience making Web pages.
Mrs. Becker:	Impressive. How would you describe yourself?
Sam:	I am hardworking and organized and I work well with others.

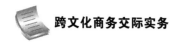

Mrs. Becker: Where do you picture yourself in five years?

Sam: I want to be in a senior sales position with a high-tech company.

Mrs. Becker: Do you have any experience in sales?

Sam: Actually I don't. But I believe my personality and the ability to learn fast will enable me to become a good sales rep.

Mrs. Becker: I appreciate your honesty. It's really quite refreshing. Some interviewees tend to exaggerate.

Sam: I prefer to be truthful. No one likes to be misled, including potential customers.

Mrs. Becker: OK. I've asked you a lot of questions. Now do you have any questions about P&T or the position?

Sam: Yes. Can you tell me about the company's future plans?

Mrs. Becker: Sure. Our big focus now is on the Internet sales. It is all explained in our company brochure. Here.

Sam: Thank you. And who will be my supervisor?

Mrs. Becker: As a sales representative, you will be working in the sales department. You report to the assistant sales manager.

Sam: Does the job require much travel?

Mrs. Becker: Yes, our sales people are on the road a lot visiting perspective customers. Anymore questions?

Sam: No, I can't seem to think of any others this time.

Mrs. Becker: Well, let me give you some information about our compensation package. We offer all entry level sales people an annual salary of 80,000 yuan plus health coverage, and two weeks paid vacation.

Sam: That sounds good.

Mrs. Becker: Sam, I certainly enjoy meeting you. You seem like a strong candidate for this position.

Sam: Thank you.

Mrs. Becker: Good luck and feel free to call me if you have any questions.

Questions for discussion

1. What is the role of an interviewee and how should he or she behave during an interview? Please comment on Sam's performance.

2. How should the interviewer ask questions? Please comment on Mrs. Becker's performance.

2. Job Interview

Language Points

Job interviews never seem to get any easier — even though you have gone on more interviews than you can count. You are meeting new people, selling yourself and your skills, and often getting the third degree about what you know or don't know. Once you have been selected for a job interview, the best way to reduce the stress is to prepare properly. The following are some interview questions you will most likely be asked. They will help you prepare the interview effectively.

- Getting started:

How would you go about establishing your credibility quickly with the team?

How long will it take for you to make a significant contribution?

What do you see yourself doing within the first 30 days of this job?

If selected for this position, can you describe your strategy for the first 90 days?

- Basic interview questions:

Introduce yourself: name, age, nationality, etc.

State when you are available.

Describe your relevant experience — or justify your lack of experience.

Describe your skills in your own language, English and other languages.

Describe how you meet the requirements of the job.

Say when you are available for interview.

Does your present employer know you've applied for this job?

How would you describe the ideal person for this job? What has been your most valuable experience?

What are your strengths and weaknesses?

When did you last lose your temper?

Describe what happened. What was the worst problem you have had in your present job and how did you solve it?

Describe your present job — what do you find rewarding about it?

What do you do in your spare time? Describe your ideal boss.

What can you do for us that other candidates can't?

What makes you think you'd enjoy working for us?

How would you describe your own personality?

What worries you about the job you're doing now?

What is the best idea you've had in the past month?

Are you willing to relocate?

If you were me, what other questions would you ask?

- Career development questions:

What are you looking for in terms of career development?

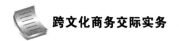

How do you want to improve yourself in the next year?

What kind of goals would you have in mind if you got this job?

If I were to ask your last supervisor to provide you additional training or exposure, what would he/she suggest?

● Salary questions:

What salary are you seeking?

What's your salary history?

If I were to give you this salary you requested but let you write your job description for the next year, what would it say?

Business Know-how

How to be a good interviewee?

Listen carefully. You will be judged on the basis of your answers to questions, so listen to them carefully. Pick out the key details of the question and pause briefly before answering, keep answers on target. Never interrupt the interviewer.

Take care to use correct expressions. Interviews, especially those for jobs, tend to be fairly formal occasions, so utilize language suitable for the situation. At all costs avoid slang and expressions like "you know", "sort of", "er", etc. Speak clearly and distinctly.

Observe etiquette. Even if you are invited to do so, don't smoke, eat, or drink during the interview. Address the interviewer as "Mr." or "Ms." unless he/she indicates otherwise. Never touch objects and papers on the table.

Maintain eye contact. Look directly at the interviewers and project that you are confident. Situp straight, control nervous habits and smile naturally as you are greeted. These are all nonverbal behavior that you will be observed.

Be honest. Do not say what you think the interviewer wants or expects you to say. Putting your views and your personality across as courteously as possible is better than giving bland, non-committal responses to the interviewer's questions. Also do not pretend you have qualifications or experience which you do not — you are bound to be caught.

Ask questions. A good interviewer will give you the opportunity to ask questions. This does not mean you should ask about holidays and salary. Find out about potential for the future, your responsibilities, training and other work-related questions.

- For interviewees:

Research. Find out as much as you can about the company — goods or services they provide, how long they have been established, top management/branch, company policy, past, present and predicted growth patterns, special programs the company is involved in, etc.

Punctuality. Be sure of the person you are to see, the address and the time of the interview. Plan how you will get there and know the length of journey. Aim to be there at least 10 minutes early so that you can relax and compose yourself before the interview.

Documentation. Don't forget to bring original and copies of documentation such as certificates, assessments, reviews, etc. The original copy will validate your claims while copies may be asked for reference/filing purposes.

Presenting yourself. Dress for success. Wear to the interview what you would wear on the job. Do not overdress or over accessorize. Be neat and clean.

- For interviewers:

Your aim is to put the interviewee at ease and help him/her to relax by being friendly and reassuring.

Create a climate of confidence. You can do so by giving the interviewee your undivided attention.

Smile, nod, use appropriate gestures to exhibit genuine interest in the interviewee and what he/she has to say.

Beware of closed questions; instead use open questions.

Keep an open mind and don't just stick to your prepared questions; allowing the interviewee to speak freely.

If your interview meets a dead end, you should redirect the conversation back toward your subject matter.

You must also be precise in your questions and project your point of view such as giving examples of answers needed.

Portfolio

Please put your coursework into the file according to the checklist.

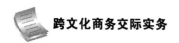

File 1 The employee requisition form of your department

File 2 The job advertisement of your company

File 3 The recruitment flowchart of your department

File 4 The personal resume for job application

3. Cross-cultural Awareness for a Job Interview

Cross-cultural differences can have a significant impact on job interviews, as they can affect communication, perception, and understanding between the interviewer and the candidate. In today's globalized world, it is essential for both parties to be aware of these differences and adapt accordingly to ensure a successful interview process.

Language Points

One of the most critical aspects of cross-cultural differences in job interviews is communication style. Different cultures have varying norms regarding directness, formality, and tone of voice. For example, in some cultures, it is considered polite to use indirect language and avoid confrontation, while in others, directness and assertiveness are valued. Interviewers should be aware of these differences and adjust their questions accordingly to avoid misunderstandings or offense.

Another important factor is nonverbal communication. Gestures, facial expressions, and body language can vary widely across cultures, and what may be considered polite or appropriate in one culture could be seen as rude or disrespectful in another. Interviewers should pay attention to these cues and avoid making assumptions based on their own cultural biases.

Perceptions of time and punctuality also differ across cultures. In some societies, being late to an appointment is not considered a big deal, while in others, it is seen as a sign of disrespect or unprofessionalism. Interviewers should clarify their expectations regarding arrival time and be flexible if necessary.

Cultural differences can also affect the way candidates present themselves during an interview. For instance, in some cultures, modesty and humility are highly valued traits, while in others, self-promotion and confidence are essential. Interviewers should be aware of these differences and evaluate candidates based on their qualifications rather than their cultural background.

Questions for discussion:

Cross-cultural differences can also influence the types of questions asked during an interview. Some cultures may place more emphasis on education and academic achievements, while others may focus more on work experience and practical skills. Interviewers should tailor their questions to each candidate's background and avoid making assumptions based on stereotypes or cultural biases.

---

1. Do the interviewees need to have an immediate answer when they are asked a question?
2. Do you think bringing a to-go cup of coffee to a job interview is a great idea?
3. How do you sell yourself in a job interview, directly or indirectly?
4. If you are going to participate an interview, is it necessary to carry a pen and paper in your portfolio or briefcase?

Tips:

When you're asked a question, you don't need to have an immediate answer. In fact, it can be a turn off for an interviewer to feel as if you've given no thought whatsoever to a complicated question. Slow down and think about it. Pause, say, "That's a great question, let me think about a good answer".

Another common mistake in an interview is talking too much and too quickly. You don't need to fill awkward silences with chatter. Especially if you're a nervous talker, don't feel the need to fill the space with talking. Sit back and listen. Don't give away too much.

Your go-to answer in a job interview should be "Yes". Are you willing to work nights and weekends? Yes. Are you comfortable taking on multiple clients? Yes. Do you have experience working in a high-paced environment? Yes. Most jobs provide enough on-the-job training for skills that are essential to conducting the day-to-day operations that you'll be able to pick up anything you're unfamiliar with after you get the job. Don't disqualify yourself ahead of time. Be agreeable and sort out the details after you get the job.

Don't lie about some things. Being willing to do what's necessary for the position doesn't mean that you should stretch your experiences or tell fibs that'll get you outed the first day on the job. If you've never cooked a meal in your life, you shouldn't tell the kitchen manager you're a great cook.

Business Know-how

Don't show up with coffee. For some reason, lots of people think bringing a to-go cup of coffee to a job interview is a great idea. To an interviewer, this looks informal at best and disrespectful at worst. You're not on your lunch break, so treat yourself to a latte after the interview, not before. Even if the interview is early, or you might end up waiting a long time to get through with it, don't show up with a cup of coffee. The plus side is you won't have to worry about spilling it.

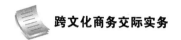

Turn off your phone and put it away. Biggest faux-pas of the mobile phone age? Using yours in a job interview. Never ever take your phone out and look at it at any point in the job interview. As far as your interviewer is concerned, you should be a troglodyte who's never even heard of an app. Turn your phone all the way off, keep it in your car, and never, under any circumstances, give the interviewer the impression that a text message takes precedence over getting this job.

Sometimes, you'll be prompted to provide a base salary requirement for the job. The best answer for this is that you're willing to work for the lower end of the average salaries for your position. Express that you really want the job and that you'll be fine with what's being offered in the legal limit.

Treat your interview like a conversation, not an interrogation. Never get defensive in an interview, even if you feel like you're not getting on perfectly with the interviewer. It's supposed to be a conversation, so try to assume the best in people. Nobody is trying to antagonize you on purpose. Treat it as a chance to prove yourself and come up with a good explanation, not a defensive snark.

Don't knock your previous boss. Making petty comments about previous coworkers, superiors, or other job in general should be avoided. Even if you're applying for a rival business, avoid painting yourself like someone with a grade, or like someone who'll be difficult to work with. It's bad form to gripe about your previous job.

If you're asked why you're leaving your current job, say something positive. "I'm looking for more out of my work environment and I'm excited about getting a fresh start. To me, this looks like a great place to do it."

Avoid pre-interview cigarettes and alcohol. Even if you indulge in the occasional smoke, avoid smoking before a job interview. A recent study revealed that up to 90 percent of employers would hire a nonsmoker over a smoker of equal qualification. Right or wrong, smoking makes the interviewee looks nervous.

Likewise, having a few drinks to soothe tense nerves should always be avoided. You want to be sharp and on point, not sloppy. Interviewers will expect you to be nervous. It's a job interview.

Tips:
Avoid clichés. Interviews are a time to let your potential employer get to know you, the real you, not a pumped-up, cliched version of yourself who's giving canned answers to try to get a job. The purpose of the interview isn't to suck up, show off, or tell the interviewer what they

want to hear. The purpose is to give sincere answers, not to insult the interviewer's intelligence. Avoid interview lines like "My only weakness is that I'm a perfectionist", or "This company needs someone like me to turn it around".

Cultural Awareness

Working effectively with different cultures is a necessary skill for anyone in a culturally diverse work environment. Immigration, technological advances, and the emergence of global virtual work teams have increasingly exposed workers to other cultures. Cultural variations in the workplace may range from simple regional differences, such as varying dialects, to divergent perspectives on timeliness, productivity, and communication. There are several steps you can take to work effectively with people from different cultures.

<u>Become Self-aware.</u> If you have never worked with someone from a different culture before, it can be an adjustment. While you might encounter some challenges, you will likely find it a rewarding experience. Your first step is to put yourself in the right frame of mind.

- Work on becoming more aware of your words and actions. What seems appropriate to you may not be a cultural norm to another person.

- Before you give someone at work a high five or a pat on the back, take a moment to consider your actions. Based on what you know about that culture, is touching in the workplace appropriate?

- A good rule of thumb is to take a moment to consider your words before you speak. Is what you're about to say possibly offensive? If so, figure out a way to rephrase.

<u>Practice patience.</u> It may take a while for you to get used to working with people from different cultures. Don't worry, that's normal. It probably took you awhile to acclimate to your current co-workers, too.

- Try not to get irritated if communication takes a little extra effort at first. For example, maybe you are now working with someone whose first language is not English.

- Instead of getting impatient if they don't understand your point, try to treat it as a learning experience. Try saying, "Ok, I can see I'm not making myself clear. How can I help us get on the same page?"

- Be patient with yourself, too. It may take you some time to adjust to working with your new co-workers or clients, and that is ok.

<u>Use humor.</u> Remember that working in a new environment might be intimidating for someone from a different culture. Whether you are on a conference call, or traveling to meet someone face to face, the initial meeting can feel stilted or awkward. Don't be afraid to lighten the mood.

- Humor is an excellent way to ease tension in the workplace. It can serve as a way to make people feel comfortable and even more connected to each other.

- Remember that different people have different senses of humor. Before making a joke, try to make sure that it won't be construed as offensive.

- You can try making a lighthearted joke about something situational. For example, if it's a nasty, rainy day, you can jokingly say, "Lovely day, isn't it?" It may not be the most original comment, but things like that can lighten the mood.

Look at issues from a different perspective. Remember that not everyone will come at a discussion from the same angle. Difference in perspective are coming when working with people from different cultures. Don't assume that you are all looking at the issue from the same perspective.

- Clarify what important terms mean to each individual. For example, in a meeting you could ask, "What does efficiency mean to you?"

- It's possible that you might think you're working with the same goals in mind, but that you have a different understanding of the process or outcomes. A simple question can help resolve any issues.

- Once someone explains their perspective, take some time to reflect. Looking at an issue from an alternate perspective can help you find solutions that you might not have considered.

Accept differences. Part of choosing the right frame of mind means that you are open to differences. If you go into a new situation aware that people might have different customs than you, you will find it easier to be accepting. Go to work knowing that people from different cultures might work differently than you, and that's to be expected.

- Be aware that there will likely be differences in communication styles. For example, in some cultures the word "yes" means, "Certainly, I'm in agreement". To others, the word "yes" can mean, "I heard you".

- Accept that there might be differences in addressing conflict. In some cultures, a face to face conversation might be the norm. For other people, written communication might be more appropriate.

- When you encounter differences, be willing to be adaptable. You might need to alter some of your habits in order to make the work relationship more constructive.

Get to know individuals. When you take time to get to know someone, you can find new ways to strengthen your work relationship. Put some effort into building individual relationships. Your work life will be more productive and pleasant.

- Don't lump people together in a group. For example, avoid making general comments such as, "Those Australians don't have the same work hours that we do".

• Instead, say, "I need to talk to Anna and Steve about how we can resolve this issue". Thinking of people as individuals is a great way to show respect and build relationships.

Tips:

<u>Listen to stories.</u> One of the best ways to learn about a new culture is by hearing some personal anecdotes. Ask your new co-workers or clients to tell you some stories. Listen with an interested and curious open mind.

Perhaps you have some new clients from South Africa. You can ask them to tell you stories about what life is like there.

You can say something like, "What do you typically do for fun after work?" Then you can offer examples of your own experiences.

Listening to stories is a great way to form bonds. You'll learn something new, and likely find more commonalities than you expected.

Many cultures maintain a high degree of formality with strangers. Some cultures are more casual than others, but you can never go wrong with being overly polite. If you're being excessively formal, the person you're talking to will correct you — but they certainly won't be offended by it.

Generally, refer to strangers by their surname and "Mr. " or "Ms. ". In many cultures, it's a big deal to be on a first-name basis with someone. If they prefer that you call them by their first name, or by something else, they'll let you know.

Remember your manners! Regularly use words such as "please", "thank you", "excuse me", "pardon me", and "I'm sorry". If you know some of these words and phrases in the person's native language, they'll appreciate it all the more.

<u>Keep eye contact brief</u> to show respect and attention. Different cultures treat eye contact differently, so it's best to keep it brief if you're trying to avoid miscommunication. In some Asian, Latin American, and African communities, prolonged eye contact is seen as rude and challenging. In pairs, searching and discussing eye contact differences among cultures and present your findings before class.

In more hierarchal cultures, such as many Asian cultures, avoid eye contact if you're speaking to someone older than you or in a position of authority. This communicates respect for their position.

In Middle Eastern cultures, prolonged eye contact is common if you're speaking to someone of the same gender, but if you're speaking to someone of another sex, eye contact should generally be avoided.

A simple search with the name of the person's culture or nationality and a phrase such as "cultural etiquette", "social norms", or "customs and norms" will get you the information you need. If you're talking to someone in a particular context, find out cultural norms that are applicable there as well. Take the time to get to know your coworker so you can understand how they like to communicate.

Keep in mind that cultures can be extremely varied, so be as specific as possible. For example, while you'll get some information by searching for "Asian culture", you'll get better information if you look specifically for "Chinese culture", "Korean culture", or "Japanese culture".

For example, if you're meeting someone as a business representative to negotiate a contract, look up cultural norms both for business and for contract negotiation.

Picking up some common words and phrases in someone's native language also helps a lot! For example, polite words and phrases such as "I'm sorry", "please", and "thank you" can help smooth out any missteps.

Task 2: Furthering Your Understanding

Please research and prepare for a simulated job interview with diverse interviewers, adapting their communication strategies to demonstrate cross-cultural awareness.

Materials needed:
- Research materials (internet, library).
- Interview preparation worksheet.
- Reflection journal.

Steps:
- Research company culture and potential cultural backgrounds of interviewers.
- Prepare interview answers and plan cultural adaptations.
- Role-play mock interviews with cultural nuances.

4. Recruitment Flowchart

Introductory background: When preparing for the new employees recruitment, the Human Resources Department in P&T has drafted a selection process for the event.

Task 3: Understanding the Concepts

Put the following boxes in correct order to make a reasonable recruitment flowchart.

The correct order: _____ .

Task 4: Preparing for the Unit Project

Read the following recruitment strategies and discuss in groups to see whether you have anything to add to the list.

Recruitment strategies

1. Selection will be based on merit, which is determined through an assessment of an applicant's qualifications, experience, standard of work performance and personal qualities relevant to the requirements for the position and relative to the credentials and attributes of other applicants.

2. Applicants may be interviewed either in person or, where this is not possible or practicable, by telephone or video conference.

3. Applicants should be asked similar core questions based on the requirements for the position. Supplementary questions may be asked to clarify issues or to obtain further information deemed by the panel of interviewers to be relevant to identifying the best applicant.

4. Recruitment strategies that may be considered include, but are not limited to:
    a) external advertising;
    b) use of a search agency;
    c) internal advertising;
    d) direct appointment;
    e) application by invitation;
    f) appointment from eligibility list;
    g) application by expression of interest.

Language Points

Besides internal discussions within the company, employers also need to contact the potential candidates to inform them the progress of each stage. The following are some sentence patterns usually used on the phone between them.

Inquire results
— I am just calling to see if you have made any decision concerning...
— We haven't made any decision yet.
— Do you have any idea/know when you might arrive at a decision?
— If there is any additional information you need, please call me at any time.

Respond to invitation
— Thank you for calling. /It was really good to hear from you.
— I really appreciate your invitation, but...
— I just accepted another offer that I feel is more suitable to my needs/more right for me/more interesting to me.
— I really think that position suits my education background better.
— Thanks for your time. /Well, it's been nice talking to you

Notify result:

— This is... from... Company.

— Thanks for your application/first interview on···

— I'm pleased to tell you that your application for X is under consideration/has been accepted.

— We would like to invite you to attend a formal/second interview at...

— Congratulations! You have passed the test/second interview.

— We warmly welcome you to join us.

Business Know-how

Job recruiters should select candidates who are ready to work as team players and team leaders, with a personality that matches the company's corporate culture. Candidates Ability Tests are useful for selecting candidates according to the level of their intelligence, verbal ability, numerical ability and mechanical ability. These tests are popular because they select candidates based on standardized methodologies which are considered less prone to human error. Make selection processes fair, open and transparent. Fair hiring practices that give all applicants equal opportunities to meet the job requirements help to protect against discrimination claims and typically give you the best candidates. Open communication and transparency with applicants on how the hiring process works establish your organization as an ethical recruiter and employer.

- Multiple interview steps confirm the consistency of the employee's abilities.
- Reference checks are important to verify accuracy in a candidate's resume and background.
- If your company's recruiting process is tediously slow and out of your control, take it upon yourself to call your short-list candidates and frequently reassure them that things are progressing.

Task 5: Furthering Your Understanding

Scenario: As a newly established organization, your company is in need of numerous new employees for each department. You work in the Human Resources Department of the company.

Group discussion

Discuss with your group members about the recruiting process and recruitment strategies according to the situation of your company.

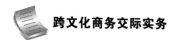

Individual work

Based on the discussion above, draft a flowchart of recruitment process and a list of recruitment strategies. Email the documents to your departmental manager for evaluation.

Part B   Sales and Customer Service

1. Cross-culture Sales

International business comprises a large and increasing portion of the world's total trade. Companies involved in international business deal with sales transactions or negotiations which span national & cultural boundaries. That means sales negotiations interact with individuals from unfamiliar cultures that exhibit different negotiation styles, behaviors and expectations about the normal process of negotiation. This presents several potential culture – related obstacles that confront the international negotiators.

Individuals having the same cultural backgrounds tend to display common patterns of thinking, felling and reacting in line with their cultural heritage. As a result, behavior in sales negotiations is consistent with within cultures and each culture has its own distinctive "style".

Language Points

People who are accustomed to different contexts of communication shall rely on quite different cultural dimensions. North Americans rely heavily on the precise meaning of the words exchanged. While people from Asian countries rely heavily on the context of situation to communicate meaning.

Case Study

Sugimoto, a Japanese salesman, was praised in a monthly sales meeting by his American manager Mr. Huge for his outstanding sales performance recently. The conversation is listed as follows:

Mr. Huge: Mr. Sugimoto, I have noticed that you are doing an excellent job on the assembly line. I hope that the other workers could learn from you.

Sugimoto: (*He is uneasy*) It's my duty and I am only doing my job.

Mr. Huge: You are one of the most excellent and dedicated workers in our company.

Sugimoto: ... (*He blushes and nods his head several times, and keeps working.*)

Mr. Huge: ... (*He seems confused about Sugimoto's reaction to his praise.*)

Sugimoto: Excuse me, Mr. Huge. May I leave for ten minutes?

Mr. Huge: Sure. (*He looks a little uncomfortable when Sugimoto walks away. He thinks Japanese workers are so rude and impolite.*)

Q1: Please describe the cross-cultural conflicts in this case.

Q2: What are the possible solution to these conflicts?

Q3: Please evaluate this case with cross-cultural theories.

Tips for Reference

There are three conflicts between Sugimoto and Mr. Huge.

The first conflict happened when Sugimoto was praised by Mr. Huge in public but Sugimoto felt uneasy, which is a conflict about individualism and collectivism.

The second conflict happened when Sugimoto responds to Mr. Huge's praise with silence. The third conflict happened when Sugimoto asked for a ten–minutes leave to evade Mr. Huge's question. The second and third conflict are related to high context versus low context.

Business Know-how

Barbara is an American working for United Technologies, a Chicago-based company. She is talking on the phone to Abhinav, an Indian manager of one of United Technologies' vendors for customer service outsourcing.

Barbara: We really need to get all of the service representatives trained on our new process in the next two weeks. Can you get this done?

Abhinav: That timeline is pretty aggressive. Do you think it's possible?

Barbara: I think it will require some creativity and hard work, but I think we can get it done with two or three days to spare.

Abhinav: OK.

Barbara: Now that our business is settled, how is everything else?

Abhinav: All's well, although the heavy monsoons this year are causing a lot of delays getting around the city.

Two weeks later...

Abhinav: We've pulled all of our resources and I'm happy to say that 60% of the customer service representatives are now trained on the new process. The remaining 40% will complete the training in the next two weeks.

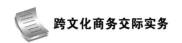

Barbara： Only 60%? I thought we agreed that they all would have been trained by now!

Abhinav： Yes. The monsoon is now over so the rest of the training should go quickly.

Barbara： This training is critical to our results. Please get it done as soon as possible.

Abhinav： I am certain that it will be done in the next two weeks.

Q1： Please describe the cross-cultural conflicts in the case.

Q2： What are the possible solutions to those conflicts?

Q3： Please evaluate this case with cross-cultural theories.

Tips for Reference

There are 3 conflicts between the above dialogue.

The first conflict happened when Abhinav responded "OK", however he was not sure about the project deadline, which is a conflict about power distance.

The second conflict happened when Abhinav explained the delays caused by monsoon without telling the precise delays of the deadline, which is a conflict about high/low context.

The third conflict happened when Abhinav responded "... in the next two weeks" after Barbara's request for finishing the training project, which is a conflict about time concept.

Task 6: Furthering Your Understanding

The Chinese girl Xu Han was going to study in an American high school. But when she arrived there and began her school life, it was hard for her to adapt to American teachers' styles of teaching and methods of tutoring. She found that the teachers dressed casually and often sat on the table during class hours. Teachers rarely lectured like Chinese teachers, but always asked students to discuss questions and make reports themselves.

Q: In this situation, how can Xu Han resolve the intercultural conflict?

Task 7: Telling China's Stories in English

Translate the following article into Chinese.

A Tale of Resilience and Entrepreneurship — The Spirit of Shanxi Merchants

In the heart of China, nestled within the historic province of Shanxi, lies a story of entrepreneurial prowess that has captivated generations. This tale is not merely one of commercial

success but of a spirit that has become synonymous with resilience, innovation, and community —
the spirit of the Shanxi merchants, or Jin merchants as they are known in Chinese lore.

Historically, Shanxi was not a land blessed with abundant resources or favorable climates for
agriculture. However, it was rich in coal and salt, commodities that were vital for the daily
lives and industries of ancient China. It was this strategic

advantage that propelled the Shanxi merchants to the forefront of trade and commerce during
the Ming and Qing dynasties.

The Jin merchants' journey was fraught with challenges. They traversed treacherous terrains
and braved bandits to establish trade routes that spanned from the Silk Road to the tea houses
of Russia. Their caravans were legendary, often consisting of hundreds of camels and mules
laden with goods. The risks were high, but so were the rewards. And reward they did, by
building a commercial empire that rivaled those of their contemporaries.

What made the Jin merchants stand out was not just their business acumen but also their
adherence to a code of conduct that prioritized integrity, mutual support, and a long-term
vision. They understood the importance of collective strength and often pooled resources to
finance large-scale ventures. Their partnerships were based on trust and respect, values that
permeated their interactions both within and outside their community.

Moreover, the Jin merchants were known for their philanthropy. Wealth was not hoarded but
reinvested into the community through the construction of schools, temples, and public
facilities. They recognized that their prosperity was intertwined with the well-being of their
society and acted accordingly.

Their business practices were characterized by adaptability and innovation. The Jin merchants
were early adopters of sophisticated accounting techniques and management systems that
allowed them to operate efficiently across vast distances. They also pioneered financial
instruments such as promissory notes and letters of credit, which facilitated trade and reduced
transaction costs.

However, perhaps the most remarkable aspect of the Jin merchants'spirit was their ability to
confront adversity head-on. During times of drought or famine, they did not wait for aid but
organized relief efforts and funded infrastructure projects that provided employment and
restored livelihoods. In doing so, they demonstrated a deep sense of social responsibility and
an unwavering commitment to their homeland.

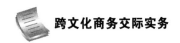
The legacy of the Jin merchants extends beyond their commercial achievements. It is a testament to the power of human resilience, the potential for collective action, and the enduring value of ethical business practices. As we face our own modern challenges, the spirit of the Shanxi merchants reminds us that with vision, cooperation, and moral fortitude, even the most daunting obstacles can be overcome.

Today, as China continues its meteoric rise as a global economic powerhouse, the lessons of the Jin merchants remain relevant. Their story serves as an inspiration for entrepreneurs everywhere, illustrating that success is not solely measured in profit margins but in the ability to uplift communities and leave behind a legacy of progress and prosperity. The spirit of Shanxi merchants, therefore, is not merely historical lore but a timeless narrative of ambition tempered with altruism — an eternal flame guiding the path of enterprising spirits towards a brighter future.

2. Cross-culture Customer Service

Dealing with customer service for a specific company or service can often be a very frustrating experience. While some companies are more customer – friendly and pride themselves on making their customers happy, other companies don't care as much and often take their customers for granted. As a result of this, it's a little tricky dealing with customer service and customer service representatives. Luckily, there are a number of things you can do to improve your chances of receiving quality customer service.

Cusomer Service

Language Points

Your first step is to know exactly what it is you want and be able to explain it fully. For example, if you have a technical issue with an electronic or online service, make sure you can clearly state what it is. Technical support usually needs as much information as possible to help provide you a solution. If you are disputing a charge, make sure you've gone over the bill and come up with a rationalization for why you think the bill is wrong. In any event, make sure to have it clear in your mind what resolution will make you happy, and what resolution is reasonable.

The second thing you need to prepare is to reserve a sizable chunk of time to deal with your issue. Dealing with customer service will probably take a substantial amount of time, so you need to think about this before you call or visit them. There are a number of things you should consider. For example, maybe you need to keep waiting 10-20 minutes to talk to an agent, then escalating your issue to a supervisor, waiting for the supervisor, and then explaining your issue to the supervisor.

Thirdly, prepare yourself to navigate through many voice prompts and be prepared to wait on hold, if calling. You probably need prepare to enter or say your account number, ticket number, or the last four of your social security number. If you prefer to make a phone call, make sure that you could speak in a friendly tone of voice and have a positive attitude. You are supposed to maintain a professional attitude and tone of voice that is conducive to business no matter how frustrated you are. Say "please" and "thank you" when appropriate.

Finally, while being polite, you need to be assertive and confident. You should articulate your dissatisfaction in a forceful way and communicate that you want the best service possible. Consider statements such as:

"I believe that my business is being taken for granted. "
"As a loyal customer, I deserve the best customer service. "
"I'm sure that you (the customer service representative) will go above and beyond in order to make me a satisfied customer. "

Business Know-how

Customer service experience can be a valuable skill in many jobs. For example, skills like addressing customer complaints: checking customers out, "encouraging repeat business through diplomacy".
Addressing Customer Complaints:
Engaged with the public to address issues and problems.
Placated customers until their issue could be addressed.
Designed and implemented solutions to solve customers' problems.
Followed up with customers to ensure issue was solved.

Task 8: Preparing for the Unit Project

Read each of the following statements and choose the best answer to resolve the Cultural Conflicts Effectively.

Hall, a nine-year-old boy who grew up in the United States, came to China with his parents to visit his Chinese grandfather. One day, at the dinner table, Hall seemed to have no interest in the food and stick chopsticks uprightly in rice. If you were the grandfather, what would you do?

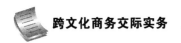

A. Get annoyed and blame your grandson directly.

B. Smile and tell Hall that sticking chopsticks is thought to bring misfortune in China.

C. Feel hurt and leave the table immediately.

D. Ignore Hall's behavior but criticize his parents.

跨文化交流技能主要包括以下 6 种。

（1）对比关联技能：具有跨文化差异敏感性的能力。

（2）多视角观察技能：从多角度看待其他国家和地区的政治、经济、宗教等事件。

（3）合作技能：能通过交流协调保持交流的顺畅，如回应对方、避免打断、转换话题等。

（4）回避冒犯技能：与外国人交际中，尽量回避成见、偏见、隐私或者冒犯（如在言语、行为、穿着等方面）。

（5）冲突管理技能：出现交流障碍和误解时与对方进行有效的协商和解释。

（6）评价技能：理性评价本国和他国的文化观点、文化事件和文化产品。

Part C　Accounting Management

Accounting management refers to the process of overseeing and managing the financial aspects of a business or organization. This includes tasks such as budgeting, forecasting, financial reporting, auditing, and tax planning. The goal of accounting management is to ensure that the company's finances are accurately recorded, monitored, and analyzed in order to make informed decisions about the organization's financial health and future growth.

Understanding
Corporate Cultures

Language Points

How to pay the bill at a restaurant? There is a big difference between China and the United States. In China, of course, it's normal to fight over who gets to pay the bill, which doesn't really happen in America.

By default the waiter will bring you the bill and ask "Would you like it separate?". So you usually you have the option, the default option of paying separately. The restaurant will split your items into two lists, and you will have separate totals. If this happens and you want to pay the bill, you can say to the waiter, "I'll get it"; or you can say to your companions, "It's ok, I'll get it"; or you can say to your companion "Do you mind if we do it separately?"

It's a dedicate situation, if you put it as a question, it will go over smoothly. What happens if your companion that you are eating with offers to pay the bill before you do and you feel awkward? What would you do in response is probably "Well, let me get it next time"; or

"Well then, next time drinks are on me!"

Business Know-how

He Yuan-man is the newly appointed director of the subsidiary of IKEA in Chicago. He requires his staff member John Smith to work overtime to complete a project, but John Smith refuses. Which of the following do you think is appropriate?

(1) He Yuan-man allows John to complete the project the next day.

(2) He Yuan-man cuts John's bonus that month.

(3) He Yuan-man finds another one to do John's work.

(4) He Yuan-man promises extra pay for John's work.

Task 9: Preparing for the Unit Project

Read each of the following statements and choose the best answer.

1. Which of the following is typically viewed as a characteristic of Chinese management style?

    A. High power distance between managers and subordinates.

    B. Delegation of decision-making authority to lower levels.

    C. Individual performance bonuses and rewards.

    D. Direct communication regardless of hierarchy.

2. In Western management, which of the following is often considered a best practice?

    A. Centralized decision-making by senior management.

    B. Avoidance of conflict through indirect communication.

    C. Standardization of processes and clear job descriptions.

    D. Emphasis on group harmony over individual achievement.

3. How does Chinese management typically handle decisions compared to Western management?

    A. With more collective involvement and consensus-building.

    B. With more individual autonomy and personal accountability.

    C. By relying heavily on external consultants and experts.

    D. Through multi-departmental competition and internal bidding.

4. Which of the following is true about authority in Chinese management?

    A. Managers frequently rotate roles to avoid power concentrations.

    B. Authority is often decentralized to teams and individuals.

    C. Decisions are usually made autonomously by middle management.

    D. Subordinates rarely question superiors' decisions due to cultural etiquette.

5. In Western business culture, what is a common expectation regarding leadership?

    A. Leaders should be accessible and approachable to all employees.

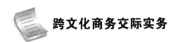

B. Leaders make all key decisions without consulting others.

C. Leadership is based on seniority and experience alone.

D. There is a preference for leaders who maintain distance from employees.

Assessment

Read each of the following statements and choose the best answer.

1. Prof. Lee attended the M. A. thesis defense of his department yesterday. During the thesis defense meeting, he found a male Pakistani student wearing slippers. How do you think of the Pakistani student's behavior?

　　A. He wanted to be cool and attract other's attention.

　　B. He wore slippers to show for religious reasons.

　　C. He used to wear slippers in his country.

　　D. He didn't take the thesis defense seriously.

2. Shirley Wen is a Chinese who has been studying in Germany for almost one year. Her German friend Leon has invited Wen to a small dinner party at her house this Saturday. Which of the following do you think is the most appropriate for Wen if she goes to Leon's house?

　　A. She brings a bunch of lilies.

　　B. She brings a bottle of whiskey.

　　C. She arrives at Leon's house a quarter ahead of the agreed time.

　　D. She arrives at Leon's house a quarter later than the agreed time.

3. Wen Zhongchen travelled in Mongolia. He booked a traditional ger in advance. When he got there, the host of the ger offered him a dried cheese and a cup of tea. But Wen didn't like cheese. Which of the following do you think is the most appropriate?

　　A. Wen refuses the host's cheese politely.

　　B. Wen takes a token bite of the cheese.

　　C. Wen accepts the cheese with his left hand but doesn't eat it.

　　D. Wen accepts the cheese with his left hand and eats it up.

4. One day, your Turkey colleague invited you to eat dinner together after work. Because you were busy with your accounting work at that time, you posed an "OK" gesture. But your Turkey colleague became somewhat angry. What can you learn from this conflict?

　　A. In Turkey, people avoid non-verbal communication with colleagues.

　　B. In Turkey, when someone talks to you, you should respond verbally.

　　C. In Turkey, gestures are not allowed.

　　D. In Turkey, the "OK" gesture is very insulting.

5. You had been dating Tania, a Russian girl, for a few weeks, and things were going well. You decided to surprise her on Saturday morning by bringing her a beautiful pair of her red and

white roses. However, as soon as she saw the roses, she became upset and started to raise her voice. You were confused, and the situation became tense. What can you learn from this conflict?

    A. In Russia, roses are not a proper gifts because they are cheap and easy to get.

    B. In Russia, flowers are not a good gift.

    C. In Russia, roses refer to something rude.

    D. In Russia, a pair of roses is only for a funeral.

Unit Project

A Finnish company was going to meet an Italian company for the negotiation of future cooperation. After arriving in Italy, the Finnish manager wanted to go straight to business and talk about the orders when the Italian wanted to have dinner and take the time to get together first. The Finnish manager seemed a little bit uncomfortable but said nothing about the cooperation. During the dinner, the Italian manager kept approaching, while the Finnish manager kept standing slightly apart. The Finn thought the Italian manager was rude but the Italian did not notice. The next day, they started their negotiations. However, the Italians also felt unhappy when seeing the chief negotiator of the Finnish side was only an employee. The negotiation seemed not to go well.

Q1: Please describe the cross-cultural conflicts in this case.
Q2: What are the possible solution to the conflicts?
Q3: Please evaluate this project with cross-cultural theories.

Case Analysis

You are working in the accounting department of a foreign company in Guangzhou. Micheal (British) just joined your work group eight days ago and was assigned a seat next to you. Liu Jie (Chinese) is your colleague at the opposite seat. With the Chinese New Year approaching, you discuss holiday arrangement with them in the office. Here is the conversation:

You: Where are you going during the Chinese New Year holiday?

Liu Jie: I will go back to my hometown to reunion with my parents. What about you?

You: I'm going to take my parents to Dali for a trip.

Micheal: Chinese New Year? (*He looked puzzled*)

You: What's up?

Micheal: Is it this one? (*showing a picture of moon cake in his picture*)

You: That's Mid-Autumn Festival.

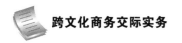
Micheal: And this one? (*showing a picture of dragon boat in his phone*)

You: That is Dragon Boat Festival.

Micheal: So what is Chinese New Year? Is it "Chinese Christmas"? Could you please explain it to me?

You: Sure!

Q: What are the differences between the Chinese New Year and Christmas?

(Note: please focus on the origins and beliefs, legend, decorations, activities, and food)

Further Reading

In today's globalized world, businesses are no longer confined to their domestic markets. With advancements in technology and transportation, companies have the opportunity to expand their operations and reach customers across the globe. However, this also means that they must navigate a complex web of cultural differences and adapt to diverse business practices. Intercultural business is the study of how companies can successfully operate in different cultural environments and build relationships with clients, partners, and employees from various backgrounds.

The first step in intercultural business is understanding the cultural context in which one is operating. Culture encompasses a wide range of factors, including language, customs, beliefs, values, and social norms. It influences how people communicate, make decisions, and interact with others. Therefore, it is essential for businesses to research and familiarize themselves with the cultural nuances of their target market or partner country. This can involve learning about the local language, history, politics, religion, and economic conditions. By doing so, companies can avoid misunderstandings and conflicts that may arise from cultural misinterpretations.

Once businesses have gained an understanding of the cultural context, they must develop effective communication strategies. Communication is a critical aspect of any business transaction, but it becomes even more challenging when dealing with individuals who speak different languages or have different communication styles. To overcome these barriers, businesses should invest in language training and translation services. They should also be mindful of nonverbal cues, such as body language and facial expressions, which can convey meaning beyond words. Moreover, businesses should adopt a respectful and open‑minded approach when communicating with people from different cultures. This means being aware of potential biases and stereotypes and avoiding assumptions based on cultural differences.

Another crucial aspect of intercultural business is building trust and establishing strong relationships with clients, partners, and employees. Trust is essential for successful business interactions, as it fosters cooperation, reduces uncertainty, and enhances mutual understanding. To build trust, businesses should demonstrate integrity, reliability, and transparency in their dealings with others. They should also show respect for cultural differences and be willing to adapt to new ways of doing things. This can involve negotiating contracts, setting expectations, and resolving disputes in a fair and equitable manner. Additionally, businesses should prioritize relationship‑building activities, such as networking events, social gatherings, and team‑building exercises, which can help create a sense of community and shared identity among diverse groups.

Furthermore, intercultural business requires flexibility and adaptability. As companies enter new markets or collaborate with international partners, they may encounter unfamiliar business practices or legal regulations. To succeed in these situations, businesses must be willing to learn from their experiences and adjust their strategies accordingly. This can involve adopting new technologies, modifying products or services to suit local preferences, or changing management styles to accommodate different work cultures. By embracing change and being open to new ideas, businesses can stay competitive and innovative in the global marketplace.

Finally, intercultural business demands ethical considerations. As companies operate across borders, they must ensure that their actions align with universal ethical standards and respect human rights. This includes issues such as labor practices, environmental sustainability, and corporate social responsibility. Businesses should strive to minimize negative impacts on local communities and contribute positively to the development of host countries. By doing so, they not only fulfill their moral obligations but also enhance their reputation and brand image globally.

In conclusion, intercultural business presents both challenges and opportunities for companies looking to expand their reach in the global marketplace. By understanding cultural differences, developing effective communication strategies, building trust and relationships, being flexible and adaptable, and considering ethical implications, businesses can navigate the complexities of intercultural business and achieve success in diverse environments. As the world becomes increasingly interconnected, the ability to manage intercultural business will become a vital skill for any company seeking long-term growth and prosperity.

单元小结

1   学习目标

学完本单元后，你将能够：
- 创建员工申请表格；
- 创建招聘申请表；
- 起草职位广告；
- 申请工作并参加面试；
- 在工作面试中应用跨文化意识。

2   学习情景

学习本单元后，根据以下情景完成单元项目。

假设你是一位名叫亚历克斯的求职者，在申请一家国际公司的职位，该公司的总部设在与你所在国家不同的地方。该公司以其多元化的员工队伍和全球化的业务运营而闻名。你受邀参加面试，面试将通过视频会议进行，面试小组由拥有不同文化背景的代表组成。你需要为即将到来的面试做好充分准备。

3   导入

介绍背景：P&T 是一家高科技公司，即将在下个财政年度启动新的员工招聘计划。以下文件是其某个部门的一份员工需求申请表。

3.1   招聘与选拔

3.1.1   工具包
员工需求申请表。

3.1.2   语言点
员工需求申请表用于特定部门需要填补职位时。它包含职位空缺的描述以及该职位所需的资格条件。该表由存在空缺的部门准备，并主要提交给人力资源部门，由其发布职位空缺广告。以下是员工需求申请表中应包含的详细信息：

3.1.3   商务知识
雇用新员工时，第一步是填写员工需求申请表并提交给行政经理审批。员工需求申请表的目的是确立新职位的合理需求，并为发布职位提供一个源文件。

3.2   工作面试

3.2.1   语言点

工作面试似乎永远不会变得更容易——即使你已经参加了无数次面试。一旦你被选

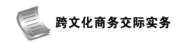

中参加工作面试，减少压力的最佳方法是做好充分的准备。

3.2.2 商业知识：如何成为一名优秀的面试者

- 仔细倾听。

你将基于对问题的回答而被评判，因此请仔细听问题，找出问题的关键细节，在回答之前稍作停顿，确保答案针对性强。千万不要打断面试官。

- 注意使用正确的表达方式

面试，特别是工作面试，往往在比较正式的场合进行，所以要使用适合这种场合的语言。无论如何都要避免使用俚语和"你知道""有点""呃"等表达。说话要清晰、明确。

- 遵守礼仪。

即使你被邀请这样做，也不要在面试期间吸烟、吃东西或喝酒。除非对方另有指示，否则请以"先生"或"女士"称呼面试官。千万不要触碰桌上的物品和文件。

- 保持眼神交流。

直视面试官，表现出你的自信。坐直，避免过分紧张，并在被问候时自然微笑。这些都是你将被观察的非言语行为。

- 诚实。

不要说你认为面试官想要或期望你说的内容。尽可能礼貌地表达你的观点和个性，这样会比对面试官的问题给出平淡、无承诺的回应要好。同时，不要假装拥有你实际上不拥有的资格或经验——否则一定会被发现。

- 提问。

一个好的面试官会给你机会提问，但这并不意味着你应该询问关于假期和薪水的问题；但可以了解未来工作职位的可能性、你的责任、培训和其他与工作相关的问题。

3.3 工作面试的跨文化意识

跨文化差异对工作面试可能产生显著影响，因为它们会影响面试官和候选人之间的沟通、感知和理解。在当今全球化的世界里，双方了解这些差异并适应是确保面试过程成功的关键。

3.3.1 语言点

工作面试中跨文化差异的一个最关键的方面是沟通风格。不同的文化对于直接性、礼节和语调有着不同的规范。例如，在一些文化中，使用间接的语言和避免冲突被视为礼貌，而在其他文化中，直接性和自信是被重视的。面试官应该意识到这些差异，并相应地调整他们的问题，以避免误解或冒犯。

另一个重要因素是非言语沟通。手势、面部表情和肢体语言在不同文化中可能大不相同；在一种文化中被认为是礼貌或适当的行为，在另一种文化中可能被视为粗鲁或不尊重。面试官应该注意这些线索，并避免基于自己的文化偏见做出假设。

对时间和守时的看法也因文化而异。在一些社会中，约会迟到并不被认为是什么大不了的问题，而在其他社会中，却会被视为不尊重或不专业的行为。面试官应该阐明他们对到达时间的期望，并在必要时保持灵活性。

文化差异还可能影响候选人在面试中的自我展示方式。例如，在一些文化中，谦虚和谦卑是非常受重视的特质，而在其他文化中，自我推销和自信是必不可少的。面试官应该意识到这些差异，并根据候选人的资格而非他们的文化背景来评估候选人。

3.3.2　商业知识

● 不要带着咖啡出现。不知为什么，很多人认为带着一杯咖啡去参加工作面试是个好主意。对面试官来说，这看起来至少是不正式的，而最坏的情况是被视为不礼貌。这不是午休时间，所以面试后再享受你的拿铁吧。即使面试安排在早上，或者你可能会等很长时间才能完成面试，也不要带着一杯咖啡出现。好消息是：没有咖啡，你就不用担心咖啡会在面试中洒出来。

● 关闭手机并收起它。移动电话时代最大的失礼是什么——在工作面试中使用你的手机。在面试的任何时候，永远不要拿出手机看它。就面试官而言，你应该是一个从未听说过应用程序的穴居人。将手机完全关机，放在你的车里，在任何情况下，都不要让面试官觉得你把一条短信看得比得到这份工作还重要。

● 有时，你会被要求提供一个基本薪资要求。对此最好的回答是你愿意接受该职位平均薪资范围的低限。你应该表达出你真的想要这份工作，你会对法律允许范围内的任何薪资满意。

● 把你的面试当作一次对话，而不是一次审问。即使在面试中你感觉和面试官相处得并不完美，也永远不要表现得过度防御。这应该是一次对话，所以尽量往好的方面想。没有人故意试图激怒你。将其视为一个证明自己的机会，给出一个好的解释，而不是进行防御性的反驳。

● 不要贬低你以前的老板。避免对以前的同事、上级或其他工作发表负面评论。即使你正在申请竞争对手的公司，也要避免把自己描述成一个有偏见的人或难以共事的人。抱怨你以前的工作是不恰当的做法。

● 如果你被问及为什么要离开当前的工作，说些积极的话。"我希望从我的工作环境中获得更多，我对于新的开始感到兴奋。对我来说，这里看起来像一个做这件事的好地方。"

● 避免面试前吸烟和饮酒。即使你偶尔喜欢抽烟，也要避免在工作面试前抽烟。最近的一项研究显示，多达90%的雇主会选择一个不吸烟的应聘者而不是具有相同资格的吸烟者。无论对错，吸烟会让面试者看起来紧张。

同样地，为了缓解紧张神经而喝几杯酒这种事应该始终避免。你应该保持敏锐和专注，而不是邋遢。面试官会预料到你会感到紧张——毕竟，这是一场工作面试。

4　销售和客户服务

4.1　跨文化销售

国际商务占据了世界总贸易中的一个庞大且不断增长的部分。参与国际商务的公司

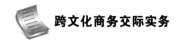

处理跨越国家和文化界限的销售交易或谈判。这意味着销售谈判与拥有不同文化背景、不同谈判风格的个体进行互动。这给国际谈判者带来了几个潜在的与文化相关的障碍。

具有相同文化背景的个体倾向于展示出与其文化背景一致的共同思维、感受和反应模式。因此，销售谈判中的行为在文化内部是一致的，每种文化都有其独特的风格。

4.2 语言点

习惯于不同沟通环境的人会依赖截然不同的文化维度。北美人非常依赖交换的词语的精确意义。而来自亚洲国家的人则严重依赖于情境的上下文来传达意义。

4.3 商业知识

处理客户服务常常是一种非常令人沮丧的体验。虽然一些公司更加以客户为中心，会以使客户满意为荣，但其他公司则不那么在乎。因此，处理客户服务和客户服务代表有点棘手。幸运的是，你可以做一些事情来提高获得高质量客户服务的机会。

- 第一，确切知道你需要什么，并能充分解释它。例如，如果你对电子或在线服务有技术问题，确保你能清楚地说明遇到了什么问题。技术支持通常需要尽可能多的信息来帮助你提供解决方案。如果你对某项费用有争议，确保你已经查看了账单，并想出了一个合理化的解释：为什么你认为账单是错误的。在任何情况下，确保自己清楚什么样的解决方案会让你满意，以及什么是合理的解决方案。

- 第二，预留一段时间来处理你的问题。处理客户服务可能会花费大量时间，所以在你打电话给他们或拜访他们之前需要考虑这一点。有一些事情你应该考虑：例如，也许你需要等待 10~20 分钟才能与代理交谈，也可能你的问题需要由主管来处理。

- 第三，准备好通过许多语音提示进行导航；如果打电话，准备好等待接听。你可能需要准备输入或说出你的账号、票号或社会保障号码的最后四位。如果你更喜欢打电话，确保你能用友好的声音说话并保持积极的态度。无论你多么沮丧，都应该保持专业的态度和有利于业务的语气。在适当的时候说"请"和"谢谢"。

- 第四，在礼貌的同时，你需要表现出自信和坚定。你应该以有力的方式表达你的不满，并表示你想要尽可能最好的服务。可以考虑以下这样的陈述：

"我相信我的生意被当作理所当然。"

"作为忠实的客户，我应得到最好的客户服务。"

"我相信你（客户服务代表）会竭尽全力让我成为一个满意的客户。"

5 会计管理

5.1 财务问题

会计管理指的是监督和管理企业或组织的财务方面的过程，包括预算、预测、财务报告、审计和税务规划等任务。会计管理的目标是确保公司的财务状况被准确记录、监控和分析，以便对公司的财务健康和未来增长做出正确的决策。

5.2　语言点

● 在餐厅如何付款。这方面，中国和美国之间有很大的不同。在中国，客户间争着付账是很正常的，而在美国则不太会发生这种情况。

● 默认情况下，服务员会将账单给你，并问："您想要分开支付吗？"通常你也可以选择别的付账方式，但默认选项是分开支付。如果你想付账，你可以对服务员说"我来付"或者对你的同伴说"没关系，我来付"。

● 如果你的同伴在你之前提出付账，而你感到尴尬时，该怎么办呢？你可能的回答是"好吧，下次让我来付"或者"那么，下次饮料就由我请了！"。

5.3　商业知识

案例：何元满是芝加哥宜家子公司新任命的董事。他要求他的员工约翰·史密斯加班完成一个项目，但约翰·史密斯拒绝了。

＊本单元智慧职教线上课程：https：//zyk. icve. com. cn/courseDetailed？ id ＝obbaaaqvo4doejfjffeicq&openCourse＝obbaaaqvw79e5opp1bwbg.

Unit 11　习题参考答案